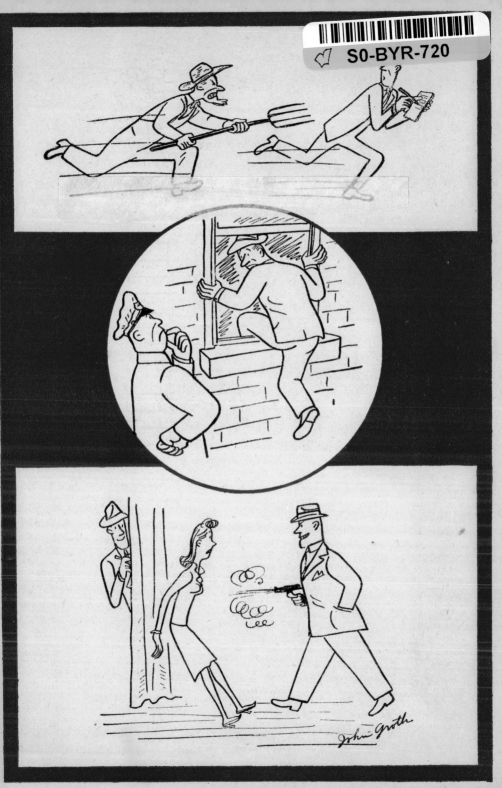

John Groth

SUCH INTERESTING PEOPLE

WITHDRAWN

By ROBERT J. CASEY

WAR
  The Cannoneers Have Hairy Ears
  I Can't Forget
  Torpedo Junction

MYSTERY
  The Secret of No. 37 Hardy Street
  The Secret of the Bungalow
  Hot Ice
  News Reel
  The Third Owl

TRAVEL
  Four Faces of Siva
  Baghdad and Points East
  Easter Island
  The Land of Haunted Castles
  The Lost Kingdom of Burgundy

ROMANCE
  The Gentleman in Armor
  Cambodian Quest

SATIRE
  The Voice of the Lobster

TECHNICAL
  Manual of Radio Interference

VERSE
  The Vest Pocket Anthology

Such Interesting People

by

ROBERT J. CASEY

Joseph 1890—

THE BOBBS-MERRILL COMPANY

INDIANAPOLIS   NEW YORK

Dedicated

IN THE ORDER OF

THEIR APPEARANCE

TO

HAZEL KNOWLES

BETTY CASEY

PAUL QUAY

PHILIP NEWMAN, JR.

ROBERT KEARNEY

ROBERT CASEY LANE

AND

(BY ELECTION)

KRISTIN TRAUTMAN

JUDY BURKE

CONTENTS

CONTENTS

Foreword

AND AREN'T THEY ALL?

THERE once was a newspaperman—he has had a thousand names in as many chronicles of the incident—who by odd chance was invited to sip tea in the home of a wealthy gadget manufacturer on the right side of the tracks. His hostess looked at him wide-eyed as she tried to make him feel at ease. And she said, after the fashion of hostesses to newspapermen since the invention of movable type: "It must be fascinating to be a journalist. You meet such interesting people."

And the reporter answered mechanically: "You certainly do, and they're all in the newspaper business." *

This book is the report of a lot of research along the lines of that general proposition. The oddments of history presented here have not been altered in any way from the form in which they now find circulation in the trade.** In most respects they are true. If they seem to support a theory that the newspaper business and bedlam are the same thing one must remember that the resemblance is purely accidental.

---

* Stanley Walker and Walter Winchell both claim authorship of this *bon mot*, but it is the opinion of your investigator that they were both a little late.

** Reserving, of course, a copyreader's right to misspell a few names.

SUCH INTERESTING PEOPLE

1

"THE ODD ONES ARE FAR VOYAGERS"

～～～～～～～～～～～～～～～～～～～～～～～～

HE WAS a nervous little man in a suit of heavy gray tweed and a straw hat the color of mellowed meerschaum, and he was easily the strangest exhibit that a pair of tired eyes had discovered in Cairo. The noon sun was bright as it can get nowhere else in the world save in Egypt in midsummer. The air was filled with the smells of camel dung and cooking asphalt. The little man was red-faced and steaming and that was the only thing about him that seemed normal.

He was in a hurry, which, of course, would have marked him as something unusual even aside from his odd taste in clothes. Nobody hurries on a hot day in Cairo, or for that matter on a cool day—when there is one. Nobody (even in wartime) has found anything worth hurrying for in these parts since the days of Rameses II. But the little man didn't seem to have heard anything about local customs. He came striding from the terrace of the Continental Hotel with quick, short steps, his arms swinging and his chin snapping up and down at every stride. It made one dizzy to watch him—especially one who had been wandering for days in the blazing mirages of the Syrian and Sinai deserts.

[13]

His middle was ornamented by a heavy gold watch chain from which hung a Masonic charm somewhat smaller than a horseweight. A pencil and fountain pen of the fifty-cent variety stuck out of his breast pocket. And to the lapel of his coat was pinned a little American flag—a celluloid badge such as one used to find in the popcorn balls that were so important a part of one's childhood. He halted his dash suddenly as the *gareh* driver dumped my suitcase onto the sidewalk, his face lighting with what was startlingly like a smile of recognition.

"Hello," he said. "You are also an American."

How he arrived at that diagnosis after a brief inspection of an outfit of soiled and wrinkled linens and a battered cork hat is difficult to say. Perhaps the shoes gave him a clue. They had come from Honolulu, which, after all, is by way of being American. At any rate he seemed sure of himself.

"You have been to Baghdad," he said. "I know that. They told me at the hotel you were coming in today. I must talk to you about it. The British run Baghdad, don't they? They run Iraq? Well, then I must talk to you about it. I am a journalist." He looked about furtively, saw nothing moving except the sleazy heat waves rising from the pavement, and lowered his voice to the pitch and timbre of the stage conspirator. "They're after me," he went on. "The British are after me. They follow me everywhere."

At the moment it appeared that the British were busy elsewhere because he was certainly uncrowded on the sidewalk. The only human beings in sight were the *gareh* driver, some hopeful dragomans loitering about the steps, I, the freshly returned pilgrim from Baghdad and a few tourists whose faces were hidden in tall sweating glasses on the terrace.

[14]

"They're after me," he repeated casually. "The British. I'll be back and tell you about it. My name is Eddy . . . Captain Eddy."

He went away under a full head of steam, easily the most incredible person in a land where the impossible is commonplace.

Nobody in his right mind would have laid a bet that Captain Eddy would ever get back from his walk in the noonday sun. He was a cordial invitation to sunstroke, if indeed he might not be considered fresh bait for the alienists. Such people, as a rule, have short life expectancies, bad memories and an affinity for trouble. They come across the horizons of more or less normal people only briefly—which is probably fortunate. But none of the rules ever seemed to fit Captain Eddy. He came back. He lingered. There appeared to be no end to him.

The conniving British were still on his mind when he returned to the hotel two hours later although it was obvious that if they were shadowing him they must be doing it by remote control. He was only a little hotter than when he had started out. His eyes were no more glassy. The sun which probably would have killed any other white man in a straw hat who ventured into that seething street had been kind to him. He lowered himself with great dignity into a wicker chair on the terrace and ordered a large beaker of cognac, a drink which, in the circumstances, might seem to lack something as a refresher.

Then he began to talk.

Taufig Bey Maufarigge, an Americanized Egyptian with some sort of job in the government, was present at that first meeting with Captain Eddy. At the table also were a Cairene doctor named Achmet and a local poet whose English works consisted mostly of sonnets in praise of Herbert Hoover. These people took little part in the conversation either then or later. They sat popeyed and in silence at the unfolding of a tale the like of which had probably not been heard in the Near East since Scheherezade was a girl.

"I am a journalist," said Captain Eddy. "I was military adviser to the late Dowager Empress of China. I am a graduate physician. My father was once Mayor of San Francisco. I have a news bureau in Peking [or maybe it was Shanghai]. I cable reports of news affecting industry and commerce to the great corporations of the United States. . . ."

"And what are you doing here?" somebody wanted to know.

"I am here," he explained a little petulantly, "because the British stole my passport. I can't go any farther until I get another one." He went into some detail about that. He had been robbed on shipboard somewhere between Aden and the canal. His loose change and his letter of credit had been left to him together with other personal articles of great value. But in the final inventory the passport was gone. He was keen enough to guess at once who had taken it and why. It was the nefarious British, of course. They wanted to delay him, to prevent his accomplishment of an important mission.

"I am a press delegate to the League of Nations," he said, as if that clarified everything. "I have things to tell the League about commercial conspiracies in the Far East."

"You're a little late," commented Mr. Maufarigge, joining the discussion for the first—and only—time. "The League of Nations adjourned last week."

"We would have had reason for a special session if I had been allowed to go on to Geneva," said Captain Eddy unperturbed. "As it is I am temporarily defeated. I know many things that the British would like to remain secret. I have many connections in the Far East. I shall tell you something about myself."

And he did. Some of the things he told about himself were really difficult to believe.

"I have had an adventurous life," he said. "I have done a lot of good in the world and it has been very profitable. When I got my degree in medicine many years ago, an old aunt of mine who lived in the Germantown section of Philadelphia said she would set me up in business if I came to live with her and forgot my notions about traveling. But I figured that people got just as sick in China as in Philadelphia and I might as well see something of the world. So I went to Manchuria and opened an office in Harbin. . . ."

Captain Eddy did very well in Harbin. He made a specialty of visitors who contrived to get sick in the hotels, which, if the usual run of hotels in Harbin is any criterion, should not have been at all difficult for the visitors. The captain was always strictly professional about it. He never solicited any business personally. But he overcame the handicap of such ethical conduct by hiring runners who went about meeting people and recommending his services.

Even in those years when the Dowager Empress ruled in China and the World War was still far in the future, there was an undercurrent of trouble across the border in Russia. Bright-eyed young zealots were continually scrambling into Harbin to escape the rifles of the Czar's Siberian troops. Little revolutions were being incubated in every alley. World-shaking philosophies were being preached in every café. The better to acquaint himself with what was going on about him, the young doctor learned to speak Russian. He also learned other languages, though his gift of tongues did not keep him in later years from tingeing his English with a hint of German.

"One of my best runners," he said, "was a Russian. He was a gruff, serious-minded fellow. He was always telling me about the dawn of a new day in his country when the *mujiks* would be free. I didn't care much about that. I thought he might earn bigger commissions for himself if he paid more attention to his work. But I didn't have much complaint. He got to know everybody and, fortunately, a lot of his friends were in bad health. Our association paid us both very well.

"I had no way of knowing at the time that this young man would be any different from the other revolutionaries I was meeting every day. When, after two or three years of association, we said good-by and he went back into Siberia, I actually shed tears for him. I tried to persuade him to stay in Harbin with me and get rich. I thought surely the Czar's spies would be waiting to kill him. Not until years later did I learn how silly my fears had been. . . . The man's right name was Stalin."

Captain Eddy achieved a fine dramatic effect with that reve-lation. Taufig Bey Maufarigge hastily ordered another drink. The Egyptian laureate of the Hoover administration opened and shut his mouth without finding words. Old acquaintances of Stalin came seldom to Cairo and when they did they were hardly ever little men with American flags in their buttonholes.

[18]

Without further effort Captain Eddy would have been assured of a prominent place in local gossip for weeks to come.

Stalin, as it turned out, wasn't the only important personage he had met while piling up his fortune as a medical practitioner in Harbin. Another lad had come wandering far afield because of doctrines that his conservative countrymen did not appreciate. He too found employment with Dr. Eddy as a runner, and like Stalin he had got the knack of the job almost at once. The doctor had to learn another language in order to converse with him, but such things come easy when one is young and ambitious. The new man was brilliant, well informed, determined. He became more than an employee with an eye for cases of ptomaine poisoning and indigestion. Friendship grew out of that association, a friendship that continued on down through the years.

The runner eventually went away as Stalin had gone to do deeds of high emprise and change the course of a nation. But he never forgot his benefactor in Harbin, you may be sure of that. He was an Italian, the captain recalled. And good showmanship would have ended the discussion right there. Nobody needed to be told the name of this pill salesman. He couldn't have been anybody else but Mussolini.

"That," said the captain, "was what gave me the idea for my news service. I have two friends at the top in the two countries from which it is most difficult to get accurate commercial reports. In addition to that I have numerous connections in China as a result of the years I spent as military adviser to the old empress. I am in a position to tell the heads of great corporations what they want to know about three of the world's greatest markets. Also I am in a position to find out things that

[19]

might be embarrassing to the British. That is why they interfere with me."

He rose suddenly after that and went away with a promise to return again some other day and tell more about his career. His audience sat for a long time in silence after he had disappeared behind the potted palms in the lobby. His contribution to the day's small talk somehow had made ordinary conversation seem like a waste of time.

That was not the end of Captain Eddy. He turned up day in and day out and in the oddest corners of Cairo—in the office of the U.S. consul arguing about his lost passport, in the hotel lobby whispering into the ears of odd-looking Europeans whose amazed expressions showed that his talent for narration was still pretty good, in the bazaars, in the banks, in the steamship offices. Never did one see any signs of a British spy at his heels but that may have indicated only that the spies were unusually good at their job. Always he seemed pleased with himself and disdainful of everybody else. Always, no matter how hot the day, he was in his customary hurry.

One morning he paused on the terrace to display a Chinese umbrella. It was one of those things with which the tourist shops are littered from Port Said to Yokohama, a green, sticky affair on bamboo ribs with decorations in the technique of a sign painter and a vigorous smell of fish glue.

"A present for you," he said, "from one journalist to another. It is very valuable. It was painted by a Chinese princess who is a special friend of mine. I want you to have it because you will appreciate it."

In such little meetings as that, cheery high spots in hot, monotonous days, he revealed other things about himself. . . .

[20]

He had made a fortune as a physician, invested his money wisely, and, by strict frugality and close attention to his work as military adviser to the empress had come to be a man of fabulous wealth.

Late in life, one gathered that it was shortly after the finish of the First World War, he had fallen in love. It was not entirely a new experience. Soon after his coming to Harbin he had married. But his wife had gone into a decline, probably accompanied by vapors, and had left him to carry on his great work alone. After that her beautiful memory had stood between him and all other women until the fateful day when he met a girl in Paris. . . .

The story of his romance was delivered piecemeal because it involved his daughter whom he had previously neglected to mention. The daughter, he explained, had been cared for by relatives in the United States since the death of his wife and had married a high official in the Standard Oil Company of New Jersey. He thought it only fair to let her know that he was about to provide her with a stepmother. So he did. He was heartbroken when she failed to send him so much as a picture post card in reply.

"I really loved that little girl in Paris," he said dreamily as he raised his blood pressure fifteen or twenty points with a double order of brandy. "I really did. I bought her jewels and furs and an automobile and she said she thought we would be very happy together. She wanted a marriage settlement but I didn't think much about that. I was a rich man and that was the French way of doing things. . . ."

Then had come a denouement that might have had a tragic effect on his life save that he had always been essentially a realist. Without any word to him his daughter had come to Paris. She had followed him from his hotel to a café and there had got a close look at his fiancée. She had followed the fiancée and had seen her meet another man. She had trailed them to a hotel. . . . It was a sordid story that she had come at length to lay before the infatuated captain but her proofs had been good.

"My whole life seemed ruined," he admitted. "But what was I to do? I could see how I had been tricked. Almost I had thrown away the wealth that I had intended someday to leave to my daughter.

" 'There's no fool like an old fool,' I told her. 'But I'll not put your rights in danger again.' So we went to a bank that afternoon and I turned over all my property to her . . . that is everything but my news agency. I went back to China a poor man."

That, of course, might have been the end of the story had Captain Eddy been like any other man. But Captain Eddy was different. Back in Germantown was the old aunt who had urged him to practice medicine in Philadelphia. None of the family, save Captain Eddy, had ever paid much attention to the old aunt. None had suspected her of owning anything more than enough for her simple daily needs. But just about the time the captain got back to Shanghai or Shangri-La she died and left him a million dollars in bonds. . . . So everything turned out all right.

So it went during the captain's stay in Cairo—every day a new surprise—every day an increasing fear that the psychiatrists might get to him ahead of the threatening British. The heat did not seem to bother him, nor the cognac; and, whatever the mysterious business that kept him scurrying about odd corners of the town, nothing interfered with the charm and quality and convincing detail of his reminiscences.

Yet, as so frequently happens in the case of people one meets aboard ships or over bottles, Captain Eddy and his sprightly stories might well have drifted into the file of the things one hopes to remember but seldom does. Even in a few fleeting days he had come to be more boresome than entertaining. It was becoming more difficult to laugh behind his back, more easy to feel a bit sorry for him. After all he was such a little man in such a strange and inhospitable country.

There came another day when he talked of his daughter and of his abiding love for her. Taufig Bey Maufarigge who was at the table with me when he came hurrying from the blazing street to the terrace was in no mood for this recital—nor was anybody else. As usual we listened.

"For years," the captain said when he got around to it, "I have been collecting pearls for a lavaliere for my daughter. I have traded here and there, always trying to get better ones. Now I have three that are as beautiful as anything in the world. They cost me a fortune but I don't care. Few people have ever seen anything like them."

Maufarigge sniffed.

"And where do you keep them . . . in your pocket?"

Captain Eddy did not seem to notice the Egyptian's impoliteness.

"They are in a vault at the bank down the street," he said. "The British didn't get them when they took my passport."

"All right," said Maufarigge, "let's see the pearls. Go and get them. That oughtn't to be much trouble."

The situation was unpleasant and promising to get worse. But Captain Eddy saved it.

"All right," he said, rising from his chair. "I'll get them. I'll be back in fifteen minutes. Order another double brandy for me."

He went out into the street and Maufarigge, too, pushed back his chair.

"Excuse me," he said, "but I've got an idea. I don't know anything about pearls but I know a man who does. He imports the things. I'll bring him here. . . ."

The jeweler, a hawk-faced Egyptian, was at the table when Captain Eddy came back. He was obviously annoyed at being dragged out of his shop and just as obviously convinced that he was wasting his time. He sipped ice water and drummed on the table with lean fingers.

The captain hardly noticed him as he sat down. He took a considerable gulp of brandy, then extracted a wad of tissue paper from his vest pocket. He unrolled it carefully and spread on the table three pear-shaped pearls as big as marbles, the loveliest things that anybody at the table had ever seen. The jeweler picked them up reverently, studied them one at a time against the light and set them down again. He looked at Captain Eddy and his straw hat and his rumpled tweeds in deep amazement.

"If you would sell them," he said in slow, careful English, "I shall give you fifty thousand pounds for them. . . . They are worth more but that is all I can afford."

The captain wrapped them once more in the wad of tissue

paper, put them back in his vest pocket and went away in silence.

That, so far as this chronicler is concerned, ends the saga of Captain Eddy. For days afterward he was about the hotel still whispering to people behind the potted palms, still wearing his straw hat and tweeds, still dashing in great haste out into the sun. But somehow he had changed. He was a man who told strange stories but he was also a man who carried a fortune in pearls in his vest pocket.

2

"WHENCE COME THESE STRANGE
PEOPLE?"

~~~~~~

IT PROBABLY serves no good purpose to bring up the story of Captain Eddy except that it may illustrate why people stay in —if not why they get into—the newspaper business. You meet such interesting people.

Journalistic memoirs of the past decade (one excepts, of course, those of the war hawks) are not very illuminating in this regard. The special correspondents, the foreign correspondents, the loftier minds of the press normally live, if one may judge from their sprightly reminiscence, in a rarefied atmosphere inhabited by kings and queens and noble statesmen and commoners above the rank of major general. Their ordinary tasks are fraught with intrigue and danger. Their ears are molded to fit the keyholes of the chancelleries. Their eyes are focused on the various equivalents of Darlan's grave. Their social routine is circumscribed by affairs of world import. And, all in all, one suspects that they must have a pretty dull time. They never see the Captain Eddys who wander about the earth with pearls in their pockets, or at least they never remember when it comes time to write an autobiography.

"THESE STRANGE PEOPLE"

The picture of the so-called Fourth Estate as a conclave of earnest men in frock coats whispering good advice to prime ministers is, perhaps, just as true as the cinema theory of the business, but, alas, no truer. Despite the growing popular belief it is not given to many reporters to enjoy the confidences of the great and meddle with international affairs. One or two—notably Junius B. Wood, of whom more later—have displayed remarkable talents in this direction. But the majority meet more policemen than grand dukes. (You will shed no tears for them if you know anything about grand dukes.) Their world is the world of folks in trouble—a world inhabited for the most part by people of only ephemeral importance. Their days are spent interviewing odd characters and their nights in forgetting about them. They work without animus or personal concern and, in time, see nothing unusual in their clinical material. They are not at all disturbed by the quirks and idiosyncracies of the human phantasmagoria with which they are kept in unending contact, nor should they be, for, of all the strangely contrived persons in the world, any number of puzzled critics will admit that they, themselves, are the strangest.

It is part of the fable of this queer trade that one starts into it with a great singleness of purpose. Urging him on are the spirits of countless crusaders who righted the wrongs of mankind with flaming words. Ahead of him are the paths of sacrifice that he will pursue heroically until he has accomplished his great mission and sits down in Omsk or Nagasaki to compile his personal record. . . . Well, maybe. . . .

The sawmill in which I went to work when I found out that there were reasons why I could never be a chemical engineer was about as far from a city desk as the most inveterate visionary could imagine. But it turned out to be the reason why at least one person got into the newspaper business.

There is plenty of action in a sawmill with wheels constantly turning, danger always at one's elbow. Unless one is deaf he cannot but thrill to the unearthly noises, the clank of the bull chain, the snarl of the big bandsaw, the crash of the "nigger," the grumble of the "hog." There was plenty of drama—as for instance when Challo John was pushed through the side of a box car by a plank hot off the planer, or when a millwright removed Dick Bruce's hand from the gears of the edger with a cold chisel. Probably there is romance in a sawmill, too. As to that I couldn't say.

This mill was in Rapid City, South Dakota, at the gateway to the Black Hills. In those days that was where old sawmills went when they died. This one had completed a long and useful life somewhere in Wisconsin and in its resurrection had developed miseries and frailties that made its operation a constant adventure. Its bandsaw came apart periodically and tore things up. The slasher had a habit of biting off more than it could chew and whenever it did everything stopped for hours. Every union in the steam lines leaked and on cold days—which were pretty frequent—it snowed inside the mill. But there was one thing about it that wasn't secondhand: the accounting system. We had a fine collection of bright new journals and ledgers and cash books and such—enough books to run a courthouse. And I was the bookkeeper.

As I remember it I became a bookkeeper through no heroic or romantic impulse. I hadn't wanted to be a bookkeeper any more than I had wanted to work in a sawmill. I didn't know anything about bookkeeping. But even in the few months that had intervened between my college diploma and the first snow I had learned a great deal about economic necessity. I have since come to the belief that economic necessity plus opportunity may explain why most men are what they are and not something else.

Bookkeeping, many of my friends tell me, is not such a bad profession. Perhaps my puzzlement over the essential differences between a ledger and a journal may have kept me from a thorough appreciation of its more interesting features. But I am forced to admit that I found it lacking in variety save for the totals which never came out the same way twice.

It was bitter cold that year, eighteen and twenty below most of the time, and I lived a mile and a half from the mill. The walk was bad enough in the wintry twilight when enough folks were abroad in the town to lend first aid if you slipped and broke your leg. At ten or eleven at night (which was the time you usually arrived at a balance if you arrived at all) it was an expedition. I began to hate bookkeeping with considerable intensity.

Emancipation was always sufficiently close at hand to keep me bent over my books. That may not meet the approval of current business philosophers but it was true in my case as I have found it to be in many others. The reason I didn't quit my job was because I had hope of getting out of it. There was one lad—his counterpart is in a thousand sawmills—who wanted me to go with him to a gold mine in a warm climate. There was another who said he could get me a berth with a seal-poaching expedition presently to start from San Francisco. In the end, however, I managed to achieve liberty without any outside help.

One night, when everything seemed to be working out beautifully, I found that I had one cent in the cash drawer more than I had on the books. Other, better, bookkeepers no doubt have had similar experiences. I am informed that in such cases it is customary to tinker with the books until they come out even with the cash. But I had had enough of tinkering with books. I struck a balance by the simple trick of throwing the penny into the coal scuttle. After that I went home. I didn't know it until a week later when the auditors got through their work but I was even then on my way into the newspaper business. The mill superintendent when he heard my intentions turned out to be something of a prophet. He said I had the right temperament for it.

Perhaps the oddest thing about the newspaper business is the homogeneity of its personnel. Towns differ and editorial policies and circulations. Nobody would expect the Podunk *Daily Enterprise* to resemble, say, the New York *Times*. But it is a fact that the men in one local room are the men in another save for variants in names and geography. Why it should be so I cannot say unless it is because humanity itself is the same wherever found and folks who deal constantly with humanity draw into themselves and develop their own protective coloring. Whatever the reason, reporters are definitely marked by their trade as policemen, soldiers, clergymen and actors are marked by theirs.

Not so many years ago a Little Theater group in Sydney, Australia, produced *The Front Page* by Ben Hecht and Charles MacArthur. A visitor from up yonder could not have imagined a worse play for an Australian audience. *The Front Page* was less of a drama than a stenographic report of routine doings in the Chicago Criminal courts press room. If ever characters should have been indigenous to a given locality such were the people who marched through this highly realistic opus. Not even the names of the original dramatis personae had been changed. None of their interesting habits had been overlooked. And one might have excused the suspicion that Sydney would get little out of the exhibit save the rough idea that American journalism is a prize product of bedlam.

However, the show was what the local critics called a "wow," the Little Theater's greatest success to date.

"Just like our own press room," observed one commentator, and that seemed to explain everything.

Then there was a day in Paris. . . . The boat train was about to leave for Cherbourg. Some three hundred and fifty passengers for the *Majestic* were milling about the station platform bidding good-by to about two hundred friends. Through the mob elbowed a slim young man with an envelope in his hand—a Parisian obviously, and just as obviously a Parisian who had had much contact with Americans.

"I beg your pardon," he said, "but aren't you a newspaperman?"

I admitted that I was.

"Then," he said, "will you please deliver these photographs to the International News man at quarantine?" I took the envelope, scribbled my cabin number on a card and advised him to cable New York where the International News messenger could find me. He thanked me and was starting away when I caught his arm.

[31]

"Wait a minute," I said. "How did you know that I'm a reporter?"

He shook his head.

"I don't know," he said. "I just thought you might be."

Evvie Fort, wife of William Fort, our New York correspondent, gave one simple solution to this puzzle when I got to port.

"It's your hat," she said. "All newspaper men wear the same hat." But perhaps her husband came closer to the true inwardness of the situation.

"All reporters are screwballs," he said. "Any screwball ought to be able to recognize another one." Whether or not there is anything to this philosophy it makes a good working hypothesis for a book.

The city editor of the Des Moines *Register and Leader* must have been too tired for argument when I came in to see him after my career in the sawmill. There could have been no other reason for his hiring me.

"What makes you think you could be a reporter?" he inquired.

"Because," I told him frankly, "I don't know anything about keeping books."

"Were you the editor-in-chief of your college daily?" he wanted to know.

I told him the truth about that, too. "Our college didn't have any daily."

He was pleased and said so. "That's a break. Everybody who's been in here in the past two months has been editor-in-chief of his college daily. Do you feel that a job as a reporter is what you want most in the world?"

"I want to be a chemical engineer," I said. "But I've only got one lung."

"One lung's enough," he commiserated. "And besides if you haven't patience enough to keep books you wouldn't do much with chemistry."

"I didn't say anything about patience," I reminded him.

"You don't have to," he said. "You haven't got any. You'll probably be a rotten reporter but I'll put you on. Next Saturday you'll get $18 for the week or you'll be fired."

In retrospect, this meeting doesn't seem to have followed any of the rules of the textbooks on journalism and, for that matter, it was never paralleled in my own subsequent experience. Probably nobody ever got a job just that way before or will again. And yet there are numerous incidents to illustrate that anything can happen in the newspaper business and usually does. A. R. Decker, a thoroughly competent correspondent, was a steel engineer until World War I caught up with him somewhere east of Verdun. Jim Mulroy, who won a Pulitzer Prize for building up the case against Loeb and Leopold, came to the Chicago *Daily News* straight from a steam laundry. One talented youth rose to considerable importance in the United Press office to which he had delivered milk for several years. I think of these things when hopeful boys and girls come asking advice on how to break into what has become a highly competitive trade and I tell them frankly that I don't know the answer.

Save for a case of amoebic dysentery life on the *Register and Leader* doesn't seem much different in retrospect from that on any other newspaper. The hours were long but nobody had to do much work. The criticism of the desk was biting but undoubtedly deserved. The pay wasn't much but it was better than it had been in the sawmill. The paper was prosperous, influential and well edited as, indeed, it has been ever since. The plant, as I came to know afterward, was like any other plant. And if the local staff seemed to me something like a collection of Homers and Richard Harding Davises that was possibly because I hadn't had much chance to find out anything about reporters.

Bob Wright, the city editor who had hired me for reasons that he never made clear, had serious, even forbidding manners but innate patience and a great gentleness. He may have felt like firing me many times but he never got around to it. He never made any pretense of running a school of journalism but he had a few simple rules, easily mastered, such as: Write on only one side of the paper. Tell something of what the story's about in the first paragraph. Try to get the names right —some people are sensitive about such things. Don't leave the office to go chasing after fire engines unless you are sent.

From Rolly Bales, his assistant, I learned some other interesting things. One day came a police report about a burglary in a minister's home. The burglars hadn't found much except a silk dress belonging to the minister's wife. I wrote perhaps twenty-five words about it, which represented my considered news judgment at that time. Mr. Bales was kind in his comment.

"We ought to have more on this," he said. "Novelty is what makes news and this is novelty. A minister's wife very seldom has a silk dress, a newspaperman's wife never."

It was from Parker Lowell, a reporter whose experience was little broader than my own, that I got my most valuable instruction although he didn't know he was giving it to me at the time. He taught me by demonstration how to a write a feature story and, what was even more important, that a fake is good only if you can protect it.

Summer came while I was still in Des Moines and, like all Des Moines summers, it was a hot one. The town was full of dogs and the dogs, displeased with the weather, began to go about biting people. The overworked dog-catcher was loud in his complaint.

To meet this emergency the city commissioners decided to make every citizen his own dog-catcher. It was announced that a dime a head would be paid for dogs escorted to the police station and, despite the modesty of the bounty, the plan worked. Half the cells in the police station were speedily filled with dogs which yelped all night and drove the night captain into nervous prostration.

At this period there was little or no crime in Des Moines but there was one character who kept the cops from stagnating. He was entered regularly on the blotter as "Freddy, the Village Drunk," a sobriquet that he had devised for himself. Nobody knew his last name.

Freddy took one of his periodic rides in the patrol wagon during the dog mobilization and alone of all the station inmates he found nothing bothersome in the noise. On Monday he was arraigned, fined and released as usual, and the story of his sojourn might have seemed a matter of no importance to any artist less gifted than Mr. Lowell.

"There's a fine human interest bit in this," he observed to Mr. Hal O'Flaherty of the *Capital*. "On account of the public hysteria about dogs."

"There aren't any dogs in the life of Freddy," responded Mr. O'Flaherty. "He wouldn't bite a dog and a dog wouldn't bite him. They're both too fastidious."

"I shall put the dogs into his life," explained Mr. Lowell. "I have a theory that little fictions like that are defensible in a story if they serve to emphasize the basic truth. And I shall prove it." So he sat down and typed a story that went something like this:

> For three days, without food, water or outward signs of cheer, Hector, a long-haired, misshapen pooch owned by "Freddy, the Village Drunk," sat on the steps of the city police station waiting for the release of his master. Freddy, a well-known character about town, was in a cell on a charge of intoxication. Hector refused alike the relief offers of the kind policemen and overtures of friendliness from reporters and was obviously in a weakened condition when Freddy was released with a warning by Judge Whosis today.
>
> Freddy did not notice the little dog as he came down the steps until Captain George Jackson directed his attention.
>
> "Isn't that your dog?" inquired the captain.
>
> "So it is," said Freddy. "You take him and give me my dime. I need it to buy a drink."

Mr. Lowell brought this masterpiece to the office and laid it before Mr. Bob Wright with the self-conscious smile of an artisan who knows that he has done well. Mr. Wright's immediate explosion was something that is still a legend about the local room of the Cowles press.

"I'll not print such a story!" he roared. "What is the world coming to when they let a buzzard like this live? You go get me that dog, do you hear? You get me that dog! Here's a dime. You go get him."

So the discomfited Mr. Lowell went out to pass a hot afternoon in a town virtually denuded of dogs trying to find a "long-haired, misshapen pooch" of suitable dimensions at an outside price of ten cents. That he eventually found one and saved his job is proof of his native resourcefulness and also of the fact that he had five dollars of his own money to add to Bob Wright's dime.

It may be a matter of passing interest that the editorial departments of Des Moines howled, as loudly and continuously as other editorial departments elsewhere seem to have been doing ever since, for more space in which to print the essays of the local staff. Then, as since, the front office would reply with a stock joke dating back to Guttenberg: "There are only seven columns to the page, you know. [There were at that time.] And you can't stretch paper."

There seemed to be no answer and so far as we were concerned there probably wasn't. The stories worth telling ran too long and the stories that you condensed never got into the paper. Yet, over in the shop of the Des Moines *Capital* the boys made some beginning toward a solution. Their effort was not so much a matter of paper stretching as a demonstration that large forests are being despoiled every day to make paper to carry messages that nobody wants to read.

Every Sunday the *Capital* carried a full page of religious notices, paragraphs outlining the Sabbath services for every church in town, and there were many churches. This department was the pet of Colonel Lafe Young, the publisher, who made it the personal responsibility of John Ball, the managing

[37]

editor. Mr. Ball, in turn, transferred the editing and make-up of the page to a competent secretary and everybody was satisfied.

Mr. Ball had long been skeptical about the reader-interest of the material but he argued in vain with Colonel Young when he suggested that it be cut. He pointed out that any church news of importance was covered by staff men and handled in the regular news columns and that the weekly programs were largely repetitious. But the colonel didn't care anything about that.

Then, one Friday—make-up day for the church directory—the secretary was sick. An office boy with a long record for intelligent service took over the job and finished it quickly and without complaint. Mr. Ball, working day and night on a political campaign in which the *Capital* was interested, was not bothered with copy or proofs and saw nothing of the page until Sunday morning. The presses had stopped and the edition was on the street. He had read the news columns and was ready to go home when he chanced to glance at the church directory.

It looked just about as usual, the same symmetrical array of little paragraphs. But there was a difference. . . .

"First Baptist Church," he read. "Rev. J. M. Pollard is in fine form today and will preach a snappy sermon on Hell."

"Christian Church. . . . Rev. George J. Hadley will lead the choir in singing 'Everybody's Doin' It.' Irene McDowell, Soloist, will yodel assisted by the eight bounding Bensons. Come and bring your lunch."

The page was all like that. Every paragraph had been tinged by the office boy's imagination. And there was nothing anybody could do about it . . . nothing but sit down and wait for the lightning to strike.

But there wasn't any lightning. The office boy stayed home on Monday. In fact he stayed home for a couple of weeks. But that seemed to be the only result of the new style in religious announcements. No irate church-goer raised his voice. No outraged pastor demanded retraction. It appeared that the page was one of those things that everybody thinks are read by everybody else.

On Thursday Mr. Ball laid his report on the matter before Colonel Young who hadn't known that anything was amiss. The directory page was missing from the next Sunday edition for the first time in decades, and the city editor got seven more columns of space. Nobody in Des Moines knew the difference.

3

FANTASY AMONG THE MAGNOLIAS

NUMEROUS other things happened during those months in Des Moines: I became so engrossed in a four-alarm fire at Highland Park College that I forgot to report it. A workman tumbled into a concrete form on the new Sixth Avenue bridge where he probably remains to this day, an unseen caryatid. An elephant belonging to a local circus committed suicide in a lake. In order of importance, I got hit on the head with a brick in a streetcar strike; I was fired; I was rehired; somebody found out that I could keep a box score; I was made sports editor; the Des Moines baseball team finished last in the Western League.

Sports reporting promised well but was not an unqualified joy. The budget provided for only one sports editor for the morning *Register and Leader* and the afternoon *Tribune* and in consequence days that had been long before got longer. Save for baseball, if the local club's performance could be called that, there wasn't much going on in the way of athletic effort during the summer. Nobody thought there was any news in golf and only men with time on their hands could get out to the golf clubs anyway. Tennis was generally classed as a symptom of mental deficiency. Power-boating on the Des Moines River was suspended because there wasn't enough water to lay the dust. Prizefighting was illegal and nobody appears to have thought of calling it boxing. It was difficult to get much suspense into a story about a game of Kelly pool. Frank Gotch, Iowa's own wrestling champion, had already been interviewed on every possible subject from crop prospects to the state of the Republican Party. When, to complicate such a situation, amoebic dysentery came to occupy my time, all the evidence seemed to indicate the need for a change.

In those days, and for that matter until not so many years ago, newspapermen were a migratory lot. They were also carefree, undisciplined and independent. If you didn't like your job, if you objected to the policy of the paper or the climate or the slant of the city editor's ears, well what of it? You could always get another job in St. Louis, in Kansas City, in Akron, in Denver, in Scranton. Maybe you'd get more pay—you weren't likely to get much less. You'd have all the broadening experience of travel. And eventually you'd land in New York.

Just why New York was so persistently glamorous is another of those mysteries. Loyalty to one's current grocery supply and a certain protective coloring of pride prevented any reporter in the hinterlands from admitting that he might be able to learn something about the newspaper business in New York. Nobody in Des Moines, for example, would have dared to suggest that a New York newspaper might be better written or better edited than the *Register and Leader*. Nevertheless the eyes of all of these nervous journalists were constantly turned toward the East. Among the advantages and disadvantages of each prospective new job was calculated its distance from the Hudson River.

Some of the boys actually got to Manhattan Island but not any considerable percentage. Most of them died trying or compromised with the demands of weariness and old age on a copy desk in the sticks. But spare the tears, there are probably enough reporters in New York, anyway.

Not all of the Des Moines crew had ambition to join the eastward trek—at least not immediately. In the first place the competition was certain to get stiffer the nearer one came to the Atlantic coast. In the second place the train fare was high and no reporter ever had any money. Bankruptcy, then as now, was something of an occupational disease.

It was Chester Cogswell who first put the yearning for green fields and pastures new on a practical basis.

"All towns are the same," he contended, "and all city editors were sprouted in the same greenhouse. There's no use trying to better yourself by jumping around. But maybe if a guy traveled south he could save the price of a new overcoat."

I went south in a light-weight rubber raincoat and very nearly froze to death during the two years of my effort to find out whether or not he was right. Long before I grew tired of looking at the dizzy baseball team across the top of a paregoric bottle I had been in correspondence with one Harry Warner, managing editor of the Houston (Texas) *Post*. As the summer faded he must have begun to believe my direct-by-mail advertising, for he telegraphed the offer of a job. It arrived, fortunately, the day after I had printed a half-page portrait of Bombardier Wells, probably the world's worst heavyweight, in the Sunday sport section for want of anything better to fill the space.

It's funny how quickly a confident young man can graduate from the kindergarten class in the newspaper business. When I came to the Houston *Post* I was no longer a cub: I had had three or four months' experience. I didn't have to be told to write on one side of the paper or to refrain from chasing fire engines unless assigned. I knew enough to get the names and initials of people into the stories I wrote about them. And, so far as I could see, a managing editor didn't have to know much more. With the amazing gall of youth I would have taken on any job from dramatic criticism to the cotton market—and frequently did with results that pleased me if nobody else. When in the course of years I accumulated a bit of modesty it was a comfort to find out that this brashness had not been peculiar to me. Any young reporter knows that he can do anything. The pity of it is that so much of his life is spent in demonstrating that he can't.

Harry Warner turned out to be a shrewd operator with a wide experience in many cities, including Chicago and New York. His news judgment was unfailing, his insight into human nature uncanny. But he had one blind spot. He thought I ought to be a good copyreader.

A copyreader, as everybody who goes to the movies already knows, is a man in an eyeshade who edits, corrects, or destroys the gems of thought turned out by reporters and writes the headlines. The *Post* already had one very good copyreader whose heads had made him famous all over Texas and in parts of Louisiana. When Jack Binns was making history at the wireless key of the foundering *Republic* this lad informed the palpitant public of Houston:

SINKING SHIP SENDS OUT
S.R.O. CALL FOR HELP

And again, when a picturesque con man departed this life in New York, he wrote:

WEEPING TOMMY DEAD. MADE
FORTUNE WITH LACTEAL GLANDS

He was a pompous young man who cherished a vague and distant attachment for Lillian Russell. He was related, so he said, to a Confederate general who had escaped reconstruction by taking service as military aid to the Khedive of Egypt. He referred to President Wilson by his first name with the modest explanation that such familiarities are excusable in old friendships. Colonel House, the President's Warwick, was, one inferred, his boon companion. He let it be known that his social duties were many and onerous and some nights he came to work in white tie and tails, a regalia which he embellished with a thirty-eight revolver for use "in case of emergency." All in all he was a bright and interesting person to have at one's side during the long, hot hours from 1:00 P.M. till the presses started at two in the morning.

The telegraph room on the *Post* was about the size of a two-dollar hotel bedroom and was occupied by four operators, three copyreaders and the cotton editor. On a cool night the temperature fell off to something approximating that of the Black Hole of Calcutta.

The Associated Press report was typed on flimsy (tissue

[44]

paper) that blew out the window when the fans were turned on and mushed to a pulp under one's sweating hands when they were turned off. The "state" copy, received by mail from distant cowtowns in Texas, was written in a confusion of tongues, generally illegible and completely puzzling before or after editing. The local news grist came on sheets about two feet long, one sheet for a weather report, two or three sheets for an obituary . . . for the *Post* was printed in agate type and it takes a lot of words to fill a column of agate. There was quite a lot of this stuff, all of which seemed important at the time. And it was augmented in season by a leased-wire report from the state capitol at Austin. All in all there was generally plenty of copy to be edited and headed for a paper that it seemed impossible to fill. The work was interesting in its fashion but hard.

It was the boast of Harry Warner that he had never fired anybody during the long years he had spent as managing editor of the *Post*. However, he recalled, quite a lot of reporters had resigned by getting drunk on the job. Resignation in such cases, it seems, was automatic. He was reasonably undisturbed by the other ills that beset local rooms but that did not prevent his being an expert and loudly vocal critic when occasion demanded.

One evening I rewrote a bit of state news in which our correspondent had described a "large and destitoox family." I said somewhere in the head that it was a "poor" family and there was a prompt howl from the folks who had received the publicity and an immediate inquiry by Mr. Warner.

"What makes you think this fine, upstanding West Texas family is impoverished?" he wanted to know, waving my copy and the handwritten scrawl on which I had based my small rewrite.

"The correspondent said they were large and destitute," I said.

"He didn't say any such thing," said Mr. Warner. "He said they were large and destitoox, whatever that means. Lesson Number 1 in your job is: Never guess what a grapevine correspondent is thinking about when he writes words like destitoox."

The incident seemed a little silly at the time but that was because no cub could be expected to know much about the Texas libel laws. Warner knew about them. His profound knowledge of precedents and his uncanny foreknowledge of what jurors would do with them helped to keep him in the front rank of Texas editors. Libel suits were expensive to defend in those days and almost impossible to settle.

Only a short time before the episode of the destitoox family a Galveston publisher had learned how simple (and costly) it is to blacken the character of a good citizen. One bright young reporter had gone out to interview a local barmaid on some subject the nature of which is forgotten. In his story he had mentioned, just by way of decoration, that she was wearing red stockings. She sued for, and collected, ten thousand dollars. The outraged jury agreed with her that the mention of her stockings carried with it the suggestion that she had been immodest enough to show the reporter her legs or at least her ankles and this, of course, was to be construed only as a deliberate imputation against her chastity.

There was a case in Houston where a couple of partners in a garage business quarreled and one murdered the other. The

[46]

killer called the police, surrendered his revolver and confessed the crime. The *Post's* report was typical:

"John Doe was found shot to death last night in the Acme garage in Fannin Street. Robert Roe, his partner, was later arrested by city police." Robert Roe's confession didn't count, because, in the current interpretation of the libel law, it would cease to exist if at any time before he should be tried and found guilty he should choose to repudiate it.

There are libel laws everywhere to help the proletariat enjoy the benefits of the free press. All of the big dailies keep a stable of lawyers the year round to explain why the wrong people get mentioned in scandals and why the wrong pictures get involved with mixed-up cut lines. Some of these experts earn their fees as, for instance, in the case of the Fort Smith (Arkansas) newspaper that went to press hurriedly on the day that the mayor's wife died and the old ice house burned. The lady's portrait was two columns wide on the first page and over it was a startling tribute: "Old Eyesore Gone At Last.". . . Normally, however, the lawyers don't have to spend much of their time in court. Eastern rewrite men seem to have learned that while the misspelling of names may be a cardinal sin in journalism it makes a fine "out" in a suit. And there are enough ex-Texans scattered across the country to provide other subterfuges for virtually any emergency.

Summer had come and the bugbear of the libel situation was no longer much of a worry on the day when the staff photographer resigned automatically in the customary fashion. The managing editor came stalking into the city room with a camera in his hand.

"Do any of you so-and-sos know how to run a camera?" he inquired. The silence was unanimous.

"Well," I volunteered when the lull became a little embarrassing. "I remember enough chemistry to make the silver emulsions they put on the plates."

He looked at me sadly over his glasses.

"I guess that'll have to do," he said. "It's a hundred percent more than the rest of these mugs know. You're the new photographer." And he handed me the camera.

It was an old Hall Mirror reflex with one of those hoods on the top arranged so that the operator can keep his face covered up and get hit by flying brickbats and run down by policemen's horses when he isn't looking. It had a Cooke lens, so shallow that when you got a man's nose into focus his ears were out. The reflector had been broken and replaced by a piece of plate-glass mirror. When you pressed the button the mirror was supposed to swing up out of the way of the lens and it did. The only trouble was that its weight supplied an inertia that tended to swing the lens downward which made for all sorts of novel pictures.

I don't remember much about my career as a photographer. It is best to forget unpleasant things and one acquires the knack rapidly.

One or two incidents, however, have remained vivid throughout the years. . . . There was the time the shutter hung up at the Galveston beach races and I took a lot of interesting shots of rocketing automobiles with a two-dollar box camera. The subjects were a bit blurred but nobody said anything about it. And there was the even more unforgettable occasion when I photographed the new president of the Southern Pacific Railroad.

This gentleman, Scott, I think his name was, had arrived in town on a schedule that did not permit much time for picture-taking. He was affable but hurried, and I got one snap of him before he was dragged away by the diligent Chamber of Commerce. I went back to the office, developed the plate, and discovered that the camera had performed with its customary efficiency. Mr. Scott was there, all right. That is to say he was all there from his belt to his brow. The top of his head had been lopped off neatly from a point just below his hat brim.

Here, of course, was the spot for quick thinking. I tried to find Mr. Scott but he had gone far afield. And from the front office came the roar of Harry Warner demanding the portrait for the first edition. I made a somewhat fuzzy enlargement and took it in to Bert Blessington, the cartoonist, and explained my predicament.

"And what do you want me to do with it?" he wanted to know.

"Daub up the background and paint a hat on him," I explained. "And make it snappy."

Bert was always the one to oblige. His art required no greater inspiration than the sight of a comrade in trouble. So he hauled out some gray and brown water color and went to work while I moved onto the front office and delivered messages of assurance.

Blessington finished the retouching job in what is still a record for the premises. I knew there was something wrong with it as I made a copy and handed it to the engravers. But it wasn't until the next day that I knew the answer. I was standing in Warner's office when the telephone rang.

"Listen," came the puzzled voice of the new president of the Southern Pacific, "I'm not making any kick, understand, but I wish you'd tell me something. I came here with a straw hat and I've still got a straw hat."

"Yes," observed Mr. Warner politely.

"Well then," went on Mr. Scott, "where the hell did I get that derby I'm wearing in your newspaper?"

"I haven't an earthly idea," said Mr. Warner. "The camera, of course, can't lie."

Memories of a photographer's life may dim, and with good reason. The pictures of the old local room with its ancient, blind typewriters and the crumbling desk at which the late O. Henry had sat, and of the town in which the *Post* circulated are clearer and more poignant. There was Bill Ruggles, the sports editor, who did all his typing with the index finger of his right hand. There was the constant procession of geniuses from the big towns who treated Pat Daugherty, the city editor, with much condescension and presently moved on to bigger and better things. There was the youth (one of Warner's automatic resignations) who staggered in from a fire one night and wrote a story unique among the exhibits of American journalism. . . . He had been working on it for about an hour and a half, typing steadily, when Daugherty came to look over his shoulder.

"The fire," he had written, "the fire, the fire, the fire, the fire, the fire, the fire, the fire, the fire, the fire. . . ." And so on for about three linear feet of copy.

There was George McLendon who, in a previous existence,

[50]

had been a civil engineer. He had laid out much of the line of the National Railways of Mexico and was an authority on Mexican culture. His written works never seemed particularly inspired. But unhampered by a typewriter he had the knack of making everybody listen to his stories.

One recalls a night when a norther was blowing, and shivering reporters huddled over a radiator that was just beginning to get warm.

"You guys are getting soft," observed Mr. McLendon. "You don't know what cold weather is."

"Of course *you* do," commented one Buchanan, a police reporter from Nacogdoches. "You came from the polar regions around Corpus Christi, didn't you?"

"The weather is cold in the high altitudes in Mexico," said George patiently. "I remember the first time I ever saw snow . . ." He paused and filled a pipe.

"It was up in the mountains of Sonora," he said. "I'd got off my horse and was sitting on a log right on a peak. The sky had gone dull and mistylike and the horizons seemed to be closing in.

"Ahead of me the valley dropped down about two thousand feet. There were masses of forest in it and down at the bottom there was a sort of blue light. I don't think I'll ever see anything as beautiful as that again."

Buchanan sniffed. The other reporters looked pained. The contrast between McLendon's pipe and his poetry was all too obvious.

"But what got me most," the raconteur went on, "was the silence. I'd been up in the mountains many times before and it's always sort of quiet up there, but not entirely. Generally you can hear the wind in the pines. And the insects make little noises—and the birds. But this time there wasn't any sound of any kind. It was so still that you could feel the blood throbbing in your ears and it seemed to be coming from outside. The whole world seemed to be filled with it—like the beating of a great heart."

McLendon's voice had sunk almost to a whisper and he seemed to be looking out through the wall of the local room, his appreciative eyes resting once more on that lovely vision.

"Then all at once I knew," he said. "I felt something soft and cool on my face and then a white curtain was drifting across the valley.

" 'It's snowing,' I said. 'It's snowing!'

"The horse never said a goddam thing."

There were two good fires in Houston that year. One consumed a mile and a half of dwellings along Buffalo Bayou. Another made ashes out of the more modern part of Main Street.

Losses in the latter were reckoned in millions and the spectacle of burning skyscrapers was something that few cities have duplicated. But the fire is remembered not so much for that as for the lead that one of our itinerant craftsmen wrote about it. The first sentence was one of those things that stick in the memory defiant of time:

"It is a curious, awesome thing, a fire at night . . ."

A lot of the boys thought it was pretty good and those who didn't had to admit that the detailed account of the proceedings on page five was easily accessible.

We put the sinking of the *Titanic* on an inside page that year. There wasn't much interest in Atlantic shipping in

Houston and everybody knew that the *Titanic* was an unsinkable ship.

It is difficult to explain why one should have wished to leave such a shop. There was always something going on. The people, in and out of the office, were the right sort. Living was gracious and comfortable. The winters, after one got used to them, weren't bad.

However, one day the spring came and with it unmistakable reminders of last summer's heat. Warner offered some good advice.

"Your clothes are too heavy," he suggested. "Get a couple of linen suits and you won't mind the temperature." But I looked at the stokehold of the telegraph room where I spent the time that I didn't work as a photographer.

"Nope," I said. "I think I'll put the price of new clothes into a ticket to Chicago. I know Chicago as well as I know Houston."

"Better buy a street guide," he said. A bit sourly, I thought.

There were giants in the earth in those days—not the least of whom was Harry Warner himself. And whether the Houston *Post* was in the middle of their stamping ground or merely at the threshold of a new era we heard of them there as nowhere else in my experience.

Most of their names are forgotten, unfortunately. Some of them died too quickly to get decent obits, for it was no easy job to run such papers as the Tombstone *Epitaph* in Tombstone's prime, or the Tonopah *News* or the Deadwood *Pioneer*. Newspapers had no reticence in the cruder communities any more than the late Mr. Bonfils had at a later date in a more polished locale. And where respectability was a recently acquired luxury and skins were correspondingly thin, anything you said out loud was certain to be an insult to somebody. Even before coming south I had seen some demonstration of the theory that good editors die young.

Once Mrs. J. O. Grace offered me a job on the Lead *Daily Call* and so I was interested when she received a warning from some crimp of the gold-mining industry who disliked her editorial policy. (She was campaigning for a six-day week for the muckers in Phoebe Hearst's Homestake Mine.) She sniffed at the threats until somebody set off a stick of dynamite under her office. The story goes that the mobsters took what remained of her press and ran it through the crushers and stamp mill at the Homestake.

That Warner should have taken high rank in this company of the great—when one considered the history of the Houston *Post*—did not seem at all surprising. One evening as he was discussing something with the society editor a large subscriber who didn't like what the *Post* had said about cotton-crop reduction or the boll weevil or something strode into the office. Without warning he landed a haymaker on Mr. Warner's chin.

Mr. Warner turned groggily toward the society editor.

"Excuse me," he said apologetically. "If our friend had any manners at all he would know better than to do such things in the presence of ladies." The frightened girl recovered from shock just about that time and ran shrieking into the corridor, after which Warner turned about and reduced his visitor to pulp.

"The South is filled with inhibitions and rules of social conduct," he told me as the ambulance men came in to clear away the debris. "And you've got to pay heed to all of them if you want to get along in this business. . . ."

[54]

FANTASY AMONG THE MAGNOLIAS

It was in Houston that I had first heard the legends of Joe Leveque of the New Orleans *Harlequin*—a character who seemed to have come from the same folklore that produced Paul Bunyan.

Leveque, who probably would have had apoplexy had anyone called him a reformer, was at the throat of a succession of city administrations which seem to have been consistently like those that got national publicity in the days of Huey Long. Leveque may not have been *For* anything but he was certainly and continuously *Against* everything. Naturally he walked abroad with his life in his hands.

Our leased-wire operator told us of the climax of his career. He got the story in conversation with another leased-wire operator who had been chatting with a friend in New Orleans. On this night the chief of police came roaring into the office of the *Harlequin,* with a pistol in his hand. He was apoplectic with rage, and slavering. He tore open the door to the editor's private coop and stood facing Leveque at a distance of exactly five feet.

"I've come to kill you, you so-and-so," he announced in a scream that could be heard in the composing room. And with that he began to shoot. Six bullets went into the wall over Mr. Leveque's head, after which Mr. Leveque knocked him unconscious with a paste pot and picked up the telephone to the city editor. . . .

"That you, Fred?" he called. . . . "Well, Fred, come in here a minute. We're going to get out an extra. . . ."

A fine effort, of course, and there was much discussion of it in our office. But if there had been any voting for first place among the giants most of us would still have backed Warner.

4

THE NEWSPAPER NOBODY KNEW

~~~~~~

THE next stop was the Chicago *Inter-Ocean* (morning, daily and Sunday, Republican).

It is difficult for any modern newspaper man to envision what sort of a periodical was the old *Inter-Ocean*. Physically its offices were quiet enough. The published product was a study in perfectly edited dullness. Inwardly it was a joyful madhouse, architect's model for all the Hollywood journals ever screened. The staff had the permanence of a crowd in a railroad station. Nobody ever took his hat off or sat back in his chair. Nobody ever knew who actually worked there except, perhaps, a clerk in the pay-roll department and one never heard his testimony. His big day of the week, naturally, was payday—and on that day he was usually in hiding along with the cashier and the business manager.

Presumably the *Inter-Ocean* had some kind of circulation. It seemed best to the management never to talk about it. There was never enough advertising to make news space a problem. Any reader, if one admits for the sake of discussion that there were any readers, could see that for himself. Once in a while there would be a full page from a rubber company or an automobile concern but that was no solace to the publisher who knew how such ads were solicited. It was the practice of the advertising manager to pick up such pages when they appeared in other newspapers and then attempt a post-mortem collection from the boys whose products were mentioned. The system was good in theory as had been demonstrated in other lines. (Look we're giving you this handsome crayon enlargement free. You have to pay only the nominal cost of the fine gilt frame.) In practice—well, that's what it was, just practice. The *Inter-Ocean* would have been forced to operate entirely without money were it not for the fact that it had an electric power plant in the basement and peddled current to neighboring loop buildings. For this service it collected cash.

Nowadays, if one mentions the name of the *Inter-Ocean* where any of the brethren are gathered together, there is sure to be some observation that its staff was the last great assemblage of newspaper rumpots in the history of American journalism. That, of course, is libel. There have been larger and more recent assemblages. It is true that there were many rumpots on the uncertain pay roll. It was mere routine for the head of the copy desk to go down every evening to "The Sewer," a charming basement saloon next door, and sort out the copyreaders able to stand on their feet. It was common practice for Big Bob Maxwell, telegraph editor (and a graduate physician) to feed restoratives to such of his workmen as he happened to find within reach of his ministrations. In some years of the paper's colorful existence the office boys were busy all through the weary night rushing the can for prisoners in the local room.

Such practices may explain why occasional gems got into

print despite the microscopic eye of Bill Moore, the constantly vigilant managing editor. There was, for example, the interesting performance of Mr. James Mark who was called upon to edit a story about an Indiana farmer who had put green spectacles on his cow to make her think that excelsior was edible. Mr. Mark, who had every outward appearance of sobriety, produced a headline in due course: "Indiana Bovines Put Green Glasses on Cows." It was puzzling but undoubtedly effective.

No reporter or copyreader on the premises ever wasted much time thinking over the advantages of employment by the week or the month. Theoretically one worked seven days out of every seven but under normal conditions one toiled until he had a few dollars coming and then took enough time off to get rid of his pay. It was a sort of piecework routine that gave work to a mob of "substitutes" almost as large as the regular staff and almost as regularly employed. By and large, the directors of this enterprise were lenient toward people with hangovers and jitters and simple alcoholic fogs, but even in that golden age there were signs of a change. The night editor was heard to wish, one night, that some of the talented authors would stay around long enough for him to learn their names and memorize their faces. And it was significant that the substitutes—whether because of meager pay or generally empty stomachs—never went near "The Sewer," never got drunk within sight or hearing of a boss.

Despite the haphazard methods by which the news got itself covered, edited and eventually printed, the *Inter-Ocean* always reached the street as one of the most dignified and error-free newspapers on the continent. There was a reason for this. Bill Moore might deal kindly with an alcoholic and he never raised much fuss if half the staff went A.W.O.L. But he never tolerated mistakes. A misplaced comma meant a day's layoff, a misspelled name meant a week. And with the obscure philosophy of their kind, men who were willing to suspend themselves two or three days on their own volition felt the hardship of unemployment resulting from the orders of the management. On every post in the big barn of a city room were pasted little signs bearing the signature of H. H. Kohlsaat, the publisher: " 'I can forgive a liar but I hate inaccuracy.'—Samuel Butler. 'I concur in this sentiment.'—H.H.K."

So the *Inter-Ocean* was accurate, well printed, easy to read. By all the rules it should have prospered. Instead, the critical city turned its favor toward such morning offerings as Hearst's *Examiner* and the *Record-Herald* which weren't quite so correct but a little nearer to the public.

In Chicago at that time and for many years afterward was an inventive genius named L. (for Leonard) G. (for George) Edwardson who reported odds and ends for the Chicago *Evening American.* Mr. Edwardson has mentioned that he wasn't very well paid and that the city editors of his early career weren't impressed by his craftsmanship. But, with excusable pride, he can recall that on occasions away from his own local room he rose to literary heights.

There came a day when he had saved enough money or built up enough credit to buy a complete outfit of new clothes—hat, shirt, necktie, suit, socks and shoes—all at once. That was the day when he and a *Journal* reporter named Max found themselves together on a search for photographs of two North Side belles who had recently been presented at the court of St. James's. Oddly enough, the *Journal* reporter was also well accoutered, and the pair, as they walked up the steps of an old stone mansion near Lincoln Park, gave local journalism the most impressive front it had had in years.

They rang the doorbell, got no answer, then sat down on the top step and fanned themselves with their bright new straw hats. They had formed no plans at the time other than to rest a while. Mr. Morph, the father of the girls, might possibly show up. Anyway it was only common sense to stay out of their offices long enough to miss another assignment. The day was hot and the spirit naturally languorous and neither had thought up any good reason for moving when Mr. Edwardson observed a familiar figure turning the corner.

"That," he informed Max, "is Mr. Hal Chance, a reporter for the *Inter-Ocean*."

"Let's take him over to Broadway and get some beer," suggested Max.

"Let's not," demurred Mr. Edwardson. "He needs a story for his paper. He doesn't know either of us so we'll give it to him. You will be young Mr. Alfred Morph. I'll be young Mr. Henry Morph and I'll do the talking."

Mr. Chance turned in at the gate. Mr. Edwardson put his new ten-cent handkerchief to his eyes and began to weep vigorously. Max took his cue and burst into convincing sobs. Mr. Chance looked puzzled.

"I beg your pardon," he said, "but is this Mr. Morph's residence?"

"Yes," said Mr. Edwardson brokenly. "I am Mr. Henry Morph. This is my brother, Mr. Alfred Morph, and I suppose you're one of those reporters come to ask us terrible things about the bullet holes in the Rembrandt."

"Well," said Mr. Chance cannily, "I don't want to disturb you too much. But I think you will understand my position in the matter. Such things do get out."

"But for Mother's sake I beg you to keep it out of your paper," pleaded Mr. Edwardson. "You're a gentleman and you have a mother of your own. You must realize how we feel and I know you'll be fair to us. It wasn't Mother's fault."

"Of course not," sobbed Max with a picturesque heaving of his shoulders.

"You will keep it quiet, won't you?" pursued Mr. Edwardson. "You will do this one little favor for us?"

"Yes," promised Mr. Chance slowly. "I've never done anything like this before. But after all . . . I suppose the Rembrandt is ruined."

"It can be repaired," observed Mr. Edwardson more hopefully. "But you can't repair memory. It was such a beastly thing to see Father standing there shooting at Mother. I didn't even notice the Rembrandt till afterward."

"It kills me to think of it," said Max. "And they were always so happy together."

Mr. Edwardson nodded violently in assent.

"I'd always heard that they were an ideal couple," observed Mr. Chance, looking for a pencil and some copy paper.

"Ideal was no name for it," agreed Mr. Edwardson. "There never was a harsh word between them until that steel man came to visit us."

"Ah yes, the steel man," mentioned Mr. Chance. "What did you say his name was?"

"I wasn't going to tell you," said Mr. Edwardson. "But I guess everybody knows. That's because he's so prominent in

Pittsburgh. Frick, his name is. If you lived in Pittsburgh you'd know all about him."

Mr. Chance had never been in Pittsburgh but he knew that Henry C. Frick was a director and member of the executive committee of the United States Steel Corporation. He tried to conceal his interest.

"Father is a good man," declared Mr. Edwardson, rubbing his eyes. "But he is very proper and very austere."

"He never unbent an inch," contributed Max.

"Mother was always suppressed," said Mr. Edwardson. "She was given everything she wanted for her home. But she never had much chance for a good time."

"I think I understand," murmured Mr. Chance consolingly.

"She was just human," defended Mr. Edwardson. "You can't blame her for that. And when this steel man came around and gave her flowers and expensive oil paintings she was impressed. Father got very stuffy about it. He said she was acting like a fool and he called this Mr. Frick names. He ordered him out of the house. He knows now that it was the wrong thing to do. Mother got angry for the first time in her life and said she was tired of being bossed. Then this morning she said she was going away with the steel man to Pittsburgh where she could be happy."

"It must have been difficult for all of you," observed Mr. Chance.

"It was simply hellish," said Mr. Edwardson. "She stood there in front of the fireplace right under the Rembrandt with her little suitcase in her hand. She was wearing white organdy with a handmade lace collar. The tears were streaming down her face because she didn't really want to leave us. I know she didn't. She was just waiting for a word from Father. But he didn't give her any word. He warned her not to take a step toward the door and when she did he whipped out a revolver and shot at her five times. He didn't hit her. Father always was a rotten shot."

"But he hit the Rembrandt," moaned Max. "He made a sieve out of the Rembrandt."

"The Rembrandt can be fixed," said Mr. Edwardson. "But I don't think that Mother will ever forgive Father. When she went away she said she was going to get a divorce. . . . It's just too terrible. You can see why we were afraid some reporter would come out here who might not understand."

"I sympathize with you deeply," said Mr. Chance. "You may rely on me to be discreet."

"I knew that," said Mr. Edwardson earnestly. "Oh I knew that."

So Mr. Chance went back to the office of the *Inter-Ocean* and wrote two full columns about the domestic tragedy of the Morphs and the philanderings of Mr. Frick. The story ran in all editions and was exclusive. No other newspaper in the world had a hint of it.

Mr. Chance got a $50 bonus and three week's vacation. That in itself approached the miraculous but it was by no means the most astounding feature of the incident.

Never, from the moment the presses began to roll until the *Inter-Ocean* suspended publication two years later, did anybody complain about the story. Mr. Morph never learned that he had tried to murder his wife. Mr. Frick, who had never heard of the Morphs, died without ever being aware that anybody had pictured him as a home-breaker.

[63]

"The *Inter-Ocean's* circulation," said Mr. Edwardson, "was purely private."

George Wheeler Hinman was editor of the *Inter-Ocean* during an important period of its existence. It never got completely away from the influence of H. H. Kohlsaat whose child it was. But something of Hinman remained with it until the finish.

Hinman was an outspoken editor and a master of invective. One suspected that he had more enemies than friends. But his own employees thought well of him and those of other newspapers considered him a newspaperman's newspaperman. There was a reason for that.

A reporter was sent out one night to cover a routine meeting of a woman politician. Unexpectedly she departed from her prepared speech and made some extravagant charges. The reporter returned to the office and quoted her at considerable length.

The next day she called on Mr. Hinman, hurt and indignant. She had been misquoted, she said. Not only that, the misquotation showed every sign of having been prompted by the malice of a reporter who was undoubtedly drunk. Mr. Hinman sympathized with her, murmured regrets in behalf of the paper, and fired the reporter.

That should have ended the incident. The dicta of publishers have a way of being final. But Mr. Hinman was not like other editors. He had discharged the reporter without a hearing and when he got to thinking about the matter he was no longer so sure of himself. He reread the disputed story, then sent for a stenographic report of the meeting and he discovered that the lady had not been misquoted at all.

Next day appeared an editorial that has no parallel in American journalism: "An Apology to a Reporter."

Most of it, of course, was a blistering commentary on the lady politician who had been willing to sacrifice a journalistic nobody to save her own face. But much of it was what the caption indicated, an abject apology to a workman who had been unjustly treated. Somebody discovered the reporter in "The Sewer" and gave him his job back. Two days later he had recovered consciousness sufficiently to accept the apology and an increase in pay. He may have been fired later for something else—that would be merely a run-of-the-mill incident on the *Inter-Ocean*. But the best evidence is that he remained on the staff until we all were sold down the river to Mr. Keeley who didn't want us.

5

THE APOTHEOSIS OF OFFICER
SPIEGELBUEHLER

DESPITE the evidence of its peculiarities there were a lot of good people on the *Inter-Ocean*.

Not so long ago Oswald Schuette compiled a list of *Inter-Ocean* alumni, living, working, and out of jail. His roster wasn't complete by any means but even so it was imposing. Inmates who had trained in this sprightly madhouse and kept their sanity—or a reasonable facsimile thereof—had gone on to make names in the newspaper business all across the country. Oswald, himself, had taken considerable rating as a Washington correspondent. Charles N. Wheeler had come into national prominence as one of the foremost writers on politics in the Middle West. Bill Moore had gone east to become managing editor of the New York *Post*. Marquis James had won two Pulitzer Prize awards for his work in biography. George Hartford, after valuable experience in a shop where advertising was purely a topic for academic discussion, had become advertising manager for the Hearst papers and afterward for the Chicago *Daily News*. Jim Crown had moved on to run

the *Times-Picayune* in New Orleans . . . and there are countless others.

Head of the copy desk at the beginning of the paper's last
year was Robert ("Tiny") Maxwell, who reached apotheosis as
a sports editor in Philadelphia. In training he weighed close
to three hundred pounds. Out of training he hesitated to sit
down except in his own special chair. He had a couple of university degrees, one of them in medicine. But culture, *per se,*
seemed to bore him.

His strenuous education had been brought about as a corollary to his brawn which some unlucky people occasionally mistook for blubber. It was the consensus among sports authori-
ties that he had been the best football center in the United
States for some six years.

His term of service might be puzzling to recent students of
football. But it was quite possible and entirely legitimate. He
played three years with the University of Chicago. Then he
was eligible for three years with Eastern colleges which at that
time did not recognize the Middle West socially. He took his
wares to Swarthmore and was well received.

Somewhere in this pilgrimage he got a kick in the throat
which gave him an impediment in his speech and stifled what
ambition he might have had to practice medicine. He left college to take a job on the Philadelphia *Public Ledger* where
he worked two or three years before nostalgia brought him
back to Chicago and the *Inter-Ocean.*

One Sunday during those early newspaper days he found
himself sitting with one Charles Porter in the lounge of the
Pen and Pencil Club in Philadelphia. It was seven o'clock in
the morning, and the pair toyed longingly with the thought

of beer for breakfast. They sounded out the bartender and became aware that the urge was not likely to find material reward. Their credit was exhausted and they had a joint capital of twenty cents. In this dark moment Mr. Porter discovered a ray of hope in a newspaper announcement.

"Look," he said to Mr. Maxwell. "It says here that the Y.M.C.A. and a flock of Sunday schools are putting on a field meet."

"What of it?" asked Mr. Maxwell in a pained voice.

"It's a chance to get some money," explained the practical Mr. Porter. "They're offering prizes of $25 for first in all events and $100 to anybody who breaks a world's record. Let's go out there." So they went.

Mr. Maxwell didn't have any track suit but that was no deterrent. He stripped down to his shorts and entered his name for the shot-put.

Mr. Porter is a little dim in his memoirs but he remembers that Mr. Maxwell caused a lot of amusement.

"He hadn't been in training for a couple of years and he looked it," Mr. Porter says. "He was bigger than any other two men in the meet. He had been up all night. He hadn't had any breakfast. The sun was hotter than hot and that, or something else, made Tiny a little dizzy. Everybody grinned when he picked up a sixteen-pound shot and stepped into the ring. But they quit laughing right after that. He tossed the shot farther than anybody in the world had ever thrown it before. The record stood for years.

"He was allowed three tries and on the next two he couldn't do anything but drop the cannonball on his feet. But we had a hundred dollars."

OFFICER SPIEGELBUEHLER

City Editor of the *Inter-Ocean* was Jim Crown who had brought to the business great executive gifts and an impressive bellow. He had a genius for handling such raw material as the editorial pay roll and "The Sewer." provided. Somehow, drunk or sober, his reporters contrived to produce. They actually worked for him in their fashion. They felt that he understood them as well as they understood him.

Outstanding in his weird crew was one Si Clare who even then, in spite of all temptations, was a good reporter. Mr. Clare had ingenuity and a nice approach and, moreover, he could write. The only trouble with him was that he would get drunk and whenever he got drunk he would go to Dubuque.

Neither Mr. Clare nor anyone else was ever able to explain his yearning for Dubuque. He had never known anyone who lived there. He had never seen the place save through a thinning alcoholic haze. But he would go to Dubuque and, having arrived, would telegraph Jim Crown for enough money to come home on.

One evening he returned, sober and chastened in spirit, to hear what Mr. Crown might have to say about his most recent hegira. Mr. Crown, in his best voice, said plenty.

"I'm sick and tired of it," he roared by way of peroration. "You're no good to me in Dubuque and I'm giving you just one more chance. Get up on your dogs and go out and keep the death watch on Wayman. Don't come back until I tell you and if you get drunk don't come back at all."

Charles Wayman, who had been State's Attorney, was dying in his home far out on the South Side. In the composing room of the *Inter-Ocean* a dummy front page announcing his end and recounting his various works was in the form ready for the stereotypers. Si's job—to give the word that would release the dummy—involved the tedium of a possible all-night vigil with no prospect of reward, not even the reward of seeing one's own account of the proceedings in print. It was an office boy's job but as discipline for a reporter just returned from Dubuque it had its points.

Wayman's house stood in a new subdivision virtually alone, the boards, bricks and other backwash of building activity scattered about it. Si Clare arrived to find a quorum of reporters and photographers shooting craps under the front porch. They offered him a drink of bourbon for which they personally vouched. Mr. Clare wasn't having any. With a wave of new-found virtue he resented the offer. The boys meant well, no doubt. But he had no illusions. So long as they had liquor to give away he would not be able to trust himself to sit down under the porch. He went up the steps and rang the bell.

A detective answered the ring—a detective whom Si recognized.

"Listen," said Mr. Clare. "I can't stick around here. I've got to find a phone. Are you going to be here all night?"

"I guess so," said the detective.

"All right," said Si. "Do me a favor. When Wayman dies you'll know about it as soon as anybody. Just pull down the front-parlor shade and raise it twice to give me a signal."

The detective agreed. Si turned away to establish a base of communication.

It was a bad job. There was a telephone in the house across the street but an *Examiner* reporter stood at it keeping the line open. Near the corner, six doors away, was another telephone and Si's luck seemed to be in until he mentioned that he was working for the *Inter-Ocean* and the owner of the phone worked himself into a fine rage.

"Skidoo for you," he said. "The *Inter-Ocean* was responsible for the most iniquitous blight ever put on the laboring man of Cook County in the stereotypers' strike. Me, I know. I was a stereotyper." Mr. Clare moved dispiritedly toward the corner.

Things looked better on the corner. Opposite him and set back in a wooded lot but still within view of the Wayman parlor window was a large house with no signs of life about it. Back of the house was a garage and into the garage led a telephone line. Mr. Clare crossed the street. Through the garage window he could see the telephone on the opposite wall. He began to take heart.

The simple trick of burglary involved in opening the window was nothing to bother a person of Mr. Clare's talents. The catch, he observed, was one of the sort that can be bought in ten-cent stores and it responded readily to the gentle prodding of a jackknife blade inserted between the frames. In less than three minutes the lower sash went up and Si hoisted a leg over the sill. He was well inside when a hand was laid on his shoulder and a gruff voice mumbled in his ear. He turned about to confront a policeman in uniform.

"This," said the policeman, "is breaking and entering or I ain't John Spiegelbuehler. You come along with me."

Mr. Clare protested vigorously. He explained everything. The policeman was not impressed by the story of Mr. Clare's necessity.

"It's breaking and entering or the book's wrong," he said. "Come along."

"Listen," pleaded Mr. Clare. "This is a big opportunity for

[71]

you. You know you can pound a beat for years and the captain will never hear about you. You'll be just an ordinary cop until the day you die unless you get publicity. And I can give you the publicity. Wayman's a big man. It'll be the biggest thing in your life if you can get hooked up in this case. I'll fix it up for you. I'll get your name in the story—right there on the front page. Everybody will see it. Your captain will see it. He'll have to take some notice of you."

Policeman Spiegelbuehler considered the offer with deliberation while Mr. Clare sweated pearls.

"All right," he agreed at length. "You get my name in the paper. But no monkey business, see. No monkey business or I'll run you in." Just then the curtain went down and up twice in the living-room window of Mr. Wayman's house. Si rushed to the telephone and called his office.

He hadn't much to do except say: "Wayman just died." But he felt the thrill of the occasion even though he had had no part in producing it. Jim Crown took the call in the composing room and Clare could hear the resultant turmoil.

"Let 'er go!" he could hear Crown yell. And he held onto the phone listening to the racket as the form was wheeled across the iron floor. Now the stereotypers would be rolling a dry mat onto the type. Now they would be casting. Presently the presses would start. . . . Mr. Clare was still in something of a reverie as he put the receiver back on the hook and looked up into the face of an angry policeman.

"Listen," urged the policeman. "I heard every word you said. And you didn't say nothing about me. My name ain't going to be on no front page."

"My error," said Mr. Clare hastily. "I guess I was excited

but I'll fix it up right away." Once more he called Mr. Crown.

"Sorry Jim," he said. "But there's something I forgot to mention. I've got an add to the Wayman story. Get it right. It's important. I'll dictate:

"While the great man was dying, Officer John Spiegelbueh-ler—S for Samuel, P for Patrick, I for Isaac, E for Edward, G for George, E for Edward, L for Louis, B for Benjamin, U for Useless, E for Edward, H for Henry, L for Louis, E for Ed-ward, and R for Robert—Spiegelbuehler. You got that, Spieg-elbuehler. All right. While the great man was dying, Officer John Spiegelbuehler was walking his beat."

Mr. Crown's long-distance bellow shocked Mr. Clare's ears but did not deaden them so much that he could not hear what followed. Tenuous but sharp came the anguished cry of the city editor as he turned away from the telephone.

"Get back that form," roared Mr. Crown. "Get back that form. Si Clare's drunk again."

It was obvious that such a newspaper as the *Inter-Ocean* could not last forever. But it is human nature that one never expects the inevitable especially when it has been postponed from day to day over a period of years. We were distinctly shocked on the night when we came down to work as usual and found a neat sign on the front door: James Keeley had bought the paper and was about to junk it. The *Inter-Ocean* would go to press for the last time that night.

It was an unforgettable occasion. We were all out of jobs but nobody was concerned about that. Tomorrow we'd have new jobs. To a staff composed largely of itinerants a migra-tion to other fields was merely familiar routine. Few of us knew the traditions of the paper or much of its fantastic history. None of us could see that it would exert an influence in journalism long after it had ceased to exist.

Somebody hired a German band to stand in the lobby and tootle all during the death watch. From eight that evening until two in the morning the band played a single tune: "I'm on My Way to Mandalay." It wasn't good music but appropriate and we enjoyed it. We enjoyed everything for that matter. All jokes sounded uproariously funny. All the old humdrum of getting out the paper suddenly had become high comedy. We had a fine time until the palsied presses began their futile rattle and the last edition was in.

Then the printers began to come down the iron stairs from the composing room. For the first time we discovered that few of them were youngsters like ourselves. Most of them were gray and bent and slow of step. We remembered having heard that some of them had worked in that shop upstairs for thirty years. Nearly all of them were in tears and looking at them we began to wonder what we'd been laughing at.

6

MR. JOHN EASTMAN SITS IN HIS WINDOW

It HAS been said, not without some reason, that the late John Eastman, publisher of the Chicago *Daily Journal,* was the last of the great personal editors. There may be some argument about whether or not he was great but nobody who knew him will venture to deny that his methods were personal. His S.O.B. list—the roster of names that in no circumstances were to find themselves in print in his paper—was one of the longest ever seen north of the Mason and Dixon Line. He was continually adding to his file of enemies, most of whom he had never seen. He was a martinet and an autocrat who could read veiled insult into the transcript of a speech by a candidate for dog-catcher. He could be roused to picturesque indignation by an obscure ordinance relating to the removal of garbage. However, it must be admitted that life in his vicinity was never dull.

There were plenty of people around town who hated old John, but, oddly enough, the bulk of his employees were not included among the number. We may not have loved him but we appreciated and admired him just as one admires from afar the man who has the courage to toss eggs into electric fans. We didn't come in for much of his ire. He was always too busy taking care of more important people. And when he came downstairs to glower at us over the tops of his glasses, we generally talked back. Nobody, so far as I know, ever got fired from the *Journal* except me. And he was only remotely connected with that.

Old John was born in Easton, Ohio, in 1862. He was educated as a civil engineer at Ohio State University and came to Chicago in 1890 as a reporter for the *Herald*. What made the engineer into a newspaperman is one of the things the historians seem to have overlooked. During his life it's likely that quite a lot of people wondered. In 1895 John R. Walsh, banker and railroad promoter, founded the *Daily Chronicle* and to everybody's surprise the young reporter Eastman was signed on as business manager. In 1898 he went east as advertising manager of the New York *Journal* where he impressed Mr. William Randolph Hearst with his numerous qualities. So when Hearst decided to come into Chicago it seemed logical that he should pick Eastman to do the spade work. John returned to Chicago and founded the *American* in 1900.

Some time afterward Hearst and Eastman quarreled. We never got the straight of it. We never asked anybody. It seemed natural that people should quarrel with Hearst then just as they seem to have been doing ever since. And as for John, he wasn't any too easy to get along with.

His acquisition of the *Journal* was characteristic of him. As a reporter he had interviewed Commodore William Morton Plant who was taken with his forcefulness of manner and style and became his friend. When the Booth family of Detroit, owners of the *Journal,* indicated that they were willing to sell out he asked the Commodore for a loan. Plant gave him $65,000 and refused to take a note and security. Later Eastman sent him a personal note.

There is a legend about the Hearst-Eastman feud that has many of the marks of truth about it although years of research have failed to verify it. Mr. Eastman's mother died, so the story goes, and her obituary was printed in the *American,* forty-five words on page twenty-six. Old John's pride was hurt. He thought that an old-time friend had intended a personal affront and the name of Hearst went onto the rapidly lengthening list on the copy desk. Then Mrs. Phoebe Hearst died and Old John adjusted the score.

"Mrs. Phoebe Hearst died today," read Mr. Eastman's contribution to the obit column. "She was the mother of a newspaper publisher and weighed ninety-five pounds."

I was theoretically a reporter on the *Journal* but I came to do many things, some of which brought me into direct contact with the publisher. It was his habit to send me out to read long, vituperative and libelous messages from himself to the Mayor, the Chief of Police or the judiciary, and I would read them as ordered at considerable risk of life and limb. What saved me as a middleman in the insult business was the fact that most of the public officials had got used to John and his ways before I came into his life. They might receive me with great peevishness but they always listened to my recitals.

Once I took up three-quarters of an hour of the time of William Hale Thompson relaying a bleat about police graft in connection with the Sunday closing of saloons. I thought the piece was not quite up to Mr. Eastman's usual form, though it left no doubt about his opinion of Mr. Thompson, Mr. Thompson's integrity or Mr. Thompson's political gifts. Mr. Thompson sat in complete silence during the reading, his hands folded on the desk in front of him, his eyes closed. But when I finished he was all animation.

"That's swell," was his criticism. "John is getting better every day. Ask him to send me an autographed copy of that thing in six-inch perforated squares." I reported the comment to Mr. Eastman who put it away in his memory book for future reference.

At the time I fretted a bit over such assignments. They helped me to thicken and vulcanize a skin that had been reasonably thin when I left the sawmill, and I quickly developed a gall that I realized might someday be of use to me in covering murder stories and such. But, basically, the job of speaking vicariously for John seemed a little foreign to the newspaper business. I must admit, however, that I learned some of the basic rules of journalism from him. He made me feel that as a reporter I was the representative not of a printing plant but of a great intangible public factor described as "good will and circulation." I was the eyes and ears, and sometimes the voice, of the two-cent customers.

We had a little row with City Attorney Harry B. Miller. John thought he had been unkind to us in the matter of a libel suit that grew out of the action of one of his assistants. Years later Mr. Miller wanted the *Journal's* support in his campaign for State's Attorney. He mentioned his need in an interview that started off with smiles, handshaking and a great amount of sweetness and light.

"I think you know me, John," said the candidate. "It's hardly necessary for me to go into my record with you."

"Of course not, Harry," replied John cheerily. "I've known you for years. You're the S.O.B. who threw me down in the Whosis case."

I spoke of this afterward to Mr. Eastman—when the votes were counted and Mr. Miller's defeat was comfortably assured —and he explained his philosophy. He had lighted a cigar and was broadly expansive and pleased with himself.

"A newspaperman can get even with anybody in the world if he lives long enough," he said. "I just sit here quietly with a bouquet of roses in one hand and a sockful of nightsoil in the other. And my friends and my enemies pass under my window."

Mr. Eastman had the knack of a born editor for surrounding himself with competent help. In the coops outside the local room he had something of a heterogeneous crew—talented but funny. In some sections of his business department he was represented by lads whom only a blind man would have taken on trust. But if the slickers downstairs were slick, Old John, with his bouquet and sock in an upstairs window, was slicker. It is not recorded that anybody ever stung him for very much.

He never seemed to resent the sharp talents of some of his aids. Probably he admired them. It would have been like him.

He promoted loyalty among as hardy and definitely underpaid a lot of individualists as journalism had seen since Cadmus thought up the alphabet, by promising them rewards in a life after death—his own death. He was getting old, he would tell the restless ones. He had received bad news from the doctors. He could not live long and he had no immediate kin to whom he might leave the *Journal* when he should die. Very well, then. He would provide compensation for the faithful workers who had put up uncomplainingly with such conditions as the tough financial setup of the newspaper business had imposed upon them. He would name them in his will.

Actually he did leave the paper to employees. But there was a bleeding heart for every broken typewriter in the office when one night the widely advertised end came. Perhaps he had been completely sincere when he talked of revisions and codicils. Despite his own forecasts he may not have realized that his end was so near and he may have delayed unintentionally, as other men have delayed, to arrange for the loved ones who would live after him and keep his grave, theoretically, green. At any rate a diligent hunt through the files by searchers who did not let their grief overcome them failed to reveal more than one will. That one, which, according to the advance notices, should have contained most of the names in the office directory, mentioned only three principal beneficiaries. It caused a row which Old John, wherever he was and no matter how excusable his neglect, must have considered with great good cheer. He may have encouraged a lot of people to look forward to his passing as a desirable and profitable event, but that doesn't justify the belief that he shared any of their pleasurable contemplation.

Like all other positive characters he had definite streaks of kindliness. Working conditions in the *Journal* local room were pleasant and fair. Most of this undoubtedly was due to the judgment and thoughtfulness of Richard J. Finnegan, managing editor and later publisher. But even so a share of the credit must go to the man who despite his numerous gifts and tendencies toward troublemaking never interfered with the conduct of the staff.

The *Journal* took care of its sick. It was tolerant of human foibles and not too critical of the personal habits of its talented workers. Under Finnegan's direction it got a reputation as the one shop in the United States where a youngster could always get some sort of a job. There was an atmosphere of security about the place—anybody who wanted to could stay there forever. When I got fired for "insubordination" soon after my return from the wars in 1919, everybody thought I must have quit of my own accord, and that included the managing editor.

Dick Finnegan was probably the hardest-working executive who ever sat down to a desk. In his years as managing editor he saw every line, local and telegraph, that went into the paper. The copy desk read the copy, as is customary, but Finnegan reread it. He wrote most of the top heads. He directed all the important assignments across the city desk. He picked out the photographs. He platted the first-page layouts. He interviewed the syndicate salesmen and the politicians and the irate customers and applicants for jobs.

He had a sense of humor—we frequently wondered why—and he had a gift for nosing out talent no matter how well disguised. After the war I gave my brother Ray, who had never been inside a newspaper office, a five-day course in editing, which is to say I taught him how to mark paragraphs and count the type units in heads. Then I brought him down to the office to apply for a job as copyreader.

This maneuver was made possible only by acquaintance with John Eastman's principle that if you have brass you don't need any gold. For an ability to read copy is supposed to derive from a long experience with all branches of this odd business, and headline writing, for all its clichés and agonized combat with English grammar, is a highly cultivated art. However, the new copyreader did not know that and he outlined his qualifications with just the right lack of modesty.

"Where have you worked before?" inquired the managing editor.

"On the Newport *News,*" said the applicant.

"You ought to do very well here," said Finnegan unsmilingly. "We once had a copyreader who got his training on the Bronx *Cheer.*"

It is perhaps of no importance but makes an interesting footnote to record that the new copyreader was assistant head of the copy desk in three months—a week before he ever saw a linotype machine. Such things as that happened on the *Journal.*

In honest inventory I can see that my own contributions to the brightness and sales appeal of the paper over a period of some six years did not amount to much. When the war came I was doubling as automobile editor and sports paragrapher. After I got back from France I was a rewrite man—which is to say I put onto paper the sprightly narratives that came over the telephone from reporters at the scenes of fires, disorders and alarms.

The rewrite system, now common on most of the big newspapers in the United States, developed as cities expanded and the populace took to committing its murders and having its fires in spots far removed from the editorial offices. Reporters unable to get to their city desks with their wares had to confide in somebody over the telephone and that somebody had to arrange their confidences in a readable form. There is still debate about the merits of the system. Stories undergo changes in repetition and no writer's imagination is an adequate substitute for his eyes. The rewrite man has no opportunity to look farther than his own experience for the picture of a four-alarm fire or a weeping husband-killer at a coroner's inquest. His work must always contain a large dose of personal —and not always accurate—reminiscence. But for all that he's a permanent, and, in the case of the afternoon newspapers, an indispensible institution.

My own career on the *Journal* rewrite desk was interesting. It might have been downright pleasant save for the wave of moral laxness that spread across the town after the war. Prohibition had not yet begun to offer the opportunities and rewards that were later to attract the gangsters but old-fashioned robbery was still popular and profitable. Every Saturday we were sure to have a pay-roll holdup and always a mere minute or two before the home-edition press time.

For weeks I sweated with this problem. It is difficult to write half a column in two minutes. And always the circumstances of the robberies were so similar that one eventually sought in vain for new arrangements of words to tell about them.

In the end the monotony of these proceedings gave me a solution. I worked up a form sheet:

.... gunmen today held up shot seriously wounded shot and killed .... cashier of the ....

company, ... street, manufacturers of dealers in ...., and escaped with the company's weekly pay roll totaling $........... The cashier was killed instantly was seriously wounded is not expected to recover is at .... hospital suffering from superficial wounds and shock ....

And so on for half a column. With the blanks filled in and the right phrases crossed out the story may not have rated a place among The Best News Stories of the Year, but it was adequate. The editorial board caught up with the form system after three or four weeks but it made no difference then. By that time the factory operators came to realize that they could save themselves a lot of trouble if they paid by check instead of in cash, and the pay-roll raids stopped automatically. . . . Too bad! The standardized, chain-assembly idea for reporting certainly had its points and as one observes even at this late date how much one fine, original story may resemble another fine original story, he feels that it might have revolutionized journalism.

Perhaps, indeed, it has.

Lowell Thomas passed his cubhood with the *Journal* and remains one of the brightest memories of that odd period. In futile sequence all the reporters of the staff—the young, aged, lame, halt—anybody who had strength enough left to get to the Aurora and Elgin interurban line—were sent out to Wheaton, Illinois, that summer to interview the ubiquitous, and hilarious, Helen Morton—daughter of Mark Morton, the eminent drysalter. Helen had left her home without consulting the local society editors and had come back with a husband, one Roger Bailey, yclept the Virginia Horseman. She was kept in seclusion after her return, and, one after another,

[84]

we pestered the hot-tempered Mark for word of her without result. I came reasonably close to the story because I actually got to talk to Mr. Morton. He threatened to blow my head off and left the interview to get a shotgun.

A short time later Webb Miller, then working for the *Evening American,* arrived at the Morton farm where Mark, who appears to have been a little shortsighted, mistook him for me. Mark went berserk, called out the faithful retainers with pitchforks, captured Mr. Miller alive, trussed him up, tossed him into the back end of a pickup truck and started to drive him to the Wheaton County jail. On the way Mr. Morton overturned the car on top of his prisoner and broke two of his ribs.

Helen was moved from Wheaton immediately after that and placed under the guardianship of Colonel George Fabyan, then engaged at Riverbank, Geneva, Illinois, in proving that Shakespeare wrote Bacon's essays. And there—not in the black tent of Lawrence in Arabia—was where Lowell Thomas started toward greatness.

Mr. Thomas, being the most inexperienced reporter in the shop, was the last to get a chance to prove the extent of his charm with the Mortons. And, like the cub in the oldest relic of newspaper fiction in existence, he brought home the story.

It appeared that he had had some trouble getting it. He had been forced to swim the Fox River to reach the guarded estate of Fabyan. But once he had done all this he found Helen Morton seated in a bower and willing to talk. The interview was as fine a job of journalism as the tired city editors of Chicago had seen in many a day. Lowell got a promotion on the strength of it as well as a bonus and an extended vacation. Then the Mortons, through their attorneys Winston, Payne, Strawn and Shaw, sued the *Journal* for a quarter of a million dollars libel.

They declared that most of the matter published in the *Journal* derogatory to the Morton family could not properly be charged to Helen at all. She hadn't said the things about her father for which she was quoted. In point of fact she hadn't said anything at all to the reporter who had interviewed her in Geneva. For she hadn't been in Geneva that day. She had been in Lake Forest, visiting an aunt. . . .

The crestfallen reporter, apprised of these statements, admitted what Richard Finnegan already knew, that the story of a new swimming of the Hellespont was, as it is called in the trade, a fake. But Mr. Finnegan as usual was realistic about it.

"Well," he said, "you got us into this. I could fire you and let you forget about it but I'm not going to play it that way. Your assignment at the moment is to see Silas Strawn and get the suit dismissed."

The youngster walked out with the cheery air of one beginning the march up the thirteen stairs. He came back three hours later.

"It's all fixed up," he said. "There isn't going to be any suit. Strawn says to forget about it. And at the end of next month I'm going to be leaving you. Mr. Strawn and some of his friends are going to send me over to Palestine to get moving pictures and lecture material when Allenby finishes up the Last Crusade. . . . They're raising $25,000 as a starter."

Dick Finnegan started to ask him if this might be classed as another river-swimming performance. But he didn't go on with it. Whether you looked on Lowell Thomas as a hypnotist or miracle man or only as a nice boy who had talked himself out of a jam, it was obvious that he was telling the truth. It was just as obvious that he was on his way forward and upward. . . . When you could gouge $25,000 out of Silas Strawn you didn't need any further proof of genius. . . . Not with us!

At least once in the days of spiritual reconstruction that followed the war, I too should have noticed the breath of Destiny hot on the back of my neck. I might have been a sports writer, perhaps even a moderately good sports writer. For that fall Dick Finnegan and Sherman Duffy connived to give me my opportunity. I was assigned to help cover the World Series.

Possibly I should have been hardheaded and realistic enough to appraise what happened afterward. But—I offer it as my only excuse—I looked on Sherman Duffy as the greatest judge of sports I had ever known—and if he didn't suspect any venality in this world-shaking event, there seemed no reason why I should. I laced myself into my shining armor and went out with Joe Foley, the baseball writer, to look upon the third game of the series between the Chicago White Sox and the Cincinnati Reds.

The performance seemed amateurish, not to say putrid. I marveled at the way fly balls bounced out of the glove of shoeless Joe Jackson, and I wrote down the White Sox as a fourth-rate baseball team—no better and no worse than other fourth-rate baseball teams with which I had at times been associated. But I saw no evil.

Along about the fourth inning of that game, Foley and I got duplicate telegrams from John Eastman who was doing something in Cincinnati: "HAVE INCONTROVERTIBLE EVIDENCE THIS SERIES FIXED STOP WHAT ABOUT IT QUESTION."

I don't know what Foley said but my reply was a fine tribute to my innocence and credulity:

"SUCH THINGS ARE NOT DONE IN THE BIG LEAGUES."

One draws a veil.

Bringing back that old office with halfhearted nostalgia, I can see that the *Journal* had many features not to be found on other newspapers. Martin Hutchins, who was the managing editor when I arrived, was a great believer in ventilation. Blue-lipped copyreaders protested about his earlier experiments in this direction when he opened all the front windows on a day when—even with the discount that you give a newspaper's winter thermometer—it was about six below. Mr. Hutchins then brought on a machine to ventilate the premises without air—an ozonizer, he called it. You turned a switch on this gadget and it made the room smell like a bad thunderstorm in a zoo for hours afterward. We tried short-circuiting it but that mixed up burned rubber with the thunderstorm so we gave it up and lived for the rest of the cold weather in an electric atmosphere that may have had a great influence on our work.

Then there was a little emaciated old lad named Jimmy in the circulation department who looked like a collector of Sèvres china and seemed likely to fall apart at any time. We used to feel sorry for him until one day when a couple of hoodlums came in to threaten the city editor. Jimmy, who just happened to be passing through the local room, tossed both of the visitors down a flight of stairs before anybody knew what he was doing.

"It's jujitsu or something," he explained to us afterward. "I never did know exactly what you call it. . . ."

And, of course, there was Jimmy Peebles who set the heads in the composing room. He didn't like the current chief of the copy desk so, in the eternal warfare between the rim and the slot, he allied himself with the rim—which is to say with the working copyreaders against their exalted director. He made it a point never to send back a head because it wouldn't fit. He'd rewrite it himself, if necessary, but mostly he'd file down the type until he could fit about thirty units in a space designed for twenty. His memory will live forever.

And there was the other printer who sold the *Journal's* fire escape. Workmen had taken it down for extension and repair and a junk dealer saw it just as he saw this printer picking his teeth in the front door.

"How much?" inquired the junkman.

"Fifty bucks," said the printer without knowing what he was talking about. So the junkman gave him fifty dollars and took the fire escape away in his wagon. Such larceny occasioned less comment in that neighborhood than you might think.

There was also a rare old drunk who ran the *Racing Almanac,* a periodical which was probably the most inexpensive production in the world. Although John Eastman had nothing to do with it, it consisted entirely of tabulations of race results taken from the columns of the *Journal.* There was only one edition a year. Each day the type of the results was lifted out of the forms and put up on a little shelf that ran all around the composing room. Counting about fifty lines a day, quite a lot of it had accumulated at the end of the eleventh month when the editor-publisher came in to take a look at his "copy." And that was what went onto the floor when in a dizzy moment he started to fall and caught hold of the overburdened shelf. He took it philosophically.

"The horses are now pied even more'n usual," he said as he started back toward Johnson's saloon.

7

TOO MANY YEARS WITH A YELLOW

Mr. Hearst brought many things to Chicago: the first-page type-splash, the colored comic section, the squirrel-cage local room, James Arthur Pegler, (father of Westbrook "Bud" Pegler) and the three-platoon system of managing editors Of these Mr. Pegler was probably the most important. Certainly he exerted the most lasting influence.

James Arthur Pegler had been merely a good reporter in Minneapolis where the Hearst scouts found him. In Chicago he turned out to be a genius—easily the best reporter of his time. He was tall and gaunt and hard-faced, arrogant of manner, short of temper to everybody outside the newspaper business, and so assured of himself that no secretary then alive was willing to take the responsibility for keeping him out of august presences. He had a trace of an English accent and a voice like a dull file.

Pegler is generally credited with having been the inventor of the "Hearst style," a combination of trick idiom and beautiful phrase that is still popular with certain editors from San Simeon to the Atlantic Ocean. . . . "Fifteen foul fiends danced on the grave of this fair white girl tonight. . . ." That was the imagery he brought to pages hitherto devoid of color and poetry. He may have written with his tongue in his cheek—for no one who knew him doubted his linguistic talent or his sense of proportion. But whatever his motives or his opinion of the technique when he had perfected it, he made the Hearst organization like it. And although he is now in retirement, his spirit goes marching on.

He came to the *Journal* in 1914 or thereabouts. He had been working for Hearst something over ten years when somebody made a futile attempt to fire him. The effort was just a gesture, for Peg had a contract effective for another couple of years. But in the end it all amounted to the same thing. He was glad to quit.

Someday when he gets around to writing his memoirs he will probably dwell at length on this crisis. But it probably will detract nothing from his version to state here some of the circumstances as Chicago remembers them. Certainly no study of newspaper oddities would be complete without them. Pegler ran afoul of the high command not through any failure or omission of his own but as a result of what in many ways was the most accurate piece of reporting he had ever done.

Like many of his kind he had felt the call to outside literary work. He had written a play which was eminently successful although his collaborator seems to have picked off most of the royalties. He had written an occasional short story. Then, somewhere around 1913, he went in for fiction in a big way by selling a group of ten stories to *Adventure* magazine. The series was entitled "Ten Years with a Yellow." His friends had no difficulty guessing what "Yellow" he meant.

Only one of these stories was ever printed, but that was

enough to set Pegler in a special place among newspapermen forever. The opening scene was a local room and it was described with merciless accuracy: The squirrel wheel is in mad rotation. A managing editor whose name had been made fictional merely by the transposition of two or three letters is debating with somebody about a banner line, arguing over the choice that lies between two words equally inane.

A cub looking for a job is pushed, in spite of himself, into the middle of a wild turmoil. A city editor looks at him under the mistaken impression that he is already a part of the staff and gives him an assignment to get a girl's picture.

(Here a digression. Mr. Pegler explained that there were only three pictures of the girl in existence. Wrecking crews had raided the home of her fiancé, subsidized sluggers had held him up, tame yeggs had blown open his safety deposit box. . . . Why anybody should have wanted the picture is hazy after all these years, but anyway that was the situation.)

So the cub goes out and after a while comes back with the photograph. So far the story is one of a type that had become mildewed long before Mr. Pegler's birth. But that isn't the end of it.

The city editor, unable to believe his own eyes, asks the cub how he got it and the cub seems surprised.

"Why," he says, "I asked the girl for it." Everybody in the place looks at him in silent amazement, for nobody had thought that so radical a procedure as a direct approach could possibly succeed.

That the whole story was poignantly true in its background if not in plot turned out to be no solace to Mr. Pegler. Mr. Hearst was in the Lambs' Club in New York when the magazine was published. Somebody read the story to him under the impression that it was funny. But Mr. Hearst was not amused. Orders for Mr. Pegler's removal came to the *American* that night by telegraph and met the barrier of the contract. Mr. Pegler stayed on—he'd hired a good lawyer when the contract was drawn. But for a long time he wrote nothing more for Mr. Hearst.

Every day he would report for work as usual. Every day he would be ignored by the somewhat resentful persons whom he had lampooned in his fiction. He would sit at his desk until he got tired and then he would go home. He got permanently tired of it all after some months of inaction and came over to the *Journal*. He was not particularly happy with us. Mr. John Eastman's squirrel cage was possibly too much like the one he had left. He contributed only rarely to our private bedlam, and this infringement on his personal reminiscence might not be justified were it not for the case of Mr. Paul Hirtenstein.

Mr. Hirtenstein was an assistant city editor who did an occasional job of reporting, and Mr. Hirtenstein was much impressed by Mr. Pegler's literary ambition and what had happened to him as a result of it. Like the editors of the fictional "yellow" he gave considerable thought to the possibilities of the direct approach. One day he had an opportunity to test them.

A silk importer named Henry Finn had become suspicious of his wife and, unknown to her or to anyone else, had stationed a crew of dictograph operators in the attic of his home —a North Shore mansion of great size and pretensions. The spies remained there for a week during which they gathered up numerous records of frivolous goings-on. After which Mr. Finn filed suit for divorce.

There was naturally a scramble for first-hand information about the matter. Reporters laid siege to the house where, periodically, the police arrived to chase them off the front lawn. Other reporters camped, no more successfully, outside the offices of Mr. Henry Finn. A tipster from the detective agency that had gathered the evidence mentioned that Mr. Finn's brother Harold, a lawyer, was in possession of all the records —but he admitted that it would be useless to try to get anything out of Mr. Harold Finn. Mr. Harold was embarrassed by the whole business and, moreover, he hated reporters.

Mr. Hirtenstein, as a matter of routine, was assigned to get a copy of the dictograph record. It is hardly possible that anybody expected him to do it. As in the case described by Mr. Pegler in his short story, every ruse had been tried—that is every ruse save the direct approach, and Mr. Hirtenstein decided to see what could be done with that.

He walked over to Michigan Avenue, gave his name to a secretary, and presently was ushered in to Mr. Harold Finn's private office.

"Sit down," suggested Mr. Finn cheerily. "Have a cigar. I suppose you want to see me about this divorce business."

"That's right," said Mr. Hirtenstein, brightening. "I didn't want to bother you. That's why I didn't come over earlier. But I want a copy of the dictograph transcript."

"Glad to give it to you," said Mr. Finn. "I've got two of them right here. . . ."

The telephone rang. Mr. Finn picked up the receiver and talked gruffly for a few seconds.

"Reporters!" he explained to Mr. Hirtenstein with a laugh as he hung up. "They try to tell me they're somebody else. But they don't get away with it. I know all their tricks."

"I suppose they've been pestering you," murmured Mr. Hirtenstein sympathetically.

"They haven't given me a minute's peace for two days," said Mr. Finn. "But I don't get sore about it. Can't blame them for trying to do a job. . . . Here's the transcript."

"Thank you," said Mr. Hirtenstein. And he went out.

It is sad to have to leave such a story at such a place but nobody knows anything else about it. No other newspaper in Chicago got a copy of the Finn dictograph transcript in advance of its publication from the *Journal*. No other reporter ever got near any of the principals in the case. Who Mr. Finn thought Mr. Hirtenstein was he never revealed and Mr. Hirtenstein never asked.

Since John Kieran, recently of the New York *Times* sports department, turned out to be the best-read and best-informed man in his area, it has become something of a fashion to speak well of sporting editors. It seems that an acquaintance with birds and flowers and Sanskrit and medieval history and the Latin poets does not seriously interfere with one's critical opinions of baseball, pole vaulting or fisticuffs. Lots of sports writers, we are informed by the radio commentators, can talk English fluently—good, idiomatic English; many of them can read; quite a number are sober, honest citizens.

One might wonder at this discovery of culture in the sports departments were it not for a memory of a tradition that began before the invention of the box score and continued chiefly because nobody thought it important enough to destroy. Sports commentators, unlike any other artisans in the business, have always been permitted a free use of argot in their little compositions. Whether they thought they were dealing with a public that understands only that kind of language, or were merely attempting to get an atmosphere of originality into reports of contests that day in and day out resemble one another to the point of monotony, they undoubtedly have taken advantage of their license. It is hardly remarkable, therefore, that it became the custom to judge their education, breeding and moral tone by their published works. The resultant picture in the public eye was not always flattering and very seldom true.

And it wasn't only the public who cherished odd notions about sports writers. The error extended more or less to the people who stood with them every now and then at the cashier's window or harried them with pleas for baseball passes —and that included more than one publisher.

Maybe you remember the story of what happened when Fingey Conners, a political boss with a Ph.D. degree in backroom ethics, bought a newspaper in Buffalo. To him, one day, came his sporting editor, a hard-working, somewhat poetic youth with a decent background, plenty of experience, and justifiable ambitions. He said modestly that he thought his responsibilities as an editor entitled him to more pay.

"How much are you getting now?" inquired the boss.

"Fifty dollars a week," answered the sporting editor.

Mr. Conners looked aghast.

"Fifty dollars a week for a sporting editor!" he roared. "That's outrageous. If you can't pull down $10,000 a year out of that job, on the side, you're no damn good. Your salary from now on will be $25."

Probably there were sporting editors in Mr. Conners' day who matched him in morals and shared his philosophy about profits in graft. Maybe there still are, but that, I suspect, is a matter of individual choice and training rather than of universal necessity. Where some of the boys are willing to give, there will always be an equal and similar number who are willing to take. One who has spent about thirty years looking at the feet of idols and the mouths of gift horses is pleased to report that in his experience the takers haven't been numerous.

Nor does a graybeard get much excited over the present appraisal of sports-room culture. Its presence and extent have long been suspected by insiders. The truth of the matter is that one was always more likely to find it than not.

Nobody—or at least nobody in the newspaper business—thought it odd when Lloyd Lewis, dramatic critic, historian and biographer, was assigned to the sports desk of the Chicago *Daily News*. Howard Mann, who preceded him, was another of those lads who, years out of college, are still conversant with classic Greek and are very well acquainted, too, with differential calculus. Warren Browne of the Chicago *Sun* has a fine English style and an encyclopedic memory that now occasions no surprise among reporters who work with him on stories outside his accustomed field. The late Edward Dean Sullivan was another such phenomenon. Robert ("Tiny") Maxwell, previously mentioned in this clinical report, was one of the best-educated men in American journalism.

Sherman Duffy was sporting editor of the *Journal* during the days of the interesting John Eastman and he was architect's model for all the literate lads who have come to clutter up his profession since. He looked something like a college professor —as indeed he might have been. His undiscussed past was filled with degrees. His time, when he was not arguing with lop-eared wrestlers, maundering prize fighters and furtive race-track touts, was spent in pursuits as far from his daily routine as a prayer meeting on Mars. Mr. Duffy had a national reputation as a sports editor. He had a better one as a horticulturalist. He was probably the outstanding authority on rose culture in the United States.

His experimental garden was, and still is, in Ottawa, Illinois, his home town, too far away from Chicago for him to visit it except on week ends. As a hobby between Mondays and Saturdays he perfected himself in cookery. He invented baking dishes and heat controls for ovens and devised a model kitchen, the most efficient in Chicago. He was a constant patron of the opera and the Chicago Symphony Orchestra. He had an excellent collection of classical phonograph records before radio made phonographs popular. He had read everything. He could speak, read and write French, German and Spanish and had a fair smattering of Italian. But his acquisitive gift for languages did not stop there.

There was a day when the morning mail brought to Mr. Eastman's desk a factual account of a baseball game played between two athletic clubs on the West Side. Enclosed was a note signed (apparently) by a Jewish politician of some prominence requesting that Mr. Eastman give the matter some space as a means of encouraging underprivileged boys to take advantage of the uplifting influence of athletics. Mr. Eastman handed it to Mr. Duffy who handed it back.

"We can't print that," he said.

"Why not?" roared Mr. Eastman.

"Because," explained Mr. Duffy, "the names on those teams aren't names at all. They're Yiddish terms of opprobrium and half of them are obscene."

Those of us who appreciated Duffy's varied talents and spent most of our spare time loafing in his office suspected that there was some story behind his advent to the sports business. And it turned out that we were right.

It seems that after he had been graduated from the University of Illinois he got a job on the staff of the Chicago *Tribune*. There he was promptly miscast as a political reporter and assigned to assist the regular Statehouse correspondent in Springfield. He wasn't much taken with his work but he was intelligent and he got on with it. At the end of a year he knew every politician of importance in Illinois and looked forward resignedly to a career that would link his life with theirs forever. However, in the course of a year, he learned to do a little copyreading and that changed his whole life.

There was never anything doing in Springfield over the week end and it was the policy of the *Tribune* management to call in the correspondents every Saturday and put them to useful work. Duffy thus came to find himself a regular Saturday-night feature on the rim of the sports copy desk, editing minor stories, and writing heads for box scores and captions for one-column cuts.

One Saturday night, which seemed to be no different in its beginning from fifty others, he got up from his chair and walked out to the washroom. During his absence Joseph Medill, the editor, came in and without preliminary conversation fired everybody in the sports department. (It's hard to remember why.) The returning Duffy noticed the empty desks but thought nothing of it. He sat down and resumed his work on a telegraph communication from the Three-Eye League. He was interrupted by Mr. Medill whom he had never seen before.

"Who are you?" inquired the editor.

Mr. Duffy told him.

"Are you on the sports staff?" Mr. Medill wanted to know.

"No, sir," said Duffy. "I'm assistant correspondent at Springfield. I just help out here Saturdays. I don't know much about sports."

"Then start learning," ordered Medill. "From now on you're sporting editor."

Which makes it appear that the *Journal* wasn't the only newspaper office where strange things had a way of happening.

Nor was Sherman Duffy the only contributor to the scholarly atmosphere of the *Journal*. There was an old lad on the copy desk who prepared actuarial tables as a side line. There was a first-rate poet on the county building beat. And there was also Hermann Deutsch, Ph.D. in botany, who came to do general assignments. Deutsch is now political editor of the *Item* in New Orleans, author of several books and a magazine writer with a national reputation. In those days he was the most amazing cub who ever came into a newspaper office. He has been gone for many years but old-timers still speak in awe of the day when he attended the food show at a Loop hotel.

In the lobby of the exhibit hall he came upon a woman dietician expounding the interesting theory that palatable foods were indigestible.

"How come?" inquired Hermann.

[101]

"Well," said the woman, "take the case of baked beans. The tomato sauce on them makes them more palatable but it certainly makes them less digestible."

"What do you suppose causes that?" Mr. Deutsch wanted to know.

"It's the action of the acetic acid in the tomato sauce," she explained somewhat testily.

Mr. Deutsch seemed shocked and deeply grieved.

"Why, my good lady," he exclaimed. "Don't you know that the action of acetic acid on a complex colloidal polysaccharide is to break it down into its simpler sugars?"

One might suspect that with cultural influence so thick in the local room all copy would have been free from error, every edition a masterpiece of clear, classic English and typographic excellence. But, alas, it wasn't. That was why the style sheet decreed that no reporter, rewrite man or copyreader should ever refer to a ship as "she." Whatever a ship might be elsewhere she was "it" in Mr. Eastman's paper. And the reason, yellow and crumbling, was pasted on the bulletin board where all might see . . . a paragraph out of a society column that in hasty make-up had become mixed with a piece of shipping news:

"Mrs. Henry Garland of the Chicago Beach Hotel writes that she has had a pleasant summer visiting friends in the East. She went first to Bar Harbor, thence to Kennebunkport, Maine.

"After encountering heavy weather off the Virginia capes she put into Hampton Roads to have her bottom scraped."

[102]

There was another excellent bit on the bulletin board about a burglary in Lake Forest in which it was stated that "the thieves are believed to have entered through Mrs. White's panty" but the details are gone from us.

8

BE THERE WHEN IT HAPPENS

~~~~~~

Ask any young reporter what is his greatest ambition and he'll tell you. Every one you ask will tell you the same thing. All will smile sheepishly as they admit it is preposterous. And yet on at least two occasions the impossible has happened. The supposition is that it might happen again, although one may be permitted a doubt.

The story of Richard Hanlon is decorated with all the clichés that would prevent its being published in any fourth-rate magazine in the United States, including its truth. . . . He was a cub reporter out of a job. He'd been promised work on the *Inter-Ocean* if he would bring in just one printable story. His flat was unheated, the weather was cold, his wife was hungry, his baby was ill, it was only a few days before Christmas—and if you remember any more of the stereotyped troubles, he probably had them, too.

Despair had just about driven him into the lake when he remembered that a successful woman novelist lived somewhere in his neighborhood, to wit, somewhere around Irving Park Boulevard and Broadway.

He found the flat and rang the bell and the woman invited

him in. She seemed happy and that gave him an idea for an interview. He suggested that she tell other women her secret for a happy life. She seemed amused at that. She invited him into the living room, gave him a chair and started to tell him.

"You keep happy by pretending you don't want happiness," she said. "My husband will be here presently and I'll prove that to you. I drove him out of the house a couple of nights ago. I keep him dangling. Now he's coming back for a reconciliation and I'll make him think it means nothing to me. . . ."

"But," exclaimed the harried young man, "how much of this can I put in the paper?" She laughed at him.

"Everything," she said. "He won't see it until we've made up again and then it won't matter. . . ."

So that evening young Mr. Hanlon walked into a city room and got a very good job, but not from the *Inter-Ocean*. He made a better deal with the city editor of the *Record Herald*.

"I have a better story so I am taking it to the best bidder," he explained. "Mrs. Mable Whosis was shot and killed in the front room of her apartment this morning by her estranged husband who then shot and killed himself. And if you call up the police they'll go over there and verify it for you. . . ."

"And how do you know this?" snapped the city editor, suddenly suspicious.

"I was there," said Mr. Hanlon with that air of finality which every reporter has longed to be able to use. "I was talking to the woman when he came in and shot her. So I locked up the flat and went away and kept quiet so that it wouldn't get into the afternoon papers. . . ."

I find no record of Mr. Hanlon's having done anything else of note in the newspaper business in subsequent decades of my acquaintance with him. I don't know what became of him but it has always seemed likely to me that he fell dead one day at high noon at State and Madison Streets or Forty-second and Broadway in full view of a million people not one of whom thought to call the newspapers about it. That would be the ultimate, and fitting, irony.

The Japanese-Russian War was still a topic of conversation in local rooms during my first years in Chicago. Correspondents who had covered it were still alive, still full of reminiscence and still able to get an audience when they went about preaching the menace of Tokyo. Only about ten American newspapermen had covered that war and about five of them, including John Bass, Chris Haggerty and Richard Henry Little, came to Illinois. They used to meet with fair regularity at Stillson's where anybody might listen and ask them questions. And out of their conversation one got a pretty fair picture of how Russia had collapsed.

They didn't tell all the truth of the campaign. (I learned twenty years later the story of how one of them had discovered that you could cash duplicates of the same draft by traveling between two different branch banks on a fast horse.) But it became more and more obvious that they had known the truth. They had marched with it, lived with it. Not until long afterward when I was fighting with British censors in Cairo or with our own suppressionists in Pearl Harbor did I realize that these men had seen the last of the days of glory of the war correspondent. Not in this current war or in any war that we are likely to fight hereafter are reporters ever going to have the status that they had with both Russian and Japanese staffs. Never in any war will there be another exploit like that of Stanley Washburn, his tugboat and his ten thousand dollars worth of coal. War correspondents today are just the same as they always were. But the wars aren't.

Most of the boys in 1904 got themselves assigned to the Russian army because they wanted to be on the winning side. But Washburn didn't. He put up with the hardships of a rice-and-fish diet and learned how the Mikado's navy worked, and followed the funny little army swarming up the Korean Peninsula. He was well liked by the brass hats and politely received on all fronts, but there came a time when the Japs, with that Orientalism common to magicians and military strategists, expressed a desire to be alone. Mr. Washburn knew that something was going to pop on the Dairen Peninsula, but he didn't know what, and for once his facilities for getting to the front had failed him.

The kindly Japanese allowed him to go up to the advanced supply line where he had a chance to review a lot of Russian prisoners but (then as now, in the case of correspondents) saw little of battle. He wasn't a prisoner himself, of course, but he noticed sourly that he had no more privilege of circulation than the prisoners had, and that the same restriction had been placed on his cables as on theirs.

In those days it was customary for war correspondents to start out with great quantities of gold draped about their persons in money belts. But Mr. Lawson's correspondents did better than that. They carried blank checks signed by Lawson.

Mr. Washburn went to Chefoo and cashed one of his checks for $60,000 with which he bought the *Fawan,* a sea-going tugboat (valued at $50,000), and a deckload of coal (valued at

$10,000). Without bothering to get his baggage out of the Grand Hotel he went aboard and set out to sea.

If you remember, there wasn't much in the way of radio in 1904. Once the Washburn expedition sailed past the Chefoo breakwater it was lost to human ken. The Chicago office, which had received no advance information of Washburn's intentions, did get a cable from some Chinese banker, belatedly cautious, inquiring about the worth of the $60,000 check . . . then a long silence that had acquired a new and expensive importance. Washburn had gone out shortly before midsummer 1904 and thereafter continued to violate the cardinal rule of foreign correspondence that the reporter keep his home office informed of his whereabouts. Washburn never sent so much as a holiday greeting until he arrived in Chefoo on January 10, 1905. He'd picked up only one story in a four-month ramble.

But that story was an eye-witness account of the fall of Port Arthur and the first the world had heard about it.

Mr. Washburn sold his tug for just about what he'd paid for it. The telegraph editor of the *News* in Chicago got the story as he was preparing to leave on a Saturday night, and spiked it without a glance. The scoop of the century hung there unnoticed while Mr. Lawson's Sunday newspaper and Monday morning newspaper ground their inconsequential grist across the alley. But it was still a scoop on Monday at 10:30 A.M. when the first edition of the *News* went to press.

Mr. Little came home to ordinary newspaper work as did all of them except Washburn. Wars weren't continuous in those days and being a war correspondent might have been classed as a seasonal occupation. Mr. Little slipped into his old uniform in Russia during the last war and he came to great fame as a columnist before his retirement. He might easily rate as the journalist who was always there when it happened save for his greater fame as the man who was there when it didn't happen—and even before.

He was working for the *Tribune* at the time; I disremember how he got there. He had attended a banquet the details of which are something else I forget. Such preliminaries, of course, make no difference. What is really worth mention, however, is the fact that he awakened one morning in the Muehlebach Hotel in Kansas City without knowing where he was or how he got there.

So far this is not a phenomenon without precedent in the newspaper business. Offhand I can think of no other profession whose members habitually rush to ticket offices after the last toast is downed, but that does not diminish the tendency toward unconscious travel in journalism. . . . There was Mr. Clare who always went to Dubuque. And there was another whom I shan't identify who woke up one morning in Butte, Montana, in bed with One-Punch Kiley, the middleweight champion of Jefferson county. Mr. Little thought of these and others as he tried to recall one good reason for coming to Kansas City.

Well, the first thing to do about it was to head off the city desk. Along about noon when he began to feel a little better he put in a long-distance call for Chicago and got Bob Lee.

"Well, I got here all right," he said cheerily. "I thought for a while I wasn't going to make it. I've got a lot of telephone calls in and I'll have that story popping any minute now."

Mr. Lee with quick intuition refrained from asking Mr. Little, "What story?" He mumbled something and there was a moment of silence.

Then Mr. Little asked, "You haven't any suggestions have you?"

And Mr. Lee replied, "Don't be silly, Dick, I'm not going to tell you how to cover a story. Do it your own way."

"Thanks," said Mr. Little sadly. And he hung up.

Just to verify what was already a certainty, Mr. Lee looked up the assignment book and Mr. Little's name wasn't there. He smiled and awaited developments. About 6:00 P.M. came a telegram.

"AM HAVING TROUBLE LOCATING KEY MAN."

And there was a quick reply: "KEY MAN UNDOUBTEDLY IMPORTANT. KEEP AFTER HIM."

At ten o'clock there was another interchange:

"KEY MAN BELIEVED OUT OF TOWN."

"FOLLOW KEY MAN."

The next day Mr. Lee got a message from St. Louis. Mr. Little was still diligently hunting the Key Man. Mr. Lee advised him to keep up his excellent and tireless work.

"STILL ON TRAIL OF KEY MAN," was the last word from St. Louis. About noon the day after that Mr. Little came into the office.

"Awfully sorry about that story," he told Mr. Lee. "But that guy got out of town just ahead of me. I followed him all the way here and then learned that he'd started for Liverpool on a Canadian-Pacific boat out of Montreal. And for the life of me I don't know any other contact I could get that story from. It's a tough break."

[110]

"It's certainly tough," admitted the managing editor. "But don't let it worry you. We all know that you handled it with all your usual skill and energy."

Mr. Little looked a bit startled at that. But Mr. Lee's face was placid. So far as anybody knows the key man never came back from Europe.

9

THE EXTRA-WEALTHY PRINCESS
OF JARPUTANA

IN THE past fifteen or twenty years numerous clever authors have toyed with the idea of writing books about the *Herald and Examiner*. Nothing came of it for reasons that became obvious after the most superficial research.

"It would be easy to write such a book," was the burden of their song. "But who would believe it after you got it done?"

Who indeed! The *Examiner* was never, properly speaking, a newspaper at all, but something out of the Red Queen's dream.

It may not have exerted much influence on Chicago. Its circulation was never big enough and it was never out of the red from the day when Hearst in an optimistic moment founded it to be the morning companion of the *Evening American*. But it undoubtedly had its effect on journalism in the United States. Those who know best say that anybody who was able to spend a year in its local room and retain his sanity was *de facto* qualified to work on any newspaper in the world.

The difference between the *Examiner* and other journals began right at the top. It generally had three managing editors.

One might do well to stop and examine this phenomenon. The managing editors did not function on any sliding scale of authority, one in command and the two others answerable to him. They were of equal rank and in the period of their finest flower each had his own ideas and his own staff.

Mr. Hearst, who was certainly in his prime when he inaugurated the three-platoon system of managing editors, may have thought to pursue the policy of Louis XI who learned how to divide and conquer. It was impossible for any one managing editor to loaf on the job when he knew that two others were waiting for a chance to harpoon him. That, presumably, made for a high degree of efficiency in the executive department. It was somewhat confusing to the rank and file.

Latterly, when times got tough, there were not so many of them. Sometimes there was only one with the official label. But that did not deceive anybody. Behind the man with the badge there was always somebody to dispute his decisions and keep the plant in a state of effervescence. It had been ordered so in the beginning and so it continued.

There was one wonderful era—there seem to have been only two supreme executives at the time—when it was the custom of the day managing editor to leave a complete newspaper, written, edited, set up and in the forms ready to roll for the man who took over at 6:00 P.M. The night managing editor, without looking at this gift, would toss it into the hell-box and proceed to get out a paper of his own.

There was a night managing editor during the war years who survived despite the precarious tenure of such jobs on the *Examiner* because nobody ever scooped him. His method was simple but adequate. He would stay in his office until the final

editions of the *Herald* and the *Tribune* had come in. If they
contained anything at all that his own paper had missed he
would clip out such material, have it headed and set, remake
his front page and run off a few copies of a new and better
edition of the *Examiner*. By that time all the wagons would
be out and the newsstands would be loaded for the day's sales,
but no matter. This final-extra-final edition was private but
important. That was the edition that went into the mail to
Mr. Hearst.

Not so long ago this technique was extended farther into the
local room. Then the puzzled workers found themselves with
a day city editor, a night city editor, an executive city editor
and a roving city editor. Just what the roving city editor did
was never quite clear.

In spite of all this odd procedure one managing editor did
contrive to get head and shoulders over his competition and
run the paper just about as he pleased. With considerable justice he became celebrated in song and story because of it. One
refers, of course, to Walter Howey.

Mr. Howey, however difficult it may be to believe, got into
his stride as a newspaper editor in the conservative atmosphere
of the Chicago *Tribune*. He later lived that down. Why the
Tribune should have let him go, even against the extravagant
bidding of Mr. Hearst, is something nobody knows much
about. There were rumors that he had had differences of
opinion with Colonel R. R. McCormick. Probably he had.
There were other rumors—unverified—that the Colonel had
accused him of being a sucker for the wiles of press agents
questing free advertising. That is a bare possibility. One likes

to believe it because it would explain so well the little pleasantries that Mr. Howey extended to the *Tribune*.

One day after Mr. Howey had taken over his new duties a cyclone hit Murphysboro, Illinois, and spread ruin across the south end of the state. The *Examiner* promptly organized a relief train.

It is not so difficult, generally, to organize relief trains. You get some railroad to donate the train. You get doctors and nurses to volunteer their services. You get dealers in food, bedding and medical supplies to give till it hurts. But there is a drawback to the procedure in that it takes time. The *Examiner*, from long practice in such enterprises, had reduced the whole thing to a system. Numerous members of the staff knew just where and how and on whom to put the bite and for how much. So there wasn't any lost motion. The cyclone sufferers got speedy and efficient service.

Mr. Howey was highly gratified by the whole business. He allowed the editorial writers to skate close to the edge of modesty in bragging about it. But it must have irked his sensitive soul to discover that no other newspaper in town paid any attention to the *Examiner's* enterprise, public spirit or vicarious generosity. It must have irked him, else he would not have taken steps to gain the plaudits of the opposition, and he certainly took steps.

First he sat down and contrived an editorial—not long but not too brief—warmly praising the *Herald and Examiner* for its civic consciousness, its initiative, its broad, its almost godlike humanitarianism. You can find copies of this great work today in public libraries though they are difficult to come by elsewhere.

Having written the editorial he penciled some marks on it that might have had no significance to an *Examiner* printer. After which he called for a smart office boy whom he instructed in what might have been mistaken for a primitive quadrille.

"You turn left at the head of the stairs. . . . You go through a door—pretend this is the door. . . . You walk thirty-five steps straight ahead. . . . You turn left and walk ten steps. . . . That brings you to a desk. . . . There'll be an old guy at the desk wearing an eye shade and sleeve supporters. . . . He's the copy cutter. . . . You hand him this copy and you say 'Must. Colonel McCormick.'. . . Then you turn around and get out. . . . Now go ahead and let's see you do it."

Half an hour later he delivered his office boy in a taxicab in front of a door on the lower level of Wacker Drive. The boy, hatless and coatless, went up a long series of stairs and carried out his instructions.

The *Tribune* had run off about half its circulation before somebody discovered Mr. Howey's essay at the head of the editorial column. It was then too late to do anything about it except remake the editorial page and cultivate a deep silence.

It was many months afterward when the Hindu Princess came to town. She was the daughter of a fabulously wealthy Maharajah, well educated and darkly beautiful, a lovely subject for the feature writers and photographers if her visit to Chicago had been nothing more than a stay between trains. But hers was no casual call. She had come on a definite and romantic mission. She wanted to give away a couple of million dollars.

She arrived without any preliminary notice and was met by

PRINCESS OF JARPUTANA

no brass bands. She went to the Blackstone Hotel and established herself in a suite with seventeen trunks and a couple of dark-brown body servants. Then she called the manager and asked him shyly if he had heard of a newspaper in the town called the *Tribune*. Sometime later a *Tribune* reporter called on her. When he went back to his office he was dizzy.

The story of the Maharajah's daughter was stranger than truth. Many years ago there had been a sudden uprising in Jarputana, one of those quarrels between Mohammedans and Hindus. As revolutions go it hadn't amounted to much because there aren't many Mohammedans in Jarputana. Eventually His Britannic Majesty's troops had come through Lateekh Pass and established order. But while the fighting was going on the Maharajah suddenly found himself in a bad way. He had been on a journey far from his capital, unaware that trouble was in the offing, when a wandering band of revolutionaries surrounded the minor palace in which he had taken lodging and made preparations to kill him. In this desperate emergency he was saved by a young American engineer who had been in the palace installing a waterworks or something. The American smuggled him through the rebel lines in a bedroll.

"And that is why I am here," said the Princess. "The American went his own way the next morning, refusing to accept any reward for what he had done. When peace had come and my father's power was assured once more he had searches made for his rescuer all over India. But they were unsuccessful. We do not even know the name of this American. We know really nothing about him except that he mentioned to my father that his home was in Chicago in the United States

[117]

of America. And we know also that when he went away he allowed my father to put a gold ring on his finger as a token of remembrance.

"My father, as you may have heard, died three months ago, and he willed that the eldest of his family come to America and look for this man. He meant my brother but my brother died soon afterward and the task fell to me. My father's brave rescuer can identify himself with the ring and I shall deliver to him the two million dollars that my father wished him to have. . . . I had heard of the Chicago *Tribune*. I feel you can help me to find him. . . ."

Maybe the story wasn't exactly like that—but you get the spirit of the thing. It was printed in the *Tribune* the next day with many interesting pictures.

It was a complete scoop. The *Examiner,* apparently, hadn't heard about the Princess. And it remained a scoop. For none of the afternoon newspapers that day carried a line about her. Managing Editor Edward Beck of the *Tribune,* who appears to have been out of town when the Maharajah's daughter called his office, returned to read the piece in puzzlement. It was just too good. He chased a reporter over to the Blackstone and received the heartening information that the Princess and her seventeen trunks had departed. Then he hired a private detective to look into the matter while cables to the foreign service were failing to prove that any maharajah of the name mentioned by the Princess had recently died or, indeed, that any such potentate had ever existed. Presently the detective reported.

"I can't find any trace of the girl or the servants," he said. "They went out of town on the Century to New York. But I got some dope on who rented the suite. . . . He was a one-eyed guy named Bowie."

Not so long after that a new moving picture came to Chicago. It was released by the Hearst film interests and entitled, if memory is not in error, *The Maharajah's Daughter*.

My own tour of duty with the *Examiner* was brief and uneventful. I found my way to the copy desk there after the finish of the *Inter-Ocean* and remained only until I was able to get a job as a reporter somewhere else. But short as was my stay I learned much about high-tension journalism.

The *Inter-Ocean's* ghost and Associated Press franchise had been absorbed by the *Record-Herald* (morning) which rejuvenated itself as the *Herald*. The *Herald* under James Keeley's direction started out bravely to gain control of the morning field and undoubtedly took a fair slice out of the *Examiner's* circulation. However, we didn't mind that. Until the *Herald* was finally taken over by the *Examiner* it was looked upon sometimes with annoyance but generally with great tolerance. Nobody in the city room ever thought of wasting his animosity. We were gunning for the *Tribune*.

I recall one illustrative incident. A young lawyer named Dunne had been mysteriously killed. A brace of *Examiner* reporters, assigned to get his photograph, looked up his address in the telephone book and presently arrived at a South Side flat building. Nobody answered their ring at the Dunne doorbell and they appealed to the janitor. They were friends of the Dunnes, they said. They were expected. And if the janitor would let them in with his passkey the Dunne family would be deeply grateful.

That, and possibly more tangible evidences of good will, convinced the janitor. He let them into the flat. One kept him in spirited conversation. The other collected all the photographs in the place and hid them under his coat.

They departed then and all would have gone well save for the fact that they got to the lobby just as a man and woman came in from the street.

"Well, ain't that nice," said the janitor, "there's Mr. and Mrs. Dunne, now. . . . Mr. Dunne, these fellows was wanting to see you."

Mr. Dunne was friendly. He didn't seem to hear the reporters when they told him he wasn't the Mr. Dunne they were looking for—that their Mr. Dunne was dead. He wanted to tell them about a moving picture he had just seen. Charlie Chaplin was in it and he was the funniest guy in the world. The reporters stood attentive until one of them noticed that Mrs. Dunne had become restless and had started upstairs toward her flat. With no prearranged signal they dashed for the open air.

There remained, of course, the problem of returning the borrowed photographs of the wrong Mr. Dunne, which is the only point in this narrative. They took a cab to the Tribune Building, found a telephone and called for a messenger boy. He arrived to find them in front of the elevators.

"Here," was the message they gave him as they handed over the pictures, "take these things to Mr. Joseph Dunne at this address. If he asks you anything about them just say we gave them to you in the Tribune Building. He'll understand."

Anyone wishing to make a study of vigorous methods could

have found no better clinic than the *Examiner* in the days of its glory. An ability to write or sense the news in a story was only incidental to a reporter's equipment. He also had to have quick wits and initiative and determination. It must be admitted that these lads were able workmen with pride in their paper and a willingness to tackle any problem from a locked door to a platoon of police. They took unbelievable punishment without ever learning what it meant to be discouraged. Sometimes they got what they were sent after. But one who knew them intimately has been toying with a heretical thought ever since he went out of their lives: Maybe one who steps softly gets farther.

Anyway for one reason or another the management of the *Examiner*—not to mention the minor personnel—made a lot of little mistakes.

For many years Herman DeVries, a scholarly soul who deserved a better fate, was tied up with the *Examiner* as music critic. It is understandable that the customers who made up the paper's circulation didn't know this, but a little less understandable that a large part of the lads in the local room didn't know it either. So one night when a bright reporter was dispatched with a couple of opera tickets for Mr. DeVries he delivered them instead to Cy DeVry, the keeper of the zoo at Lincoln Park. Mr. DeVry, highly flattered, put on his high hat and tails and sat through Rosa Raisa's version of *Tannhäuser*. Then, slightly bewildered by the whole proceedings, he came over to the *Examiner* office, asked for a reporter and dictated a review of the proceedings. Apparently nobody in the *Examiner's* cultured circulation noticed the difference.

After Theodore Roosevelt was shot in Milwaukee he was

brought at once to Mercy Hospital in Chicago and squads of reporters were assigned to keep watch over him. Every newspaperman of more than two-months' experience knows the irksome futility of such a job. You can't overrun a hospital. You can't develop private news sources. You have to content yourself with such bulletins as attending physicians care to give out. And between bulletins you just sit on curbstones and fan yourself with your hat.

Prominent among the mob that milled about the sidewalks in front of Mercy Hospital was young Mr. Kent Hunter of the *Examiner*. Mr. Hunter knew all about the vigorous method and like all men of action he resented monotony. While other reporters lined the curbs, he walked impatiently about the building studying its entrances and its exits and the disposition of the police guard that patroled it. On one of his tours he discovered a flash of bluish light in an upper window identifying the X-Ray laboratory. That gave him an idea.

Soon afterward he was over a stone wall and creeping up the back fire escape. He lay outside the laboratory window until the roentgenologist had left the room. Then he went over the sill and made a quick survey.

He knew that Roosevelt had been in the hospital just about long enough to have had an X-ray picture taken. He knew that the plate must be still in the drying rack. He found what he was looking for and went out again. He tore his pants going over the wall but he saved the plate. He escaped the police and had to run halfway to the loop before he could find a taxi. But, eventually, he got to his office. The portrait of Mr. Roosevelt's chest (X marks the bullet) was printed as the greatest pictorial scoop of the year. Mr. Hunter got a neat bonus and a vacation and a new pair of pants, not to mention the grudging plaudits of rival reporters.

Two months later he met a doctor friend who had heard something of his accomplishment.

"But that," said the doctor, "that wasn't Roosevelt."

"It certainly was," declared Mr. Hunter stormily.

The doctor shook his head.

"Roosevelt's older," he said. "What you printed was the picture of a six-month-old fetus."

Mr. Howey left the *Examiner* eventually for fields where his skill and nervous energies would have a wider usefulness. But his spirit lingered despite the fact that no succeeding managing editor ever approached anything like his individuality. New executives promoted new ideas and new batches of reporters carried them out in the true *Examiner* tradition.

One managing editor, building no doubt for the future, got the idea of putting the *Examiner* into freshly laid cornerstones. It fell to the lot of Frank Hagen to make all the contacts, attend all the ceremonies and report all the speeches. . . . "Today's edition of the *Herald and Examiner* will be a document of historical significance at some distant date when archeologists pry into the cornerstone of the Glotz Building, laid today by President Mmph of Feitelbaum's Loan Bank. . . ." The work kept Mr. Hagen out in the open air but there was a lot of building going on and he got tired of it.

He was still brooding when a pair of hoodlums named Scalise and Anselni beat a murder rap and were given a victory banquet by the outstanding luminaries of the South Side mob. Just before they sat down to the soup course they made the mistake of letting somebody know that they intended to kill Al

Capone. It was not surprising, therefore, that they were found dead the next day. They had been beaten to death apparently with a baseball bat.

An autopsy was performed on them and Mr. Hagen was assigned to watch the autopsy. It was a messy affair but Mr. Hagen was experienced and reasonably hard. He stayed until the end and then telephoned to his managing editor.

"This is Hagen," he reported. "I've been covering the autopsy on Scalise and Anselni. Doc Whosis of the coroner's office cut them open and sewed them up again. . . . And I just called to tell you that you've got copies of your damned paper where they won't come out till the day of judgment."

10

LIFE AMONG THE MULTIPLE MANAGING EDITORS

~~~~~~

MULTIPLE managing editors and kindred blights may have been a sore burden to the constantly changing local staffs of the *Herald and Examiner* but they never caused any lasting woe. If a reporter hasn't the ability to adjust himself to queer conditions he shouldn't be a reporter. The logical reaction from the pontifical seriousness of the front office was a wild hilarity in the city room, and serfs without a sense of humor speedily moved elsewhere.

The lads had a downright affection for Mr. Sam Makaroff who was by turns office boy, assistant city editor and "roving city editor." Mr. Makaroff's education was sketchy and his acquaintance with the English language was purely platonic. To the best of his ability he maintained a dignified front and he seemed conscious of his position. But he made a nice foil for the stuffed shirts and so came to enjoy lasting popularity.

He became something of a legend around Chicago when he tried to board a special train bearing a lot of society notables on an errand which the world, unfortunately, has forgotten. A

calm and dignified gentleman tried to shoo him off the observation platform.

"I'm Charles Harkness Harkness-Clifford," said the gentleman sternly.

"You're a son of a bitch-bitch," returned Mr. Makaroff.

His gifted repartee naturally made him famous overnight.
But it was really his sense of phrase in the routine exercise of a
desk job that got him his lasting place in the sun.

A weeping woman had appeared at a coroner's inquest into
the death of her husband, and Mr. Makaroff wanted to make
sure that the rewrite man understood the story's pathos.

"Soften it up," he directed. "Get in something about her
widow's tweeds."

And once there was the matter of a story that had suddenly
blown up.

"Not much on this," he ordered. "Give me half a paragraph."

One of the itinerant managing editors appeared one night
with acidosis and an abiding scorn for the talents of his staff.
"The trouble with this paper," he informed Mr. Makaroff, "is
that nobody dares to be original. Every story in the proofs tonight is filled with old expressions—platitudes."

So Mr. Makaroff went out and shot the adrenalin into his
loyal workers.

"The boss says we got too many old platitudes," he told
them. "You gotta snap out of it and get a lotta new platitudes."

He uttered other aphorisms:

"The convention is waterlogged."

"We want pictures of the Big Figureheads of the American
Legion."

"You don't have to write this if you don't want to. It's purely mandatory."

"Get something in about the doctors' oath of hypocrisy."

And so *ad infinitum* while the rewrite men patiently recorded all the bright things he had said, all that he might have said, and many, probably, that he never said at all.

Delos Avery, a quiet-mannered man of varied talents and a bitter wit, was a rewrite man who watched the procession of executives pass in and out of the office for many years. As dean of the office he acquired skill and privilege as a sniper and he was a constant source of worry to Mr. Makaroff. That was because of his willingness to stick into every story little comments intended for Mr. Makaroff's eyes alone. He was carefully watched by editors and copyreaders standing behind Mr. Makaroff but that did not prevent the appearance of some of his gems in type.

Once the pundits decided that no story in the *Examiner* should begin with *A, An,* or *The*. And shortly after the promulgation of the rule Mr. Avery was called upon to write a piece about the finding of the body of an unidentified woman in the river. That did not bother Mr. Avery.

"Hello everybody," he wrote. "Take a look at this! The body of an unidentified woman . . . etc." That got into type and the rule was changed the next day.

Then there was the occasion when William Powell, the actor, was very ill. Somebody in the front office thought it might be a good thing to cash in on the sentiment with which this star was so generally regarded.

"Here," said the city editor to Mr. Avery. "Stick in a suggestion that this guy's fans write him cheering notes in care of the *Herald and Examiner*."

"Okay," said the imperturbable Mr. Avery. And his carefully worded account of Mr. Powell's illness came to this end:

"Mr. Powell's associates have informed the *Herald and Examiner* that messages of cheer from his numerous friends in Chicago would undoubtedly hasten his recovery. This newspaper will forward immediately all letters addressed to him.

"Write to Mr. Powell in care of the *Herald and Examiner*. Or say a little prayer."

That one got printed in a nice position next to pure reading matter and a few hours later the phone on the city desk began to ring.

"I was deeply touched by your story of Mr. Powell's illness," said a woman's voice. "And I notice that you recommend prayer. Just what sort of prayer would you suggest?"

The city editor hastily looked up Mr. Avery's work and for the first time noticed the last sentence. He went into conference with the great minds about him, then returned to the telephone.

"As for the prayer," he said with the intonation of an undertaker, "the *Examiner* approves no set formula. Just say whatever is in your heart."

Si Clare, biographer of Policeman Spiegelbuehler, came to the *Examiner* with other wreckage of the old *Inter-Ocean* and rose to great prominence. He no longer went to Dubuque when he got drunk, or rather he went there only once. On that occasion he went through his routine of telegraphing for help to Jim Crown, City Editor, the *Inter-Ocean*, Chicago. But there was no *Inter-Ocean* and there wasn't any Jim Crown in Chicago. He had gone away to New Orleans months previously. So Mr. Clare arrived at sobriety in a police station and was two days convincing anybody that he ought to be brought home. From then on, Dubuque seems to have lost its glamor.

Mr. Clare's life in the ensuing years was considerably more temperate than it had ever been before. He announced publicly that he would welcome a stomach ulcer to insure a permanent change in his habits. Once he almost became a teetotaler.

The desk next to Mr. Clare's was occupied by Mr. Earl Ackroyd, another of those geniuses who drift unsung through the newspaper business. Mr. Ackroyd in some previous existence had learned how to take a typewriter apart and put it together again and his mechanical skill had remained with him when he became a rewrite man for the *Examiner*.

One afternoon with time hanging heavy on his hands he noticed the sad state of Mr. Clare's typewriter and was seized by a generous impulse to fix it up. He sent a boy across the street for a ten-cent screwdriver and went to work. When he had finished the typewriter was mechanically as good as before but it was different. The ingenious Mr. Ackroyd had changed the position of quite a lot of the type bars without disturbing the keys. He put away his screwdriver and sat back expectantly. He had the feeling that Mr. Clare, fresh from the inspiration of a cooling saloon, would have a lot of fun with his typewriter.

Mr. Clare came in at five o'clock as expected and in the cheery state that Mr. Ackroyd had foreseen. He sat down and wrote:

By Si Clare
Gang guns blazed again today on Chicago's West Side
and in the thinning smoke of black powder the police discovered the bodies of Tony ("The Flea") Raspucci and
John ("Bowlegs") Iskovitch . . ."

Or at least that is what he thought he was writing. When he
looked at his copy he read:

Qn Lo Eswkt
Uwfu uxfl qswmtr wuwof zgrwn gf Eioewug'l Vtlz
Lort wfr of zit zioffofu ldgat gy qswea hgvrtk zit hgsoet
rolegctktr zit qgrotl gy Zgfn ("Zit Ystw") Kwlhxeeo wfr
Pgif ("Qgvstul") Olagcozei . . .

Mr. Clare showed alarm. He tore the copy paper out of the
typewriter and handed it to Mr. Ackroyd.

"Look at that," he urged. "Does that make sense?"

"Certainly," said Mr. Ackroyd, who knew in advance what
assignment Mr. Clare had been covering. "It's about Raspucci
and Iskovitch. They got shot."

Mr. Clare tried it again with no better result, arose in sudden
panic and started out of the office.

"The hooch has got me," he announced hollowly. "I can
think swell but I can't write anything that I can read. I'm going on the wagon right now." But he didn't. Instead he got a
new typewriter.

Mr. Clare, despite his failings, came in time to rate as a
Hearst ace. He was shrewd, volatile and filled with a fine
sense of the dramatic. He never saw things exactly as less
imaginative reporters saw them but his visions were always interesting and looked well in print. No wonder, then, that he

figured largely in all the policy stories, solved all the mysteries, conducted all the relief trains.

One of his expeditions became a classic among students of the Vigorous Method.

Down in middle Illinois one day a banker came back to his bank after lunch and noticed that his clerk ("teller" by brevet rating) was missing. The door of the teller's cage stood open. Some $2,000 in cash was gone. But that wasn't the worst of it. The big vault was closed and in front of it lay the clerk's hand-kerchief.

The banker sent out an immediate call for help.

"My bank has been robbed," he reported. "I don't know what the loss may total. The robbers must have overpowered Jimmy and shoved him into the vault. The door can't be opened until tomorrow morning because of the time lock. It's an airtight modern vault and he'll die there. He'll die!"

The wire services brought this sad news to the *Examiner* office and Mr. Clare was assigned to see what he could do about it. He rushed into the office of the current managing editor, got full authority to proceed and thereupon launched a campaign which for speed, vision and daring surpassed even the *Examiner's* own past performances.

Mr. Clare began as usual by calling a railroad president. The railroad president, as usual, donated the use of a special train. It consisted of one locomotive and one coach but that was enough.

Then Mr. Clare called the warden of Joliet penitentiary.

"I want to borrow a safe-cracker for a few hours," he explained lucidly.

"A what?" demanded the warden.

"A safe-cracker," repeated Mr. Clare. "This is the Chicago *Herald and Examiner* and we need a safe-cracker to save a boy who's dying in a vault. You can send guards along with him if you want to but we've got to have him. It's a matter of life and death."

"You ought to have a court order," mentioned the warden. "This is all very irregular."

But one never got anywhere talking about irregularities with Mr. Clare.

"I've got a special train waiting for me now," he said finally. "You have your yegg down at the railroad station in an hour and we'll pick him up. And you'd better find us a good one because this is a tough vault."

Within an hour after he had received the assignment Mr. Clare was on his way. Messages of good cheer were sent by the *Examiner* to the banker, the boy's worried parents and the local constable. The safe-cracker, well pleased with his prospect for a holiday, was waiting at the Joliet station with a kit of tools taken from the penitentiary museum.

Two hours later the train rolled into the banker's town. The stationmaster came out to point the way to a convenient siding. But there was no other reception committee. That annoyed Mr. Clare who had pictured himself leaping with his photographer and a safeblower into the arms of an anxious populace. But the station agent told him how to get to the bank and he went.

There he discovered what had become of the citizenry. But he no longer cared. A garage mechanic was trundling out an oxyacetylene welding outfit. The air was filled with the reek of something burning. The vault door stood open.

[132]

"I'm sorry," said the mechanic apologetically. "But we didn't think you'd get here in time. So I cut out the lock with a torch. The kid wasn't there. He took it on the lam somewheres with about twenty thousand bucks."

11

ADVICE TO WRONG-WAY CORRIGAN

~~~~~~

THE *Evening American,* when I came there after leaving the *Journal* in 1920, was not so wild a place as the *Examiner* had been seven years before but it was no place for anyone with sensitive ears. The tempo was keyed two notches above hysteria. Nobody moved even to the water cooler except on a dead run. The city editor and his crew yelled at the copyreaders, the copyreaders yelled at the copyboys and the copyboys yelled at one another. Every story, from a triple murder to a purse-snatching in the ghetto, was a big story and greeted with quivering excitement by everybody who had anything to do with it. All the typewriters were clattering all the time—although I am still of the belief that most of them never turned out anything more thrilling than "Now is the time for all good men to come to the aid of the party." All of the telephones rang incessantly. In short the *American,* save for its lack of artillery, was vividly reminiscent of the Argonne.

I got used to the din long before I could assign a reason for it. Individually the editors were quiet-mannered, well-balanced, good-humored men. As I observed to Heck Elwell, the news editor, when in a moment of sheer exhaustion I left them, they were like parts of a Seidlitz powder, harmless until mixed. The trouble with them was that they had all come up from the ranks. None of them had ever worked anywhere else and their ideas of how a newspaper should be run had been derived from the gay old days when Hearst first came to Chicago and competition had been desperate, and delirium had been a blessed escape from disheartening reality.

I was hired as a rewrite man, one of a theoretical three. Actually there were only two of us and, inasmuch as no reporter was ever called in to type out a record of his observations on a spot-news story, we wrote the entire front end of the paper. There were ten editions each day and there had to be a new lead on every front-page story for each of the ten editions. The theory seemed to be that people who read the *American* read every issue of it. One could envision them loitering about the newsstands slaver-mouthed with expectation as the wagons approached to replace the "Opening Markets Edition" with the so-called "Afternoon Edition" and so far into the night.

The leads had to be rewritten whether there was any more news or not. For the all-edition readers apparently were just as stupid as they were eccentric. One gathered that they agreed with the editors that by changing the wording of a sentence you gave it added worth and novelty.

My daily average output was between fifty-five and sixty typewritten sheets of copy a day. Joe McHugh who had the desk next to mine was just as prolific, possibly more so. And writing was only part of the work. We had to listen to reporters telephoning what they had learned about their assignments. We had also to cover assignments of our own by telephone. All in all one had little leisure to discover what was going on in the office save what he could see over the top of his own typewriter or what broke like the tide of Fundy on his numbed ears.

I got frightfully tired of telephone assignments.

"Here's a piece of I.N.S.—says skirts are going to be shorter this year. Call a lot of clergymen and reformers and get a symposium on it. You get it: What do they think about short skirts as a menace to morals."

"Here's a guy says clubwomen are bad cooks. . . . Call up a lot of clubwomen."

And so *saecula saeculorum.*

Eventually I left the *American* because a man named McSwiney starved himself to death in Dublin. My going wasn't as a gesture of protest against the wrongs of Ireland or anything like that. I never got it quite straight in my own mind what Mr. McSwiney was hunger-striking for. But, sometime during his ordeal, I had made it clear to the city desk that I would resign when and if I should ever be asked to compile another symposium. Then Mr. McSwiney died and I set about calling up all the quotable Irish in town. But I also quit as I had promised.

Despite my resentment toward the *American* system, a resentment that nineteen years of perspective have not mellowed, I shall admit that fantastic shop has attracted and fostered a lot of good help. Then as since, *American* reporters have generally been not only smart but literate.

Wallace Smith, whom we looked upon as the Richard Harding Davis of our time, was briefly with us between Mexican wars and Hollywood. Bart Cormack was one of us before he contrived a play called *The Racket* and passed on to better things. Bill Curley did so well managing us that he became editorial supervisor for a lot of Hearst newspapers which no doubt needed it. Harry Reutlinger, whom I remember as a cub with a cherubic countenance, gentle manners and widely varied talents, came into the company of the great in those days by turning up a story that the World's Series between the Reds and the White Sox had been fixed. He, however, was not one of the *American's* passing stars. He stayed on to become (a) a highly successful city editor; (b) custodian and guide of some of the strangest editorial exhibits in the record of this fascinating business.

There has been much discussion in the trade regarding Mr. Reutlinger's working philosophy and methods: Is he a genius or just lucky, a child of God or a child of Hearst? The argument, of course, gets nowhere and Mr. Reutlinger goes on doing his tricks with whatever fantastic raw materials happen to be at hand. It would not be worth mentioning were it not for the fact that it brings attention to his complete sympathy with what has been called "the Hearst reporter." And why not? Come to think about it, he was a pretty good specimen of that class himself. He helped to clean up baseball with his discoveries about gambling in Cincinnati and Chicago. He helped annoy the "big-shots" of the Capone era (which is about all any journalist did in the gin-and-gun era). And he had a fine appreciation for the true the good and the beautiful —not to mention the dramatic—in all worldly affairs.

In recent years he upset his competitors in the city-editing business with a demonstration that the telephone could be used for telephoning. At the same time he contrived to turn

Douglas Corrigan, a good but not too-colorful flier, into the most amazing figure since Icarus.

Mr. Reutlinger had come to his desk at an early hour on the morning of July 29, 1938, and saw in the clippings laid out for his inspection a brief note saying that a plane, believed to be Corrigan's, had been sighted off Ireland. Languidly he picked up the telephone and put in calls for the three principal airports in Northern Ireland and Eire.

"I want to talk to Douglas G. Corrigan," he said. "If he hasn't arrived tell 'em to hold the wire. He ought to be down any time now."

In less than half an hour he was chatting with Corrigan who seemed glad not only to have a chance to talk but to be able to. Filled with such detail as the use of a pole shoved out the window to de-ice the wings, an overweight gas tank in the back seat, a motor that he'd rebuilt himself, the story of Douglas Corrigan had already begun to sound like plagiarism from *Alice in Wonderland* when Reutlinger asked him how come he'd turned up in Dublin when he'd said he was going to Los Angeles. He hesitated and the young city editor in Chicago picked Mr. Corrigan right out of the ranks of workaday transatlantic fliers with a question:

"Fly the wrong way?"

Corrigan laughed and said, "I sure did."

"Fair enough," Reutlinger advised him. "Stick to that. It's the best story you can get."

And he turned around to a typewriter to make a national figure out of "Wrong-Way Corrigan."

This technique of making a scoop out of a story that was open to every editor in the world wasn't exactly new to him.

ADVICE TO WRONG-WAY CORRIGAN

His exposé of the Black Sox with its attendant effect on baseball and the future of Judge Landis was an earlier example of it.

Everybody in town, including at least one ex-sports writer, had heard rumors of bribery in the Cincinnati (National League)-Chicago (American League) World Series. Dispassionate analysis of the box scores after the series had fostered a growing belief that there might be something to these stories. But nobody did anything—or at any rate nobody did anything until Mr. Reutlinger decided that the matter was worth looking into.

His only evidence of fraud was that a South Side acquaintance who for many years had been an ardent White Sox fan had made several thousand dollars betting on Cincinnati in the series. That, coupled with Joe Jackson's odd antics on the playing field, seemed to Mr. Reutlinger just about enough for an indictment but still, as he saw it, he had nothing that he could print. He called up a friend on the sports desk.

"Say," he asked, "who's the dumbest guy on the White Sox team?"

The friend didn't hesitate. "Happy Felsch is the dumbest guy on anybody's team," he said. Mr. Reutlinger went to call on Mr. Felsch.

"Look," he said. "The other guys in this are going to confess and leave you holding the bag. They say you're the brains of it."

Mr. Felsch did not seem to be much concerned. "Naw," he said. "I ain't the brains. But I got mine."

Reutlinger pulled some more details of his story together and called the city desk. He got Eddie Mahoney who at the moment was all tangled up in one of the periodic alcohol-ring exposures and who had heard all about the Black Sox rumors anyway. Mr. Mahoney didn't seem much impressed.

"Call in with it later," he advised.

The cherubic cub exploded.

"Call back nuts!" he announced. "I'll call the *News*. . . . They'll take it. . . ."

Mr. Reutlinger had a change of heart as soon as he stepped out of the telephone booth but so did Mr. Mahoney. A hurry call was sent out to all *American* distribution centers on the South Side and the trucks were called off circulation jobs to hunt down Reutlinger before he could get to the *News*. He was picked up in front of an elevated station where Mr. Mahoney asked his forgiveness with a truck driver as proxy.

Early in his experience about the courts, Mr. Reutlinger came to realize that while nature sometimes imitates art, its performance is not to be depended on. Such details as birds let loose in courtrooms where beautiful women are on trial for their lives seemed a definite improvement on the usual bird-less routine in such affairs. Sound effects like racking coughs and half-stifled sobs were obviously a needed obbligato to any tense dramatic situation. Cold logic might win lawsuits, but for his money it was emotion that made newspaper accounts of them worth printing.

Which brings us around to the case of Anne Jackson who chose a dull week for her breach-of-promise suit against James Whitby, a wealthy manufacturer of waffle irons, and thereby became a person of sufficient importance to rate a biography with pictures in the *American*. Anne, it turned out, was not only a thoughtful opportunist but a raving beauty with hair, face and legs. And she was the *American's* particular property because Mr. Reutlinger had got in first with his bid for her memoirs. It was only logical, all things considered, that her lawyer should take a second place in the shaping of her immediate future. He may have furnished some legal reasons why Miss Jackson should get the $100,000 she asked for (it seemed little enough for a person of her habits), but it was Mr. Reutlinger who thought up the details of the campaign and directed the off-stage bugle calls.

It was his belief that good honest tears—tears of innocence and disappointed love—would make any jury give a woman a bonus and a vote of thanks despite the fact that plaintiffs in "heart-balm" suits hadn't been doing very well in Cook County for many a day. So he arranged for Miss Jackson to weep. The girl said that she hadn't had much experience in such matters. She'd never been a public love victim before and she wasn't certain that she would know just when to burst into tears.

"That will be easy," said Mr. Reutlinger. "I'll fix it up with your lawyer to pull out his handkerchief and blow his nose whenever he wants you to do your stuff. When he puts the handkerchief away you can quit. But do the crying naturally. Think of something you can really cry about—like the guy who gave you a diamond that turned out to be phony—that sort of stuff." Miss Jackson said that she thought she had the idea.

And very likely she had. . . . There never was any real evidence that she was a complete psychopath. . . . But when the day came for her appearance on the stand ("in her own behalf," as the leading journals put it) the lawyer had a cold in the head and, furthermore, so did three men in the jury box.

"What is your name?" inquired the lawyer. And then because he jolly well had to he pulled out his handkerchief.

"Oh dear," moaned Miss Jackson, "oh dear, boo . . . hoo . . ." And her beautiful frame shook convulsively. The three coryzal gentlemen of the jury pulled out their handkerchiefs in sympathy with the lawyer and joined in her tears.

It was a strange day in anybody's court record. Miss Jackson wept at the mention of her street address, of the school she had attended, if any, as a child, of her happy girlhood, of her hope in a hereafter. Fidgeting on his bench in the press section, the impresario theoretically tore his hair. But the jury, overlooking recent precedent, gave Miss Jackson a fine fortune. There was a generally accepted theory that three continuously weeping men on the jury were tearing their hearts out in distress for her. . . .

All in all, looking back on such episodes it doesn't seem too remarkable that Mr. Reutlinger should be able to preserve his calm no matter what happens to the news or the men who produce it.

Admittedly he has some talent on his staff of an imaginative quality hardly inferior to his own. You don't need to look farther that Mr. Randall Healy—may his restless spirit have peace wherever it is—for an example. Mr. Healy, it seems, was born to trouble and he found it in many on odd place—floods in Kentucky, Dillinger's funeral in Indiana, Chicago police stations. And if none came spontaneously he was not averse to making some of his own.

Without looking up the record it is hard to recall just what particular misfortune was afoot in Europe during the years of Mr. Healy in the service of Mr. Hearst's *Evening American*. But no matter. Some sort of menace was imminent and there wasn't a newspaperman in the United States who didn't realize that great staffs of Yankee reporters must soon be sent over there to cover one of the most tremendous stories of all time. So——

Mr. Alf Smith of the sports department of the *American* wasn't too surprised when he was called out of bed at 2:00 A.M. by somebody who identified himself as Mr. Reutlinger and told to get started for London immediately. Mr. Smith never stopped to consider his possible qualifications as a foreign correspondent. No reporter ever does. He was told to go to the La Salle Street Station and wait for a messenger who would meet him with a ticket and great quantities of money. Mr. Smith went. He reached the station at 3:30 A.M. after having said good-by to his startled wife. He wasn't able to raise anybody in the local room of the *American* until 6:30 because nobody was there.

When finally he was able to talk with Mr. Reutlinger, Mr. Reutlinger told him he was crazy and he went home deeply disappointed. Mr. Reutlinger might have taken the trouble to soothe him but at that moment every telephone on the *American* city desk was echoing through the virtually empty office and missing reporters were calling in from a variety of railway stations, bus stations and airports. All were waiting only for tickets and money and a few instructions before hopping off for Budapest, Bangkok, Sydney, Paris, Peking. The financial editor didn't call. He had been assigned to Mexico City and the train didn't go until midafternoon. So he came into the office to display his new overcoat and a lot of expensive baggage and ask for an order on the cashier.

Somebody mentioned the next day that Mr. Healy had left the office not long before, and a lot of the ex-foreign correspondents began to remember some of his vocal characteristics in the telephone calls that had sent them to the city's waiting rooms. He did not come back.

Even without Mr. Healy the pattern of life on the third floor of the Hearst Building never came very close to monotony. There was a telephone call one afternoon when Mr. Tod Sloan was on the city desk. An irritated voice informed Sloan, "This is Mr. Hearst."

"Fine," said Mr. Sloan, "this is Judas Iscariot." And he returned to his work. The phone rang again and the same voice said:

"I should advise you to call the Blackstone Hotel and ask for Mr. Hearst." So Mr. Sloan called the Blackstone Hotel and asked for Mr. Hearst and presently heard the same irritated voice.

"Okay," said Mr. Sloan, "this is Mr. Sloan submitting his resignation. . . ."

The story ought to end there, of course, but it didn't. Mr. Hearst wanted a headline changed or something of the sort and he prevailed on Mr. Sloan to stay long enough to do it. Mr. Sloan stayed for twenty years.

Buddy McHugh who took over the job of police reporter for the *American* sometime subsequent to the Haymarket riot had a similar experience with the telephone. Buddy, like others of his craft believes that a protean quality is no hindrance in ferreting news. He has played many roles over the telephone, from Jack Johnson to a Tower-Town poet, so nobody was surprised the day when, trying to get some information about a murder, he called the home of the decedent and gave himself an official identification.

"This is Chuck Reynolds of the coroner's office," he said.

"That's funny," said the voice at the other end of the wire. "So's this."

Buddy McHugh is still one of the smartest detectives in Chicago. (Don't be deceived by the line ascribed to him in *The Front Page:* "Is it true, madam, that you have been made the victim of a Peeping Tom?") But in the old days on the *American* he was not alone in his rating. Everybody was a detective except the society editor. Mr. John Delaney, for example, was a very fine detective and his discoveries were enough to justify his now famous expense account: "To magnifying glass $2.00. To larger magnifying glass $4.00." And beyond all that was Jess Krueger who had a high rating as a cryptographer.

Jess has had a firm place in the affections of many of us since he quit his job as a war correspondent and enlisted with the Thirty-third division as we started for France in the last war. But it must be admitted that his association with the Signal Corps gave him some strange idiosyncracies—among them his willingness to solve everybody's puzzles. A lot of his fellow workers got the idea that he was too proud of his talent. And they made snide remarks. It wasn't that he overrated himself. He was really good at solving cryptograms and as the lads gave him practice he got better. Mr. Kreuger's gifts as a one-man American Black Chamber might have caused no end of dissension in the *American* local room had not Mr. Reutlinger intervened. He wrote out a cryptogram, gave it to Mr. Kreuger and said he'd be satisfied with a solution in three weeks. But there never was any solution. Mr. Kreuger probably doesn't know until this moment that Mr. Reutlinger's cryptogram consisted of a sentence from a Polish-language newspaper divided up into groups of five letters each.

Such matters as that, of course, might be rated under the head of purely scientific research. For they represented the intellectual side of existence in this particular asylum. There were oddities which weren't at all scientific or intellectual. I recall a day the local-room door was locked by the city editor for fear that one of the girl reporters would run out and get married to a lad in the advertising department. We never got the explanation for this solicitude, although we were in accord with the general principle that nobody ought to marry anybody in an advertising department.

And, if you have the idea that this tender thoughtfulness was universal in the office, think nothing of it.

A few weeks later the same heroine, thwarted in some other phase of her love life, fainted dead away in the aisle beside her desk. With a fine eye for the dramatic she had picked a moment just before edition time which may have had something to do with what followed. But anyway no kindly old gentleman such as the city editor offered her aid and comfort. The kindly old gentlemen went on with their business which as usual consisted largely of running around the room like squirrels in a cage. Nobody stepped on the unconscious lovely. They leaped over her as you'd expect people of decent instincts to do. She came out of her faint unassisted after a suitable interval absolutely none the worse for the experience.

In any discussion of Woman and The Press as exemplified

in this excellent shop it might be well to recall the experience of another beautiful girl who strained all the gentler instincts of her city editor. Edward Mahoney was the city editor, and he had a phobia about people leaning or rubbing against the back of his chair. Come one day the beautiful one whose name appears to have been Helen. She wanted to borrow a pair of scissors from the copy desk and so leaned heavily not only on Mr. Mahoney's chair but on Mr. Mahoney. She was wearing a one-piece knitted dress.

Mr. Mahoney warned her to go away and she went. But she came back again—and a third time.

"Dammit, Helen," said Mr. Mahoney in a terrible voice, "you scram out of here or I'll fire you—and I mean it." So in fright the maiden fled and a thread in the bottom of her skirt caught on the copy spike alongside Mr. Mahoney's desk. By the time she reached the end of the room she'd unraveled halfway to her hips. Mr. Mahoney sent her home in an overcoat which he never saw again.

It was in the *American's* service that I first met a student of ethics whom we shall call Matt Frosch. Matt had made his reputation elsewhere but he was still glowing with it. With a dozen other high-powered reporters he had been assigned to cover the trial of a lot of members of a merchandising association for some complicated skulduggery and he was standing with his companions in a federal courtroom on the morning when the case was scheduled to be called. A representative of the defendants called the reporters aside one at a time and handed each of them a $100 bill—"as a present" he said.

What the rest of the twelve did about this crass approach is not on the record. What Mr. Frosch did is. He took his hundred dollars, ran downstairs and across the street to the

Continental Bank and changed it. In five minutes he was back and with no attempt at concealment he stepped up to the defendant's largess-bearer and put a $10 bill into his reluctant hand.

"You can't bribe me," he said loudly. And with the atmosphere of virtue dense about his person, he took his place at the press table.

"Whatever you may say about me," he announced proudly to his associates later, "you can't deny that I'm ten percent honest. . . ."

There came a time after years of retirement in a calmer, saner, local room, when I looked back on those days with Mr. Hearst's *American* as I might have looked back on a dream. I began to wonder, sometimes, if such a place ever actually existed. And then came a Christmas Eve when Mr. Reutlinger and Mr. Ray Quisno made a tour of the wealthier offices in the County Building. They accepted largess from all and sundry—"accepted" is the right word for they made no return or promise of return—no comment except to protest the small size of the donations.

Late in the afternoon a policeman came to them as they stood in an open window on the third floor. He wanted to know why they were tossing coins into the street, blocking traffic and promoting wild disturbance. And they told him.

"The money belongs to the people," was the burden of their remarks. "We're giving it back to them in the name of the Chicago *Evening American.*"

After that the *American* seemed not only possible but probable. Moreover, it seemed to be in good hands.

12

ECLIPSES ARE WHERE YOU FIND THEM

~~~~~~

ONE of the really important signs of America's Americaniza-
tion since the last war is to be found in the rapid disappearance
of foreign-language newspapers. And it is especially significant that most of them have gone from our ken without assistance from the FBI. At one time, for instance, there were five
German dailies in Chicago alone, not to mention two or three
weeklies with impressive circulations and enough influence to
worry the politicians. Today there aren't any dailies and the
weeklies if any have degenerated into something like handbills.
The rabble rousers of the Bund spread their propaganda in
English through media printed in English and, for good or
bad, the bulk of the people reached by their messages were
Americans who probably couldn't have read one of the old
Zeitungs with a dictionary.

It is significant also that in the days when they were most
flourishing no newspaperman ever looked upon the numerous
products of the German press as dangerous or even as competition. Germans generally were considered a quiet, harmless,
slow-witted people whose reading wasn't likely to change them

much one way or the other. German newspapers were looked upon as a sort of futile expression of an impossible language: "Throw the horse over the fence some hay." And for some unauthenticated reason it was an article of faith that all reporters for such newspapers were funny. To me they never seemed funny although I thought it might be easy to defend the corollary belief that they were all half-witted.

Editorial policies on these journals may have differed in different localities . . . only the unidentified few who ever read them might be able to testify as to that. But it would seem from the available evidence that in the Middle West at least they all came out of the same hopper. The editors and the reporters—the latter a definite minority—may have come at last to recognize what made a news story but they never did figure out why one yarn should be worth more than another. John Craig, about whom more elsewhere in this book, contributes a report on the St. Louis German journal once owned by the Pulitzers. One night at 9:00 P.M. he met the editor and all his brood of subeditors, copyreaders, rewrite men and reporters coming down the stairs from the editorial rooms. He mentioned that they seemed to be quitting early.

"Ja," said the editor genially. "We go home now. No room for more news. The paper is ge-stuffed."

Some such editorial attitude, some such belief that late news didn't make any difference when you once had got the early news set up in type, probably obtained in Chicago. Otherwise it might have been hard to account for the dreamy quality of the German reporters one met at riots, murders and four-eleven fires. Not all of them were phlegmatic or insensitive or unemotional but certainly none of them was ever concerned with a dead line. Jimmy Murphy once said that they all carried calendars instead of watches but didn't use them.

I recall one Herman Wentze, *"korrespondent"* for the *Illinois Staats Zeitung,* who met me on the street two days after a minor fire in a pet store on the near North Side and asked me to supply some names and addresses.

I mentioned that the story was two days old and that every newspaper in town had printed it.

"Not mine," he said. "Mine didn't print it. Now what's the name von the Herr what the store owned?"

Mr. Wentze had a varied experience. It was he who traced a report that a lion had been sighted in the neighborhood of North Clark and Center Streets and actually discovered the lion in the Lincoln Park Zoo. It was he who startled the plushy burghers of Bill Thompson's "sixth German city" with a warning of possible Indian raids in 1913. And it was he who took local journalism to a noticeably higher plane through his investigations in astronomy.

He had come one afternoon to the old detective bureau which then functioned amid a rich atmosphere of creosote and decay in North La Salle Street and there he met Mr. James Murphy of the *Front Page* and other literature. Mr. Murphy was reading a newspaper and so became the victim of Mr. Wentze's idea that American newspapers were sources of information.

"You read the paper," he observed accurately. "And what is the news?" Mr. Murphy had been through this procedure too long to ignore the question.

"There's going to be a lunar eclipse tonight," he said. "An

eclipse of the moon, see. It's going to be total, if you're interested."

"Here?" inquired Mr. Wentze ecstatically.

"No," replied Mr. Murphy. "It's going to be on the other side of the river . . . somewhere up around Lincoln Avenue and Belmont. And it won't be going good until about three in the morning. Don't miss it."

And Mr. Wentze didn't.

And then there was "The Baron." The Baron doesn't seem to have been the property of any one city. Every town in the United States with a German population big enough to support a newspaper had one of him. And so far as can be determined now his right name was never known to any of them.

In all of his manifestations, in Buffalo, Pittsburgh, Philadelphia, Cleveland, his appearance was the same. He was tall, thin, lantern-jawed, slightly stooped. He was grave of face and a little haughty of manner. His lips were thin and his eyes more or less piercing. He wore patent-leather shoes, gray spats, striped trousers, cutaway coat, a vest with braided collar, starched white shirt, wing collar, black tie, silk hat and monocle. Naturally he carried a cane.

Our specimen, despite some evidences that America was finding itself, that the United States was taking on some of the characteristics of a nation, remained unreconstructed throughout his life. He was always an intellectual explorer from civilized Prussia making a brief study of the barbarians among whom he unfortunately found himself. The jibes of other reporters never quite reached his consciousness. The reporters themselves, apparently, he considered to be part of his own retinue, loyal workers provided by somebody to gather information which he might put into shape for his paper.

It is one of the oddest things in the record of American journalism that neither his costume nor his philosophy ever caused him much trouble from the day when he first put his head into the County Building press room along about 1900 until a lot of the tolerant old-timers turned out for his funeral in 1923. The whole business was just too fantastic for the barbarian journalists of that period to comprehend. They gave The Baron his obvious title and catalogued him as a clown of considerable attainment. Thereafter they worked for him somewhat as the friends of Tom Sawyer whitewashed the fence because he permitted them to. They loved his stern censure when they weren't fast enough to suit him. They admired his uncompromising ingratitude. If ever he had given an indication that he felt he was asking a favor when he asked somebody to get him the details of a tax increase or a ripe divorce his vassals probably would have rebelled. They might have tossed him headlong into La Salle Street if ever he had said thank you. . . . But he never did.

It cannot be said that all the reporters of the town considered the sneer of The Baron worth all the trouble it took to qualify for it. One or two of the younger men murmured from time to time that he was not really a baron but an old dodo and a nuisance. And there were others, less bitter, who said that he might be a baron and still be a nuisance. And one of these was "Kid" Ashe whose memory will long be green.

Mr. Ashe was more unfortunate than the other members of the police press-room contingent in that his schedule of working hours coincided more nearly with The Baron's. And he had found that a change in schedule did no good. By odd coincidence The Baron's would suddenly change also. The law of averages that prevents lightning from striking twice in the same place or committing similar absurdities seemed to have gone out of business.

So there was one day when Mr. Ashe listened with great distaste to The Baron's greeting.

"Ah, you are here at last, are you?" The Baron said. "And what have you to tell me that I may print in my paper?"

For a moment Mr. Ashe seemed to be struggling with rebellion but nothing came of it. When he spoke it was with a soft voice and in a manner of great deference.

"There is only one story that's worth anything," he said. "Joe Muldoon of the pawnshop detail dug it up. It's about a guy who deserted his family and stayed away for ten years. And now he's come back. What do you think of that?"

"Dramatic," grunted The Baron. "These are important people, *nicht war?* I mean important *American* people?"

"Important enough," said Ashe. "The woman was half German. Her mother was named Kranz and came from Hamburg . . . on a boat, it was, I've got the name of it here somewhere. . . . Well, anyway, the guy she married had a bakery up around the park somewhere. He made all the pretzels for the North Side Turner Hall. . . . That's what makes it a good story for you."

"Zo!" contributed The Baron noncommittally.

"Well, like I said, the husband ran away. It was on Christmas Eve, 1906. . . . The woman remembers it because he went out to give a dime to an old guy who was playing *"Heilige Nacht"* on the bagpipes in the snow. He never came back. . . .

[154]

Anyway he never came back till last night. That's what Muldoon told me. He's the guy who brought in the story. He knows the family."

"What did he come back for?" The Baron wanted to know.

"Now that's where the mystery really comes in," admitted Mr. Ashe. "Maybe he recovered his memory. Maybe he came back to see if he could get the dime back from the guy who was playing the Christmas hymns. I don't know. But the point is, he came back. He went up there to Schiller Street where the woman lived. You may have seen the place. It's red brick with a little porch and a bay window with a lily in it.

"If you stand on the porch you can look in at the window. And that's what this guy did. He didn't even push the bell button. He just stood there looking into the front parlor. And it was terrible. The woman had married again and there she sat darning socks for a new husband. He was sitting at the table with her reading the *Arbeiter Zeitung*. And a couple of new kids were playing around on the floor. It was terrible."

"Ja wohl," admitted The Baron. "And what happened then?"

"The old husband went away," said Mr. Ashe. "He died this morning at two o'clock at the southeast corner of State and Division Streets. It was a broken heart, Muldoon says. And he ought to know. He knows the family. . . ."

The Baron printed the story. One is surer of this than he is about other stories in German newspapers because Kid Ashe got an interpreter out of the circuit court to translate it. All the details of the story were as Mr. Ashe had recited them including the name of the returning husband: Enoch Arden.

13

MRS. LAWSON'S CAT

THERE was a brief moment just before the latest war when there seemed to be some truth in the credo of the veterans that the days of romantic journalism are gone forever. That was the day when the milkman came to Colonel Knox's office in the Chicago *Daily News* building and asked where he should deliver the milk for the cat.

By an odd combination of circumstances the query got all the way to the Colonel who didn't know the answer either. By that time it occurred to somebody to ask the milkman what he was talking about.

"It's the cat," he explained in all simplicity. "I used to deliver a quart of milk over there in the main entrance of the old building on Wells Street every night for the cat."

"What cat?" inquired Dempster MacMurphy, the business manager.

"Well, that I couldn't tell you," admitted the milkman. "I never saw the cat, I just delivered the milk like the guy ahead of me on the route delivered it. And every two weeks I'd come around to the *Daily News* business office and collect."

"You mean to say you actually got money?" Mr. MacMurphy wanted to know.

"I certainly did," said the milkman. "But now I don't know what to do because they've just torn down the last of the building and there's no place to put the milk but a vacant lot and . . ."

"It looks like the end," said Mr. MacMurphy sadly. "And I for one think I regret it. This seems to mark the passing of some very fine phase of the newspaper business. I wish I could guess what it is." So the milkman was paid off and the research work was begun and after much patient archaeology this story, credible only to those who worked on the Chicago *Daily News* toward the end of the Lawsonian era, was brought to light.

It was a snowy evening in 1908 when the wife of Victor Lawson, founder and publisher, came to the ancient News Building to pick up her husband. On the slippery threshold she almost stumbled over a thin and famished cat. She picked it up, carried it into the business office and handed it over the counter to Harriet Dewey, cashier and unofficial watchdog of the establishment.

"A stray cat just has no chance at all here in the Loop," Mrs. Lawson mentioned. "We'll have to fix up some sort of home for her. There ought to be some space in the pressroom . . . and see that she gets a quart of milk every day."

So the milk was duly ordered. The foreman of the pressroom assumed his new duties as cat custodian. Mrs. Lawson went away and thought no more about the incident. Neither, apparently, did anybody else.

One day the cat that Mrs. Lawson had brought to the cashier

died. But there were other cats to take her place. The foreman of the pressroom said nothing. Cats were cats so far as he was concerned. He'd been asked to see that a cat was fed properly each night. So he'd go on feeding cats as long as the milk kept coming. . . .

Mrs. Lawson died. The pressroom foreman retired and another took his place. And in time he, too, went away. Victor Lawson died and Walter Strong took over the property. Walter Strong died. Harriet Dewey, the cashier, died. But meantime for more than thirty years a succession of milkmen came daily to Wells Street bearing quarts of milk for a cat that had passed not only out of this life but out of the memory of man.

The *Daily News* had moved out of the rabbit warren that had housed it in North Wells Street to a modern plant on the river. The ancient red buildings were empty and silent save for the hollow echoes of watchmen's feet. There was no longer any foreman of the pressroom in that neighborhood—no longer any pressroom. But still the quart of milk was left in the doorway and still somebody, probably the watchman, poured it out for the convention of cats that had heard about this fine soup kitchen clear across the Loop. And then, finally, the wreckers had come. The milkman, after one effort to deliver his daily quart to a parking lot, had confessed defeat and had come seeking a change in protocol as has been mentioned. The cats who had been living off a dead woman's bounty accepted the situation philosophically and disappeared.

"Well," said Dempster MacMurphy when this report had been laid before him, "there you have the story of Mrs. Lawson's cat—or should I say the story of the *Daily News* . . . ?"

Maybe it is because of the almost inexhaustible supply of

youthful energy that is pumped into the newspapers of the world every year that they can move through a wonderland capable of producing fantasia such as Mrs. Lawson's cat. But they do survive. Somehow they flourish, at times luxuriantly on top of their own dust.

Few Americans probably knew much about the circumstances that attended the buying of the London *Times* by Lord Northcliffe. Not many, for that matter, remember much about the adventures of the totally incredible Northcliffe. If they did, the cat episode might seem less absurd.

One evening after he had taken over the *Times* Northcliffe had worked late and as he was leaving the building he almost collided with a little man with a satchel in his hand who was just coming in. Northcliffe watched the little man who moved quickly along the main floor corridor, stopped in front of an unlabeled door, took a latchkey out of his pocket and let himself in. Northcliffe followed, knocked on the door and was invited in.

The room into which he stepped turned out to be a bedroom complete with old-fashioned washstand and shaving kit. The little man, who had taken off his coat and set his satchel on a table, was putting some food beside a gas plate in the corner.

"I am Lord Northcliffe," said Northcliffe. "And who are you?"

"I," said the little man, "am the man from Coots Bank."

"And what else?" inquired Northcliffe.

"I don't know," said the little man. "Frankly I don't know."

"What are you doing here?"

"I am preparing to spend the week end. That's what I'm hired to do."

[159]

"But why on earth should you do that?"

"I don't know."

"How long have you been coming here?"

"Twenty years."

"And just what do you do when you come here?"

"Well, sir, I'll tell you. I come into the bank at 3:30 when they close. They give me the satchel and I walk over here. It's always the same. I come into this room and fix myself up to stay here. I bring a few things to eat. And some more's put in here for me—sugar, tea, and the like. I stay until 9:30 Monday morning and then I go back to the bank."

"And what's in the satchel?"

"I couldn't rightly say, sir. . . . Which is to say I don't rightly know how *much*, sir. I never counted it. But it's gold —gold coin. You may look, sir." And Northcliffe looked at about twenty-five pounds weight of gold—roughly a thousand pounds sterling, $5,000. He called up the bank and discovered that other little men with satchels had been occupying that room over week ends for very nearly a hundred years. And they told him the reason:

The battle of Waterloo was fought on June 18, 1815—a Sunday—and the enterprising editor of the Thunderer thought it might be a good idea to get a man over to cover it. The distance wasn't great and plenty of sloops were available. But all the banks were closed and he couldn't raise enough money to finance the expedition. Out of that came an arrangement with Coots Bank whereby on days when the bank wasn't going to be open a man with a thousand pounds in gold would make himself available at the Times Building. As in the case of Mrs. Lawson's cat the necessity for this provision had ceased years and years ago. But in the newspaper business once you set something in motion you forget about it. Not for more than fifty years had there been a night when the *Times* didn't have enough ready cash in its own vaults to send a correspondent around the world. But by the time private vaults became commonplace and businessmen got around to putting trust in them, the deal with the Coots Bank was forgotten. If Northcliffe hadn't become aware of it the little man with the satchel would have continued his futile vigil until he ran afoul of the gold embargo that the First World War brought. . . . About that time Mrs. Lawson's cat would have been seven years old.

14

MR. LAWSON'S NEWSPAPER

~~~~~~

EVEN without such exotic connections as Mrs. Lawson's cat, the Chicago *Daily News,* when I came to it from Mr. Hearst's *American* in 1920, was probably the strangest newspaper in the world. It had long ago outgrown its original home at 15 North Wells Street and by the expedient of cutting holes through fire walls had come to embrace half a dozen ancient buildings, all of them firetraps, as far back as the west wall of the La Salle Hotel. The business manager told me once that it was possible to get insurance on these wrecks because they had "the habit of standing." . . . They hadn't fallen down in fifty or sixty years so the presumption of the actuaries was that they never would fall down. No two of them had been built in the same year or according to the same plan, so when the *News* pushed out into them you had to go up or down a few stairs to get from any one office to any other office on the same floor.

The main entrance was a single revolving door that led into the advertising and accounting departments on the main floor of the original building. Not all of these departments remained in the old quarters when I came there, of course. Like everything else in the institution, they were any place where room had been found for desks, typewriters, adding machines, etc. But enough remained in what you might call the front window to give a hint of what Victor Lawson's *News* was like.

That main-floor room looked like something you remembered having seen in a woodcut . . . golden-oak counters, curly grilles, old gas fixtures unconvincingly wired for electricity. And in the midst of this, trim, corseted and aloofly dignified, were graying women who had been girl clerks when Victor Lawson began this amazing experiment with a penny newspaper. There was an atmosphere of Dickens about it— or of Cruickshank, I never could decide which. And it was fortunate that this exhibit was right where you could see it the minute you came in from the street. It gave you an accurate idea of what the rest of the place was like.

The newspaper itself at the time was still being printed in letters a little bigger than agate but Victor's eyesight had started to fail and the type as a consequence was rapidly approaching legibility. There was a conservatism in the make-up that even a war and reluctant juggling of eight-column headlines had never quite eliminated. From the look of the outer office, the help and the front page you might have thought that the paper was turned out on a hand press and maybe it was. Circulation was limited in those days by the capacity of the venerable equipment in the basement. So was the size of the paper, and because of that restriction so was the amount of advertising that could be accepted for publication on any given day. The Chicago *Daily News* was then not only the only paper I had ever worked on but the only paper I had ever heard about that threw ads into the hellbox to make way for news.

Mr. Otis' first elevator carried the more adventurous to the fourth floor. Its movements from the day it was installed until the building was pulled down were unpredictable.

In one of the coops on the third floor Bob Andrews, now one of the more successful Hollywood scenarists, toiled all day long writing editorial-page features in longhand. Somebody asked him one day why he didn't learn to use a typewriter and he blew up.

"Sir," he said, "I was state typing champion of Minnesota for three consecutive years. . . . They won't let me use a typewriter because it annoys the other editors. . . ."

There were about four telephones in the local room aside from those on the desks of the managing and city editors. One of them had a hand ringer and was probably the last of its type in Illinois.

The walls were lined with roll-top desks that wouldn't close. . . . Somebody said that they had survived the Chicago fire. One couldn't avoid the feeling that the whole institution had survived the fire. One might be excused the belief that a plant any more archaic would emboss its news on bricks in Babylonian cuneiform.

That the news production of this museum piece should have been not only modern but probably the most modern in the world was due, of course, to Henry Justin Smith. With his theory that truth and interest did not present any contradiction in terms, he did more to make the newspapers of the United States readable than any man of his generation. His pupils, hundreds of them, went out to spread his gospel in other cities and succeeded. He was a genius, of course; otherwise he could not have done so much to alter the reading habits of the American newspaper public—and he was a miracle worker to have done it with the raw material and equipment that happened to lie at hand.

It was natural that such a place should be steeped in a tradition almost medieval and that it should be overrun with stranger people than ever came out of a folktale. The shadowy, dusty corners of our rabbit warren tended to breed and foster recluses with inflexible, not to say queer, ideas. Our exchange editor—who got up a column of filler for the early editions— had once been an acting stage manager for *The Black Crook*. And he still wore some of his Broadway finery, or maybe it was part of his costume, to work. He was a dignified, scholarly-looking old gent who never spoke to anybody and never came to much attention until one day when he got into a wordy and insulting row with our Mrs. Ford who ran a children's feature called "The Wide-Awake Club."

Mrs. Ford wanted to print the jokes culled out of the exchanges. The old man claimed them as his own. In the end Henry Smith sat like Solomon in judgment. He gave Mr. Black Crook all the seven-line jokes and Mrs. Ford all the nine-line jokes. He said that it had been his observation that all jokes were either seven lines long or nine lines. And nobody caught up with him, at least not until after the cause of the wrangle had disappeared.

The spirit of Eugene Field was thick about the premises. There was a general belief among the rewrite men that he had never been buried at all but was still making the rules for the writing of *Daily News* feature stories somewhere in Lawson's office. There seemed to be a feeling among the higher brackets of brass hats that all that was novel in newspaper writing had ended with Field's death. The musty corridors were filled with the echoes of the great poet's passing. . . . "I can remember what Gene Field said on such an occasion. . . ." "That second column story this morning reminded me of something Gene Field once wrote. . . ." "He is a good reporter. He has something of Eugene Field's nonchalance. . . ."

Henry Smith wasn't one of the memorial association although like the rest of us he recognized Field as one of the greatest craftsmen our business had ever had. He had a theory that a live second-rater was better worth promotion than a dead genius. But never so long as we were in the old building on Wells Street was he able to get the idea across.

Mr. Lawson was getting on in years when I came to work for him. If he felt that I was bestowing any boon on his declining years by entering under his roof he never gave any sign. I remember him as a quiet man with a beard who looked like some of the pictures of Garfield. He rode around in an early-model Rolls Royce and a square-topped brown derby hat of the same age. To the younger members of the staff he was just somebody who moved in and out of the building occasionally and had an "Office Hour from Twelve to One." The older retainers had a sort of filial solicitude for him. The fluttering cashiers all spoke to him as he went by the Victorian grilles on the main floor. His chauffeur used to fix him comfortably in the back seat of his car, tuck his blankets in around him and put his newspaper in his hand before cranking the motor. To such people seemingly, the old man unbent a little.

One pretty country-weekly custom stayed with us until Mr. Lawson died—two of them in fact. One was the Christmas turkey distribution and the other was the annual bonus. The exact details of the bonus are not with me at the moment because I was just about eligible for it when the efficiency engineers took it away, but roughly it went something like this: After you'd been in Mr. Lawson's employ for ten years you got a twenty-five dollar bonus at the first of the year. The bonus increased each year thereafter—I was never to find out how much.

The turkey distribution was just a turkey distribution. It probably started out as a bit of hasty remembrance when there were probably a dozen hands on the pay roll including the night watchman. But by the time I found a place in the old building something more than twelve hundred turkeys—and some of the finest ones I ever saw—were being carted over each year. If you didn't want a turkey you could take a five-dollar gold piece instead and everybody was quite happy about the whole arrangement except Frank Spalding, a quiet man who was head of the copy desk. Spalding never accepted his turkey and went into a flat spin whenever anybody mentioned it to him. He used to make an annual speech to the effect that this was a relic of feudalism and that he declined to wear Lawson's iron ring around his neck and be a serf or, as we were learning to call them then in the crossword puzzles, an esne.

The staff readily sympathized with Spalding's attitude. If a man wanted to be an individualist this was certainly the place for it. And if Spalding wanted to buy his own Christmas turkey as a matter of principle that was certainly all right with everybody. About the only thing that came of the great annual turkey refusal was that Mr. Spalding didn't get any turkey.

As a sort of footnote it may be recorded that more of these turkeys wound up in the lost-and-found departments of speak-easies than ever got home to the waiting oven—or at any rate such was the general belief. As a bit of evidence to the contrary I recall a pernicious arrangement whereby the staff divided up into turkey-eating groups. One day we'd go over to Mike's house and help him dispose of Mr. Lawson's annual gift. A couple of days afterward we'd take care of Joe's excess turkey supply. Then Mike and Joe and their families would come over and do similar service with ours.

Xavier Salerno, a talented photographer, once set a high mark for a sort of combination turkey-losing-and-disposal scheme that had not been equaled when the good old distribution custom was abandoned. Xavier did a customary round of the festive joints in Wells Street, after which it occurred to him that the turkey was no longer in his company. He faithfully retraced his steps from one barred door to another and made suitable inquiry. But nobody could give him any information, and he never saw the turkey again until the following spring when he had occasion to open up the turtleback of his car to get the jack.

It probably is needless to mention that Mr. Spalding, our only turkey-protestant, wasn't alone in his tendency to be different. It was fairly easy to be different at 15 North Wells Street because, paradoxically, if you weren't different you were quite likely to be considered odd. For a long time we had virtually all the press photographers in the business who could be classed as gentlemen. At the same time we had some reporters of high attainment who wore soiled linen and forgot to shave. We had a police reporter who was a part-time evangelist and a rewrite man who operated his own still. We had one lad covering trials and such who was perfectly deaf—a blessing that would have been of more use to him on the *American*. We had Carl Sandburg and the youthful Ben Hecht and Rube Goldberg and more briefly Henry J. Luce and Vincent Sheehan. We had a female ball of fire so lazy that she'd ask a copyboy to look up at the clock for her. As John Craig said: "It takes all sorts to make a world and they're all here. . . ."

In Mr. Spalding's little coterie on the copy desk was a copy-reader named Murchie who alone of all the newspapermen I have ever known got more salary than he knew what to do with. He lived in a five-dollar-a-week room in a West Madi-on Street hotel because it was close to his work and he couldn't eat much and definitely couldn't drink because of stomach ulcers. So every week the mob descended upon him and borrowed all but about ten dollars of his pay and so precipitated what I have always considered the finest example of the double-barreled pun.

Looking at the midweek distribution of his surplus one day, Johnny Keys, then a rewrite man, observed:

"The quality of Murchie is not strained . . ."

And John Craig added dreamily:

"He falleth like the gentle dupe from heaven . . ."

Con Rourke was also with us in those improbable times and for many a day after our transfer to quarters of chrome and enamel and matched furniture. Con was a tall, gaunt, quiet-mannered soul who moved like a ghost, spoke seldom and had more friends than anybody else on the premises. It is said that he once fell asleep in a private dining room at the Great Northern Hotel and awoke to find himself unnoticed in the middle of a strike committee of the railroad brotherhoods

[169]

contemplating war. That may be apocryphal but it is certain that he had a sort of subconscious perception that enabled him to take his rest in improbable places without missing much that was going on about him.

For example, he could sit through a whole session of the City Council apparently asleep and arise at the last gavel to give an intelligent résumé of the proceedings over the phone. There was one hitch to this talent. Once he had delivered his report he could no longer recall a single thing he had said. On an occasion when an inexperienced rewrite man called him back to verify some detail, Con didn't know what he was talking about.

He had an odd humor. Once when I was working for the *Journal,* I met him in the old Chamber of Commerce Building waiting for somebody to issue a statement. In his company I strolled about the light well of the building studying office doors and because of him came to a stop before the quarters of a law firm titled "Newman, Poppenhusen and Stern."

"You will notice," he said, "that half the offices in this place are inhabited by 'Fire Hoses' and the other half by 'Poppenhusens' . . . And I know what a fire hose is. . . ."

And he turned his attention to the tiled floor of the corridor.

"I should like to point out to you also," he said, "that the pattern on this floor is a red star surrounded by a blue circle. On the floor above the pattern is a blue star with a red circle. Below us they have an arrangement of yellow octagons. . . . If you carry a tile chart around with you you'll always know what floor you are on. . . ."

Con used to be a faithful attendant at newspapermen's funerals until the day the whole town turned out for his own.

[170]

Newspaper funerals somehow are seldom like ordinary funerals. They are either grimmer or more fantastic depending for the most part on the gifts of the strangers among the clergy summoned by the bereft families to conduct the rites. Con had a knack of getting to the fantastic ones.

On occasion he would recall in mournful fashion the obsequies of one Fred Busch, a *Record-Herald* reporter, who had died in a North Clark Street rooming house alone. Fred had no relatives nor church connections so his comrades took over his funeral without what they called professional interference. An amateur preacher from the *Record-Herald* staff undertook to conduct the services at the graveside and might have done fairly well save for the fact that it had rained all night and the clay of the graveyard was sodden and slippery. In shifting his weight from one foot to another, the preacher slipped and shot under the coffin into the grave.

"It was very confusing," Con had said. "Half the mourners didn't see where this guy had gone and the other half were in favor of burying him along with the corpse. . . ."

And there was another occasion when a printer, similarly bereft of religious ties, was borne to a cemetery on the far Northwest Side by numerous other printers and, of course, our Mr. Rourke.

The trip was long and tiresome and numerous stops were made at taverns along the route so that when the cortege passed in through the gates of the so-called Memorial Park a lot of the sadness had been dissipated. There was no chance here that anybody might fall into an open grave because the dead printer was to be kept in a vault until relatives in the East decided where to bury him.

[171]

So the hearse backed up to the door of the mausoleum and six printers from the *Daily News* chapel lifted the coffin out with great decorum. They carried it into a room where a niche had been opened in the marble wall and, despite the strain, they lifted the heavy box head high to push it into the opening. The mourners stood about holding their breath —among them the foreman who knew the limitations of his hands.

All went well until the final shove at which time the pall-bearers discovered that they had taken a bad aim. The bottom of the coffin collided with the lower edge of the opening and there was a clunk—then deadly silence broken by the foreman's bellow:

"Look out, you dumb buzzards. . . . Don't pi the form!"

The expansion of the *News* had already begun when I came there. Shortly after my arrival we moved the local room into the fourth floor of a newly vacated pants factory at Madison and Wells Streets and we no longer had to go through the Dickensian counting room to get to work. Instead we traveled in a deliberate lift that had been the pants factory's freight elevator. With the building and elevator we inherited an elevator operator—a badly shopworn little old man who looked as if he might have another month to live.

That winter was one of the coldest in Chicago's history, and the elevator shaft was warmed only by the body heat of the few people who journeyed up and down in it. We began to feel a real concern about our little old man. Sometimes we'd hear the wind howling around our corner and think of him there in his freezer and the thought of him kept our minds from our work. So we went out one morning and bought an electric heater for him. Inasmuch as he could steal all the current he needed from the elevator light socket, that seemed the logical solution to his trouble. He was much pleased with the gift and for one whole day rode up and down the shaft in something approximating comfort.

The next day, however, he was cold again. The heater was gone.

"I took it home," he explained. "Somebody would steal it if I left it down here in this place. . . ."

The *News* at its inception and for many years thereafter was one of the greatest want-ad media in the world. Until the jazz age after the war when everybody was wealthy and nobody had to work, lines of unemployed men used to gather in front of the old building every morning waiting for the first edition. They'd rush for the newsboys and leave at the trot, reading the help-wanted column as they went.

I noticed one of these job-seekers on my second day at work as I came out for some breakfast after the first edition had begun to roll. He was standing in the doorway aloof from the rest of the mob and I took him for a chauffeur waiting for somebody. He was neat and clean and well dressed. A leather jacket and cap were what gave me the idea that he might be a chauffeur . . . otherwise he was well enough turned out to fit in a bank. I was surprised when he stopped the boy with the outbound papers, bought a copy and turned to the want-ads. And I felt a little more sorry for him than for the shabbier customers. They, I felt, were probably used to this disheartening scramble, whereas my friend with the leather coat couldn't have had much experience in being out of work.

But that's where I was wrong. For eight solid years this well-kept specimen was present every morning for the arrival of the first edition. Each day he looked at the offerings in the help-wanted column. Each day he returned into whatever bourne he had left. He never found a job that suited him.

The old elevator man, who lived longer than we'd thought he was going to, said that our job-hunter lived with an aunt who had a fine position somewhere as a scrubwoman.

"He hopes to do something swell for her when he gets a job that pays enough," the elevator man said. But I don't know how it turned out. They tore down the building and anyway by that time the early-morning rush to the job market was finished.

From the inception of the *News* Miss Hattie Dewey had had charge of all the female help. Once she'd had a dozen girls to look after; now she had hundreds and her work as housemother took up more of her time than her regular job as cashier. She was getting on in years but she stayed at her post and purposefully kept out of the building all those fantastic ideas that were destroying America's good old Puritan culture. Girls who worked for the *Daily News* dressed modestly. They used rouge only in minute quantities. They never appeared in short skirts. They never rolled their stockings. They never loitered to talk with boys in the hallways. . . .

There was a restaurant in the building—a relic of the days when it had been impossible for anybody to get anything to eat in the neighborhood. It had carried on with a very good trade because it was convenient and cheap and the food was edible. And it was probably our outstanding example of Miss Dewey's influence for better things. It was the most de-

[174]

corous lunchroom in a wicked world. All of the men sat on one side of the room, all the women on the other and no waitress would serve you if you picked the wrong side.

Whisky, it is hardly necessary to say, was not even a subject for conversation inside the building. . . . Even today the *News* accepts no liquor advertising. Which makes one appreciate the fast footwork of Lional Moise who came up in the elevator with Victor Lawson himself one afternoon, stepped out of the car and dropped a package of rare old bootleg Scotch almost on the founder's toes. Mr. Lawson looked at him like Zeus preparing to let loose a bolt but Lionel never turned a hair. He stepped up to the information desk, raised his hat and asked to speak to the city editor. Mr. Lawson retired to his office. Mr. Moise went on to his desk.

That such maneuvering with the information clerk was possible is another peculiarity of the *Daily News* of that day. We always had an information clerk, principally to keep cranks from wandering into the local room. But we never had one that functioned. One of them stopped me every morning for two weeks asking me my business. I would always ask to see myself. He'd go to get me and I'd follow him into the room. It puzzled me not only that he should have failed to recognize me after repeated experiences but that he should have failed to recognize the pattern of the gag.

Then we got an old man—seventy-eight I think his age was when he first came to work. His name was Hermann Schott and he had recently lost a lot of money. He wasn't much use as an information clerk because he never even saw the people who didn't stop to ask him questions and he couldn't answer those who did. He spent all his time looking over stock reports and market letters and figuring eternally on scratch paper that he got in the local room. Occasionally he would tell you something of his prospects. Tomorrow, without fail, he was going to be rich.

There was something pathetic about him. He was so frail that he couldn't have walked up the stairs from the main floor. He had so little time left to get rich quick in, and great wealth was going to do him so little good when he got it.

There was also something very ludicrous about him, for with Prussian pompousness he gave his door-watcher's job a sort of executive classification. Because of his position in front of the elevator if not because of his position in any other rating, he was the first hurdle that ambitious kids had to pass when they came job-hunting. And always he took it upon himself to interview them.

His previous business with newspapers had been the occasional insertion of an ad in the *Abendpost* and during all the time he lingered at his desk in the corridor he never had the foggiest idea of what went on beyond the local-room door. But Victor Lawson himself couldn't have put on a more convincing act.

"Und ZO! You vish a bosition! Goot! Do you vish to be a reborter or an editor?"

Nor did he reserve his role of front-office arbiter for the questing kids alone. We got it, too, and it was plain that he expected us to treat him with proper deference because of it. Once a rewrite man quit to take a job in New York and, on his way to the elevator, stopped to shake hands with Mr. Schott.

[176]

"Und ZO! You are going," said the old man. "Ve vill miss you. Your work has always been satisfactory. I have been bleased vit it. . . ."

Mr. Schott assured us one morning that his long period of calculations was over and that the next day he would be leaving us. He fell over at his desk a couple of hours later and one of the reporters took him home where he died during the night. We wondered briefly what had brightened his prospects and when his desk was cleaned out we found the answer. He'd finally given up all hope of doping out the progress of the stock market and had switched to horses. On the horses, he had figured, you could get rich quicker. . . .

15

THE REFINANCING OF MR. LYMAN
MOOSE

THE most spectacular of the characters who helped make the *Daily News* local room what it was in those exciting days was undoubtedly Mr. Lyman Moose. Mr. Moose was—and presumably is—big in physique and mind. He was one of the kindliest souls I've ever had to sit beside day in and out, and he was always nursing black eyes and broken knuckles that he'd picked up in fights. He never seemed to figure how he got into the fights—people just picked on him, he thought.

Mr. Moose, despite some unpromising beginnings, turned out to have more foresight than the rest of us. While we were building basement laboratories and tearing the mystery out of radio, Mr. Moose was engaged in more practical research. He was taking steps to rectify the principal mistake of Prohibition. His basement laboratory was in a sort of mansard flat over a private garage and his output was about two quarts a day.

One might have thought that such a side line as this would prove a fine adjunct to a newspaper job. It looked like a certain expense cutter. There seemed to be more than an even chance that it would prove to be a fine source of additional income, providing of course that you could stay out of jail long enough to operate it at all. But our conclusions were hasty. Mr. Moose picked up a lot of new friends and a lot of new expenses. And he got into an increasing number of fights.

His first month's gas bill came to him one day at the office and we envious ones who had no private distilleries listened to his pleasant voice as he explained to an adjuster at the gas company just why he thought he shouldn't pay it.

"Of course it's preposterous," he said with a convincing laugh. "The place is a two-room apartment over a private garage and I couldn't possibly have used $67 worth of gas in one month. The meter must be leaking or maybe that bakery in Chicago Avenue was put on my line by mistake. . . ."

It was a pretty speech and apparently it did all right. The gas company was two or three months looking around for holes in Mr. Moose's meter which by that time registered $138.67 worth. In the end they gave it up but they declined to supply him with any more gas. I fail to recollect whether he put in an electric furnace or coal.

He weathered the first half-year of his experiment with the liquor supply, still a fine figure of a man and still well dressed. Fights had narrowed his wardrobe down to one suit but he contrived to keep that looking prosperous. Then he tore the seat out of his pants in some undescribed encounter and he had to stretch his resources. In a few months creditors were leaping upon him from all quarters and that didn't include the gas company.

Just to rid his telephone of inquiring bill collectors and get it back to newspaper uses, John Craig figured out a refunding process. Lyman was to borrow from the *Daily News* employ-ees' bank enough money to pay all his outstanding debts, and a few of the more hardy souls in the local room were to indorse the note. That was done. Mr. Moose took a day off and canceled out his creditors, the chief of which was the Camp Clothing Store. On his way into the Camp Building he stopped to look at some neckties, but this was purely a gesture because the department manager had recognized him and was walking over hurriedly with a sour look on his face. The store had made quite an issue out of Mr. Moose's three-hundred-dollar account and his credit was x-double zero.

He paid his bill with the quiet dignity that was so much a part of him and said a few bitter words to the credit manager. He had been put to a lot of trouble, he mentioned. He had been treated to language over the telephone that was fairly close to slander. His honesty had been impugned and in the future he would take his trade somewhere else.

The credit manager was apologetic and soothing. . . . After all Mr. Moose had been a good customer and he certainly had cleared up his account. So in the end Mr. Moose said that he might reconsider. He went out as he had come in, past the necktie counter. From there he went to other departments and saw the change in the manners of the underlings as they learned of his A-1 rating upstairs. When he left he took with him $450 worth of clothes. The Camp Store credit manager presumably got back to his worrying.

These matters admittedly haven't much to do with the newspaper business but I must contend that no study of the amazing people who went into the newspaper business would be complete without some attention to them. The indorsement of notes was one of the more dangerous hazards of the trade in those days; the appeasement of outside creditors one of the most constant worries of the cashier. Taking a hindsight on the situation it would seem that there were a lot fewer technicians in that period than there were jobs. If an obdurate creditor slapped a lien on a copyreader's salary, the copyreader always had a remedy. He packed his other shirt and took a train to Denver or St. Louis. So, in addition to keeping the creditors happy, the newspapers also had to keep the talented editorial workers happy. As I see it there were two classes of local-room help—those who were kept happy and those who indorsed the notes.

Mr. Moose after his financial reorganization had nobody to bother him but the Camp Store and the *Daily News* bank. Wisely he paid attention to the voice closest to him and cut down his debt at a rate of ten dollars a week. The note indorsers who referred to him as their "five-hundred-dollar investment" were deeply solicitous about his health. They watched over him like a Parent Teachers' Association, fed him on occasion and, so I have heard, trailed him around at night to keep him from coming out second-best in fights. In the end he paid out—that is to say he paid what he owed the employees' bank. The status of his credit at the Camp Store I don't know.

It was while the Indorsers' Committee was still concerned about him that he arrived one morning from a night assignment in what Miss Dewey described inadequately as "an intoxicated condition." John Craig, to whom as city editor Mr. Moose had to report, took one look at him and said, "My God!"

Mr. Moose was dressed in a baggy tweed suit, patent-leather shoes, a derby hat and spats. He was carrying a large yellow cane that looked something like a shepherd's crook. He was smiling upon all the world and obviously on the verge of delivering a great message. But when he started to talk he merely mumbled. John got up and started him for the door.

"Get on home before all the brass hats come down and find you here," he said. And Mr. Moose went, although it was obvious that he felt the indignity of the situation. Just as he disappeared into the old freight elevator he found his voice.

"I never throw down my paper," he said. "When I am sent to get a story I get it. . . . And I deliver it."

"Scram!" suggested Mr. Craig.

From the elevator man, the old Viking who unloaded the paper rolls at the sidewalk lift, a couple of truck drivers and other sources we learned later what happened to Mr. Moose. It was plenty.

As he stepped out onto the sidewalk a paper truck had just been emptied. The driver was somewhere in the building getting a signature on his delivery slip. When he came back he discovered a tall man in a derby hat trying to spin the crank with one hand while waving the cane with the other. As he inventoried Mr. Moose's size he thought that gentle treatment was indicated.

"What's the idea, brother?" he asked.

"I'm trying to start my car," said Mr. Moose. "I have to get over to the office of the *Evening Post* at once."

"Okay," said the truck driver who saw the futility of argument. "I'll take you there. . . ."

Long, long ago Jesse Lynch Williams wrote a popular play

[182]

called *The Stolen Story*. It had to do with a star reporter who fell into a daydream and went into the wrong newspaper office to write his great scoop. And it held top classification for newspaper ubiquity until this day in the life of Lyman Moose. He wandered into not only one wrong office but all there were. And he provided a community of interest for Chicago newspapers for the first time since they'd all been burned out in the big fire.

He was coyly received at the *Post*. He'd been city editor there once and some were afraid he might have forgotten that he'd resigned. However, he spoke politely to his successor at the city desk—a man for whom he'd never entertained any fondness—and mentioned that he had come on a delicate mission.

"I have a story to write," he said. "And on the *News,* where I am employed, all the typewriters are in use. I came over to ask if I might use one of yours." The flabbergasted city editor said yes and Mr. Moose sat down, laid his cane on the floor and went to work. When he had finished ten lines he got up again and handed the copy to a boy.

"Tube it over to the *News,*" he roared. "They're waiting for it." He picked up his cane, went back to the city desk, picked up a phone and called the circulation department.

"I should like to borrow one of the trucks for a minute," he said. "I am going over to the *American*. . . ."

Short takes of the story began to reach John Craig's desk via the City Press Association tubes ten minutes later and continued well into the afternoon . . . the *American* office, the *Journal*, the *Examiner*, the *Journal of Commerce*, the *Tribune*. It was from the *Tribune* that a friend sent an accompanying note to John Craig saying that Mr. Moose was tired and was being taken home. Craig picked up the sheaf of odd-sized copy specimens that like scraps in a paper chase told where Mr. Moose had gone. One of the puzzled rewrite men asked him what it was all about.

"I don't know," said Craig. "There's nothing in this that'd tell you."

"But what was he on?" asked the rewrite man.

"I don't know that either," said Craig. "He wasn't assigned to anything."

"Very mysterious," commented somebody. Craig shook his head and put the copy on the dead hook.

"Not with Mr. Moose," he said sadly. "Just commonplace. . . ."

There remains just one more episode in the life of Mr. Moose that ought to be mentioned here. Not that there probably isn't a whole source book of unpublished folklore waiting for anybody who will locate Mr. Moose and ask about it, but Mr. Moose went out of our lives shortly after the squaring of his account with the cashier. (We took it that the strain had been great and that he needed a rest.) And save for fleeting glimpses as he passed through town on his way to San Francisco or New York we never saw him again. . . . We remembered him though . . . always. If for no other reason we remembered him for his fantastic part in The Adventure of the Dentist's Office.

Mr. Moose one afternoon left his desk with an aching tooth which he took for treatment to a Madison Street speak-easy. There he encountered a crony, Little Harry Hochstetter, sports writer for the *Evening Post*. He admitted to Mr. Hochstetter that the treatment wasn't having much effect.

"I got a good dentist up on the North Side," Hochstetter told him. "And I might as well do my drinking up there as here. I'll go up there with you."

"First," said Mr. Moose, "we'll visit Jack Farley's place over in Wells Street." So they visited Farley's and after that they went to a number of places along a route in a direction generally north. Mr. Hochstetter, as the sequel showed, wasn't drinking too much because of nervous indigestion, but Mr. Moose hadn't any nervous indigestion. By the time they arrived in Lake View he had almost forgotten his tooth.

They delayed a moment in a speak-easy across the street from the doctor's office where Harry said he'd wait. Lyman Moose had another drink and went bravely to face his ordeal.

The dentist couldn't do much about the tooth. He gave Mr. Moose some gas and pulled it out. There would have been nothing at all to the operation if Mr. Moose hadn't taken such good care of his own anesthesia before coming in. He was so long showing signs of consciousness that the doctor was alarmed. Eventually, however, he opened his eyes, grinned foolishly, got enough money out of his pocket to pay his bill and walked with reasonable steadiness to the door.

As a matter of fact he was still only partly conscious when he came into the speak-easy. He took one look at Little Harry Hochstetter and charged at him in a roaring rage.

Harry was a possible five feet tall as against Lyman's six-feet-one and he hadn't done anything. But he didn't stop to argue. As the hulking Moose came even he hit him on the chin with an uppercut that he had lifted from the floor. Mr.

Moose went over backward and after that there wasn't any doubting his unconsciousness.

Harry mobilized some help and carried the limp victim back across the street to the nearest doctor who, it turned out, shared office space with Harry's dentist. The doctor was busy so they laid Lyman out on the dentist's floor alongside the chair and tiptoed away. When the dentist came back from whatever he'd been doing Lyman was just coming up for the second time. Slowly he got to his feet and looked about him with big burning eyes. This time he wasn't smiling. He steadied himself as he saw the white coat approaching him.

"So you did this to me," he muttered. And he put everything he had into a straight left to the dentist's chin. They were both unconscious on the floor when the doctor arrived, took one fleeting look and put in a call for an ambulance.

16

FRIENDS OF JESSE JAMES

A LOT of newspaper geniuses peeled off the old *Daily News* from time to time and quite a lot of them went far afield where, presumably, they transplanted the *Daily News* tradition. Once I met a winner of a *Daily News* oratorical contest building a bridge on the Saar out in front of the Maginot Line. He was still enthusiastic about the things that he had learned in his Chicago association.

"While I am in journalism in Paris always I speak of Truth in Journalism," he said. "Also I like the Hearst funny papers."

I met another of our former reporters selling cheese in Paris and quite enthusiastic about his work. Another went exploring in Abyssinia. Another, so I am told, ran guns on the Chinese coast.

Henry Smith took a certain pride in all these diverse wanderings from the ways in which he had led them and he kept careful note of their whereabouts.

"Once a newspaperman always a newspaperman," he said. "They may not know it, but it's in their blood. Someday they'll come face to face with a big story and all their training will come back to them. We have the finest staff of potential correspondents in the whole world. . . ."

Meyer Levin was with us in his early days—even then a boy of delicate sensitivities, a writer of clean, beautiful prose. Smith, who recognized Meyer's genius at once, fostered it, hopeful of bringing it to its full brilliance in the newspaper business, but young Mr. Levin had other ideas. He got intensely interested in the Zionist movement and eventually gave up his prospects for an important literary career to labor on a farm in Palestine. Henry Smith put him in the catalog of those whom he remembered constantly and wistfully. His name was bright before Smith's eyes the day the Arabs went berserk and British patrols seemed inadequate and bloodshed spread all over Palestine. News was meager so Smith naturally cabled Meyer Levin:

"HOW SERIOUS ARE RIOTS?"

And Meyer sent him a prompt answer:

"I AM SAFE."

The foreign service never got much attention from Smith despite the fact that he had handled it in person in Paris during the worst years of the First World War. He had no patience with the writers of "think-pieces." His was the cult of *News* as distinct from *Opinion* and for that reason he didn't think much of political reporting either. One day somebody suggested Clem Lane's appointment to a vacancy as political editor. Smith advised him against it.

"You don't want to be a political writer," he said. "In politics our side is always right and the other side is always wrong."

Nobody could be around him for more than five minutes

without understanding what he thought of News as News. And in the main, despite the fact that he surrounded himself with the most outrageously divergent lot of temperaments that ever got into a print shop, he received pretty fair co-operation.

Once he was let down by the high priests of the Truth-in-Journalism cult when the U.P. ended the World War I a week ahead of time. But he got his own back some years later when the A.P. declined to admit the death of the Pope although other wire services began to toll the bell. That was probably Smith's worst day. He stood his ground with the A.P. story through nine editions as the *American, Post* and *Journal* came onto the managing editor's desk proclaiming that His Holiness was no more. He refused to listen to the angry bleating of the circulation manager whose newsstand sales had dropped off to virtually nothing. And about time for the tenth edition he proved the value of faith and trust. The other newspapers were beginning to hedge. The Pope, in spite of editorial pressure, was still alive.

Some of the staff came eventually to share some of his own idolatry of News. All of us respected the essential verity of his philosophy, that the enlightening of the world was an important mission and carried with it tremendous responsibilities. Perhaps few of us would have summoned our last energies in a deathbed as one man did to telephone of the illness of a former sheriff in the room next door. Maybe few would have come bleeding from a railroad wreck, as one photographer did, to deliver his wares to the local room. But even without being votaries most of us went through flood waters and dust storms and mountain blizzards for him. I can recall several cockeyed airplane rides and one brief so-

[189]

journ in a leper colony as part of my own contribution to his advancement of the cause of "News above all!"

It must be admitted that our score as crusaders in a sort of newspaper religion wasn't entirely perfect. Once the good Henry's very zeal forced the concoction and publication of the most oblique piece of news that came to light during his years as torchbearer for The Truth. Again a bit of rudimentary heresy (to the effect that maybe it wasn't important what the two-cent customers found out about the day's doings in the Appellate Court) shook his faith in the fragile vessels—not to say pots—upon which he had placed reliance.

The first incident came about when Luke Hunt—who had succeeded John Craig as city editor—met a friend in Louie's bar where he had tarried for a small corpse reviver on his way to work. The friend was Lew Ferguson, dean of all the conductors on the Northwestern Railway. And with Mr. Ferguson were two other railroaders no younger than he.

"We're all from the same part of the country," he said, "all from around St. Joe, Missouri."

Luke gave some attention to Mr. Ferguson's aged friends and asked casually if they had known Jesse James.

"Went to school with him," said Mr. Ferguson. "All except Joe. He was out before Jesse started. . . . And looky here, Luke, these boys came all the way from St. Joe to see me. And I'd like to have you put their names in the paper. . . ."

"Okay," said Luke to whom long explanations at that hour of the morning were distasteful. "I'll see what I can do about it." It was obvious to him that Ferguson, despite years and years in the cities, still classed all newspapers with the home-town weekly he had known as a boy and still thought that the doings of any of God's people should be classed as news. On the other hand Luke could see no harm in a personal notice of two or three lines if it pleased Fergie. . . . He went into the office and wrote twenty-five words about "three old friends of Jesse James" who had just met in Chicago for the first time in forty years. He put a two-line head on it and sent it down to the printers. About ten o'clock Henry Smith came into the local room livid.

"Where did this Jesse James story come from?" he wanted to know. Luke began to feel uncomfortable.

"I got it," he said. "Anything wrong with it?"

Mr. Smith seemed at a loss for words.

"I can't understand why I have to tell you of all people the way a story like this ought to be played," he said. "Get somebody out on it with a photographer and let's give some evidence that we're in the newspaper business."

Luke could only gulp but that didn't prevent his thinking rapidly. While a reporter had gone out to trace Ferguson and the friends of Jesse James, Mr. Hunt was on the phone to Louie's explaining what had happened. It was desperately important, he explained, that Mr. Ferguson should protect him. And Mr. Ferguson told him reassuringly to think no more about it.

An hour later the reporter came back with an excellent story.

"I got to those guys just in time though," he told Luke confidentially. "They were all snozzled and by the time I left they were trying to throw the story down. They said the guy they'd gone to school with was Robin Hood."

And as for the backslider from the cult—one mentions it

with downcast eyes—he was Vincent Starrett who was to go a long distance in this country and England as a bibliophile, critic and writer of fiction. Mr. Smith thought a lot of him and he thought a lot of Mr. Smith, but, as I have mentioned, Mr. Starrett had interests and aspirations outside the dingy temple at 15 North Wells Street. Mr. Starrett for instance was a first-place courthouse reporter as Mr. Smith knew. But what escaped Mr. Smith was the fact that he was also a leading collector of first editions.

On the morning of the great schism Mr. Starrett was walking in leisurely fashion across the Loop to an assignment in the Appellate Court. It was nine o'clock and court didn't convene until ten. So he stopped for a moment in front of Powner's secondhand bookshop at La Salle and Washington Streets. For no reason at all he began to pick over the bargains on the ten-cent counter—those books that nobody apparently ever read or ever will read. He didn't expect to find anything of interest but he had only an hour to kill and he knew better than to go inside and get himself involved in some learned discussion with the manager. It would be amusing, he thought, to see just what sort of tripe eventually found itself in bins like this. He might be able to contrive a story about it some day. . . . And then he chanced to open a mildewed French volume and found in it a dedicatory note from Louis XIV in his own handwriting.

Mr. Starrett was sharp and he knew better than to go into the store with this book and a dime in his hand. The clerks would recognize him instantly and would be curious to see what ten-cent item had attracted his attention. After that, he feared that they might refuse to sell at the advertised price.

There was just one thing for it. He would have to wait until a friend should happen along—a friend whom he could trust enough to make the purchase.

Vincent Starrett as a reporter on the courthouse and city-hall beats had an acquaintance list as big as a suburban telephone directory. He was standing on a corner where it was said you could meet everybody you ever knew in a few hours. But that day he knew what it was to be alone and unknown in a city of 3,600,000 people. Thousands passed him hourly and never one with a familiar face. He missed his lunch. His legs got so tired that they threatened to buckle. The sun went low beyond the Loop and he began to fear the hour when somebody should come out to put the ten-cent treasures away. During all that time it never occurred to him that something had been going on in the Appellate Court—something that Henry Smith had thought important.

Relief came just about six o'clock. A police reporter bought Louis XIV's book with a couple of Elsie Dinsmores to give the purchase verisimilitude. He delivered the prize to the gasping reporter.

"Why didn't you steal it?" he asked sensibly.

"I didn't think of it," said Starrett. "I guess I was thinking of my future. . . . I'm going to be trying out a new one tomorrow."

17

THE GHOST CATCHER

~~~~~~

NOT all the genius in our shop was confined to such experts as Mr. Moose and Mr. Owen—not by any means. We had, for example, a visit from Colonel Visknisski, the efficiency engineer who went about turning out lights in the interest of economy. (The resultant touch system worked fairly well and the editorial rooms made no protest except to paste on the door of the darkened lavatory a sign: "Thomas Edison Memorial Room.") We had another expert who tried to work out a merit factor for journalists, as he called us, computed by multiplying number of hours worked by number of words produced and multiplying that by positional factors which decreased as the story appeared on pages farther and farther from the first . . . and some more of that. And we also had the Ghost Catcher.

The Ghost Catcher was probably the most permanent institution about the *News,* if one excepts a couple of broken-down presses. He remained with us until he went away somewhere shortly before the beginning of the current war. And then everybody had to remember back to the day when there had been no ghost catcher.

THE GHOST CATCHER

As a matter of fact he arrived at the old building in Wells Street one summer day in 1921 and was turned over by the doorman to Ray Quisno who appreciated him. Mr. Quisno in turn gave him to me.

The visitor turned out to be a medium-sized person, a little stooped, a little dusty. He wasn't well shaved, his clothing—which looked like a relic of somebody else's elegance—didn't fit him. He was wearing a stubble-colored straw hat which continued to top off his costume as long as I knew him. He looked in other words like the sort of crank who usually pays visits to newspaper offices. He said that his name was Professor Otto Reichmann and that he was a proofreader by profession.

Professor Reichmann, much to my surprise, had no plans for the salvation of the world or the improvement of literature . . . not then. He explained that he was a ghost catcher of considerable talent and that he'd like some work in this field.

He spoke with a pronounced German accent and sputtered somewhat at high speed but eventually I managed to make out that he had once been hired by the *Tribune* as part of a clacque that went around exposing spirit mediums. He had been paid five dollars a night for his part in this interesting crusade and had just about decided to make it his life's work when the supply of mediums ran out. He hadn't looked in on a séance for months and it had occurred to him that maybe we might think it time to revive the racket. He came fully equipped for the work, which is to say he had some little bells on thin threads, some wax to attach the bells where ghosts might trip over them, a flashlight and a lot of cards in which he described himself as a professional ghost catcher.

We couldn't give him a job but we did what was worse: we gave him a lot of publicity. After that he was a daily visitor. He had his mail addressed in my care. He invited his friends to meet him in the waiting room by the information desk. He dumped reams of blank verse about the doings of the Homeric gods onto the desks of the editorial writers on the floor below. He kept the assistant city editor moderately busy looking over news tips that nobody could ever decipher.

He was around so continuously that in time old Mr. Schott, the guardian at the elevators, thought he worked in the local room. After that he came and went ad lib. He filled his arms with our discarded exchanges—which he never seemed to leave anywhere. He wrote his letters on the rim of the copy desk and permitted the telegraph editor to mail them for him. He loitered about the local room pretty much as he pleased, chattering to anybody who would listen to him about the need for doing good in the world. He asked Arline, the beautiful telephone operator, to marry him but she said no.

During the first months of his connection with our lives he had a night job somewhere on a German weekly or in a German job-printing plant or something. But along toward winter he quit mentioning his work and began to tell us about the difficulty of getting a job. One day he confided that he was pretty hungry and I staked him to the price of a meal and after that he was ours completely.

I used to marvel during those winter months that he brought me flowers every morning. At first I thought he might be saving some of the few pennies he collected every day to buy these things. Then he told me that he was doing a little janitor work for a florist friend. And then one day I found a card on a nice bouquet of lilies: "With sincere sympathy of the Goertz family."

He moved with us to the new building where he found things much better than in the old. He might have stayed there forever, for the new local room was large and bright and there were lots of extra chairs for the use of casual visitors. But capitalism got him. He told me about it afterward with some surprise. The menace of capitalism, he said, was something that he'd never given a thought to until it was too late.

Walter Strong was then publisher of the *News*. The new building was one of his creations and he was remarkably proud of it. He was proud of the plant that turned out the *News*— cheered to hear people tell him that it was the finest in all the world.

The crowning compliment to his magnificent work came one day with a delegation of South American publishers and editors. They had visited Washington for some sort of Pan-American congress . . . but from Washington to Chicago they had come for the single purpose of looking at Walter Strong's clean and glistening print shop. . . .

The delegation, under the escort of Mr. Strong, reached the local room right after the opening markets edition had gone to press. Three copyreaders had taken the opportunity to dash down to the drugstore for a cup of coffee. Three hadn't yet reported for work. One was in the lavatory. The slot man was down in the composing room. Mr. Strong, thrilled as always at the sight of a local room that was at once efficient and as clean as a hospital, looked about him expansively. He and his guests had reached the copy desk before his eye swung back to the horseshoe. . . .

There all alone on the rim sat a soiled old man in a grease-spotted overcoat and bilious-looking straw hat writing something on a sheet of copy paper.

Mr. Strong, overcome with emotion, touched him on the shoulder and said: "I beg pardon, but who are you?"

Professor Reichmann turned around with an odd combination of surprise and indignation.

"I, sir," he cried, leaping to his feet, "I am the Ghost Catcher!"

That of course was the official end of the Ghost Catcher, although he lasted unofficially for a long time afterward. Walter Strong never quite forgave us. But we probably could have worked up a vote of thanks from the visiting publishers. I'm quite sure that they saw nothing else in the *News* building that interested them so much.

The year of the passing of the Ghost Catcher was also the year of the Tarn River floods in France, the evacuation of the Rhineland by the Allies, the fall of the Bolivian government, the closing of the Bank of the United States in New York City, and the coming of Abraham Mahoney.

Abey Mahoney isn't so hard to say when you learn that the second name is Lincoln. But it was some time before we knew that and we puzzled over Mr. Mahoney—a thing we were still doing years later.

Mr. Mahoney was large and dark and very mysterious, with a deep impressive voice and a hypnotic eye. He carried about with him an atmosphere of ominous portent and even the old-timers on the staff waited momentarily for him to toss a miracle.

Nobody was surprised when he was one of the first reporters

sent out of the office on the morning of the St. Valentine's Day Massacre. Nobody would have been surprised had he come back with all the killers or all the corpses. But that wasn't the way it turned out.

John Craig had told Mr. Mahoney what he was to do. He was to take a taxicab to the scene of the shambles. He was to spend five minutes getting what comment he could out of the officials who happened to be present. Then he was to hop back into his taxicab and return to the office. Mr. Mahoney did all that and, as might have been expected, a bit more.

"I talked to Dr. Bundesen, the coroner. I talked a little to Joe Mullins of the homicide squad. And I came away like you told me. But on the way out I got a chance to swipe this coat off the hook right above where the bodies were lying. I haven't had a chance to look at it because the taxi driver was nosey and maybe suspicious. But here it is. . . ."

He held out a gray coat from the pocket of which he extracted a wad of paper.

"May be evidence," he said. . . . And he opened the packet to read: "Care of the four-month-old baby . . ."

"Okay," said Craig. "Now you know who owns it, take it back." Mr. Mahoney, it seems, had stolen the coroner's coat.

Also, that year, we had Jack Drury, a talented investigator who dressed for his job. It is said that the perils of his work which took him past large gambling houses, speak-easies and such, made it necessary for him to wear a bullet-proof vest at all times and carry an extra large gun. As to that I can't say but I knew that he went about fully equipped with handcuffs—or at any rate he did until the day when Ray Quisno used them to handcuff his coat to his desk.

And that was the year also when the slush ice was so thick at the entrance to the harbor and a ship from Duluth got frozen up beyond the breakwater.

There was a fertile-brained young press agent out at one of the packing plants at the time—one Fred Rochester—who saw in the plight of this boat a great opportunity for some energetic meat dealer. Full of enthusiasm he brought his plan to town and laid it in the lap of John Craig. He was going to send an airplane to the rescue of that ship, he said. But it would be an expensive job and he didn't want to get his expedition aloft until he was certain that we'd send a photographer down to the harbor mouth to make a record of the great work. John said that he'd send over the photographer, and Mr. Rochester dashed out to Curtiss Field for his aviator. The brave pilot made one stop out near the stockyards to get a load of pemmican and such and then went straight to the rescue work.

Out in the ice the ship *Gustav* of Duluth nestled like a stranded whale. A lookout reported to the captain that somebody was trying to shout some messages from the breakwater but that he couldn't make them out. The captain tried also. He thought he could make out something about rescue and keeping up his courage but that sounded silly. He thought of opening up the radio and then thought better of it.

Lots of people began to collect along the shore. By that time, it appears, everybody in town knew the ship was to be rescued except the victims themselves. That is why passengers and crew all ran out onto the deck when the airplane came over.

Mr. Rochester's pilot didn't have any Norden bombsight

but he had a pretty good eye. He dropped the first ham from about a thousand feet and it went straight through the pilot house. The second missed by no more than a yard.

He never got to drop a third. By that time the victims had crawled over the side and were walking ashore on the ice. In pitting themselves against the perils of the deep they had not contemplated possible destruction by falling hams.

18

HOW TO RUN A BEDLAM

~~~~~~

IT SEEMS a matter of dubious compliment to link the name of
the best-balanced man who ever filled an editor's chair with
this virtually unending era of lunacy. But it is likewise patent
that if the circus is wonderful the ringmaster must find himself
slightly spattered by the wonder. Certainly in any study of
the Times of Mrs. Lawson's Cat it would be impossible to
overlook John Craig. Quite aside from such sentimental con-
siderations as the fact that he was the best-loved city editor
to a long procession of oddly assorted lugs he would still be
a newspaperman's choice as the world's top newspaperman.
At any rate he is the best I've ever known and I'll venture a
guess that there'll never be a better.

He was assistant city editor when I first came to the *Daily
News*. He became city editor, news editor and assistant managing editor before illness, long overdue, caught up with him.
But whatever his title, the place he sat was head of the table.
In a period of noisy dementia he was quiet, soft-spoken, assured. In a fantasia of emotional exhibitionism he was without
emotions, calm, dispassionate and eminently sane. In the most
chaotic city in the most complex civilization in history he alone

knew all the answers: Who killed McSwiggin and why. . . . Who stood behind Al Capone. . . . What time the Twentieth Century Limited got to Buffalo. . . . What was the telephone number of the desk sergeant at Grand Crossing station. . . . Who actually ran the thirteenth precinct of the fourteenth ward. . . . Who wrote that story about Charley Dawes' pipe two years ago. . . .

Somebody has said that every institution is the lengthening shadow of one man—which to my mind explained the lack of hysteria in the *News'* local room.

One February morning I came in from some out-of-town assignment and stopped at the desk to exchange greetings. . . . The telephone was ringing. Craig answered it. With no change of expression he said to me, "Wait a minute." Then one after another he gave six reporters an address and meticulous instructions about what each was to do in the five minutes after his arrival there. Each was to go in his own cab and hold it. I was amazed but kept quiet until the last reporter had gone out on the run to cover a story the nature of which had not even been divulged to him. Then I blurted a question.

"They've just killed all the hoodlums in Chicago in one basket," he said without raising his voice and he turned to the rewrite desk. "Give me what you can of that Rogers Park story," he said. "I guess maybe we'll have to put it back and lock it up." Then with the cold detachment of one to whom such things are an everyday matter he called up the circulation manager to prepare him for the story of the St. Valentine's Day Massacre.

He spoke seldom but he always had the sharpest wit in town when he did speak. One morning his assistant who had delayed a bit too long across the street put out what he thought was a reasonable explanation. . . .

"I was interviewed by a girl from a high-school paper out there in the visitors' coop," he said. "I had to tell her everything about the newspaper business in fifteen minutes."

"Go on, Tom," said Craig. "I've got fifteen minutes. . . ."

And there was the time when Henry Paynter on some assignment downstate got his pocket picked in a theater and wired home for more money. "It was a lousy movie," he said in his message, "and now I know the source of the *Daily News* comics." Craig sent him the money with some good advice: "Don't go to the movies and don't read *Daily News* comics."

And there was also the time when Clem Lane excused himself to attend a holyday Mass at noon at St. Patrick's Church. On the way back to the office he fell in with some friends in Louie's and did not show up at his desk until the following day. Craig looked at him in some surprise as he came in. "My," he said, "these Catholic services certainly last a long time."

And there was a lad on one of the departmental staffs who'd been fired and came to him for help.

"But, Mr. Craig," he said. "I love the work so much. I love to write."

"That," said Mr. Craig, "is the trouble with this damned paper."

Once I told him the ancient joke about the wheelbarrow being the world's greatest invention because it taught the Irish to stand on their hind legs. Appreciative of true wit, he took this gem over to the City Hall and told it to Marty O'Brien, Bill

[204]

Kelly, Mike Hughes and others whose names escape me, and willing hands tossed him right out into La Salle Street.

"I begin to see," he told me when he came back to the office, "that before you mention wheelbarrows in polite society you'd better take out a membership in the Ancient Order of Hibernians."

He had the most effective art of making you see his point that I have ever known. The method varied but the results were always what he wanted them to be.

I am unlikely to forget one occasion when I was aroused by something that had been done to my copy. I jumped up out of my chair, leaned across his desk and began my harangue. Along in the middle of it I began my best argument: "I am not temperamental . . ." And he never gave me a chance to get on with it.

"Good God, no!" he said and he picked up his hat and coat and went out of the office . . . and in all the years that followed I cultivated something of his own abiding calm.

19

PARADE OF THE SIMPLE BIG-SHOTS

ONLY the other day it was announced in the public prints that somebody whose name escapes me at the moment was forecasting a return of Prohibition as one of the more acceptable blessings the United States might receive as a result of the war which was then (August 1943) still being fought. And for just a moment, like a whiff of lavender and rosemary, there came to me a feeling of gladness not to say enthusiasm. Time, about to turn backward, etc., in its flight was certainly preparing to revive the greatest of the journalistic shows and to reproduce—since it could not possibly reanimate—the finest procession of small-time rapscallions the dismal human race had ever produced. . . .

The fantastic twenties! Those were the days when there were two cars in every bootlegger's garage and a corpse in every alley—when the kitchen smelled of raisin mash and the tattoo of bursting bottles marked the progress of the home-brew in the basement—when the best places to eat in the city were the speak-easies, or maybe your stomach was too paralyzed to tell—when Scotch with a Southern accent cost twelve dollars a quart and the customers all seemed to have twelve dollars—when hearts were young and gay, and livers and lights, apparently, were more durable. Those were the days when more virtuous cities, such as New York and New Orleans and Kansas City and Los Angeles, looked in great distress at the daily doings in Chicago and inquired in great alarm how long were such things going to be permitted.

Those were the days also when the sudden death of a refurbished pimp who had strayed into the hooch business seemed important. . . .

"Gang guns blazed again last night and in the acrid mists of fading smoke lay Peewee Poopopolos, the eminent big-shot!"

"The grim gray vengeance of Tough Tommy Megrim's mobsters came over the dim years last night and tore the heart out of Beetle the Blot, sometimes known as the violin-carrying mystery man. . . ."

Those were the days, also, of roaring rhetoric in the crime leads.

Hardly a man is now alive who remembers the names of any three of the ex-pickpockets who got so glamorous that they were the principal pain in the neck of all rewrite men. After the first fifty of them had been hustled through inquests it became impossible to name them without the help of a roster something like the city directory. The principal big-shots became so not through any particular talent or personality, it seems to me, but rather through the fortuitous circumstance that they lived longer than their competitors.

Despite a certain amount of scandal that attached to the shooting of a well-dressed police reporter who had shaken down not one but a pair of Chicago's less patient killers, newspapermen of that era got intimate with very few of the racketeers. Friendships like that were too impermanent to be attractive. One got a sort of speaking acquaintance with Al Capone by meeting him in courts where he was accused of things like bursting a paper bag in front of a hospital, walking on the grass in Jackson Park, failing to tip his hat in front of the City Hall. One got to know Spike O'Donnell by happening into the Randolph Street soft-drink parlor that he used as a sort of office. One met Big Tim Murphy by printing something in the paper that he didn't like.

Tim was probably the most picturesque product of that somewhat monotonous epoch. He had nothing much to do with the liquor racket except possibly as an ultimate consumer. He had come out of the bare-knuckle days in the labor-union industry surviving a lot of other emancipators who had wished him dead, and had organized the garbage collectors, street sweepers and readers of gas meters. He was also active in some corners of the building trades council with a sideline, the Federal government once made a jury believe, of mail robbery.

Tim was big, genial, handsome in a way, and wrapped in personality that might have made him one of the most successful politicians of his day if he had chosen to work at it. He had the humor and color that virtually all the rest of the extra-legal operators lacked. And, with one of the brightest minds ever directed toward the betterment of labor and the robbery of the mails, he had gifts of expression that in the eyes of tired journalists promptly set him apart from all others of his calling. As a matter of fact he invented the language that has been placed in the mouths of story-book gangsters ever since.

"The one-way ride" was one of his figures of speech; "took a runout powder" was another. "They sneezed him because his lip slipped," was his highly original report on the killing of a squealer. Capone in his parlance, frequently expressed, was "a flesh-selling S.O.B." And expanding on that theme he appears to be the lexicographer who deflated the Italian gangsters by calling them "grease-balls." The term "racket" itself is said to have been his. Certainly he was the first man to use it within the hearing of anybody able and willing to put it in print.

We all came to know Big Tim before he died. But primarily he was the friend of Editor Henry Justin Smith. There never was an odder association—if you can call it association—nor any stranger story in the newspaper business than that of their first meeting.

Tim, who, unlike any of the other big-shots I have ever known, never farmed out his battles to sluggers, came into the office in a red rage. Somebody had loosely referred to him as an associate of Al Capone and in virtuous indignation he was out for a retraction or somebody's blood. How he got as far as the local room on the fourth floor and, having arrived there, made his way virtually unnoticed to the glass partition that screened Smith's desk I don't know. Four or five copyreaders saw him at once and sent out an SOS for the strong-arm squad. I looked up from a typewriter to see Tim red across the back of his neck and hunched over like a heavyweight getting ready for the kill. And almost before I realized what was going on I saw what I afterward classified as final proof of the control of mind over matter: Smith, thin, scholarly, totally unperturbed, had risen from his desk and taken a step or two forward.

"Big Tim Murphy, I believe," he said. "Why didn't anybody out there have sense enough to show you in? Have a chair. . . ." And Tim sat down. The hard-rock men from the circulation department, the amateur fixers from the stereotyping room with lead slugs in their hands, came for a moment into the outer office and in awed silence faded away.

"And take my word for it, Mr. Murphy," I heard Smith saying, "that was the mistake of some careless and uninformed reporter. . . . The last thing I would do to my worst enemy would be to put him in a category like that. . . ." They shook hands as Big Tim went out. Both of them were calm and smiling but from that day on Henry Justin Smith might have been the biggest big-shot in Chicago if he had cared to make use of his connections. Big Tim was his. . . .

Murphy came into the office many times after that, before and after his term in Leavenworth for mail robbery, but never again in anger.

"I like to talk to Smitty," he told me later. "He's got sense. You don't need maps when you tell him somethin'. But I don't think he eats right. I brought him a big steak the other day but he wouldn't take it. . . . But gee, for a guy that eats lettuce he certainly is a good guy."

Once he came in when Smith wasn't there, but that was long years afterward when his visits had ceased to be an occasion. After a glance about the office he gave his attention to Luke Hunt, the city editor.

"Look, Red," he said with his customary lack of formality, "how long you been in the newspaper racket?"

Luke answered him just as informally. "About fifteen years," he said. "Why?"

"Well, this," said Tim displaying a late home edition. "This story here from Milwaukee says that Nicky Arnstein and I went up there and shook down a lot of building workers. Now, Red, that's the bunk."

Luke eyed him skeptically.

"That's an A.P. story," he said with considerable courage. "How do we know it isn't right?"

"If you been fifteen years in the newspaper business you know it isn't right," said Tim. "You know that in the labor racket you don't shake down the men. You shake down the contractor."

"I'm sorry," said Luke and he sent a "kill" out to the composing room.

"Not a bad guy," he said after Tim had made his exit in a sort of one-man parade. "You can put up with a dishonest man when he's honest with you."

When Big Tim came back from Leavenworth along about 1925, full of explanations of how the loot of the Dearborn Street station mail robbery came to be found in his father-in-law's attic, he decided to write his autobiography. That is, he decided to tell me the innermost secrets of his life and let me write the autobiography. Curiosity more than hope of reward made me accept the honor. We had several interviews, with a stenographer slightly offstage, and the book grew rapidly. Tim was enthusiastic as he read the copy a chapter at a time.

"Maybe I shoulda been writing books before this," he said. "I never knew I could do it." And a new dignity clung to him, whether because of his new literary status or because the town had slipped away from him during his term in the penitentiary I shall never say.

"We'll sell a lot of these books," he assured me in one conference. "But we got to be reasonable about it. We don't want to go charging any ten dollars a bite like this Colonel House is charging for his book. Five bucks is enough."

I gasped. "Look, Tim," I told him. "A book of this size will sell for two dollars and we'll get a royalty of ten percent on the first ten thousand copies which we will divide with Harry McClellan, our agent. That's what the take will be."

He sniffed. "We'll charge five bucks and let 'em keep their ten percent," he said. "That'll give us three bucks to split and at a buck apiece when we sell twenty thousand books we'll have twenty grand. . . ."

I may have shown some impatience. "And where," I asked him with an earnestness that came of long experience, "are you going to sell twenty thousand books at five dollars . . . or ten thousand or five thousand?"

"Well, there's the garbage haulers," he said. "There's about five thousand of them and every one of them guys needs a book. . . . And the electricians and the gas-meter readers, and the street sweepers. And sellin's the easiest part. I'll just go to the meetings and tell these guys how much they need a book and where they kick in with the five smacks. The trouble with you is that you don't pay enough attention to the business side of book writing. . . . Me, I see both sides. . . ."

The book when finished was an amazing document whatever else it was. I had no trouble getting the publishers interested in it. But by the time the first one had agreed to print it Tim had begun to get coy. Nothing about that first contract suited him, nor about the revised contract nor, finally, about the publisher. I found a new publisher. And after that as Mr. Murphy waxed hot and cold I took the manuscript to two others. Then I discovered what had happened. Big Tim's literary days were over. He had formed a partnership with Nicky Arnstein to open a gambling house in Chicago and he was no longer interested in vindication or any other kind of publicity. Even the twenty grand that he was to have sand-bagged out of the loyal workers didn't seem important to him any more.

I didn't see much of him after that and I was attending the Democratic National Convention in Houston, Texas, in 1928 when I got a call from the office and sent his obituary by tele-graph. It seems that Tim had been in and out of the cleaning-and-dyeing business. He had muscled in and completed a satisfactory arrangement with the musclees. In the meantime a brace of killers sent out after him when he first started to declare himself in on this enterprise had gone to a Wisconsin resort and spent their advance blood money on a long-term binge. They came out of their hangover long after Big Tim was at peace with the cleaners and dyers. But they had no way of telling that. So, on their way home, they stopped at Tim's modest home in Rogers Park, called him out and shot him.

The killers, whose names I forget, came to appropriate bad ends shortly afterward but I wasn't much interested. I hadn't written their autobiographies.

Spike O'Donnell, while less sparkling than Big Tim, was also less exacting. Furthermore he was more durable. At last accounts he was still alive and making a great hit as witness before investigating committees on the subject "Crime does not pay."

Spike resembled Tim in that he also was tall and handsome and an exemplary husband. He always felt that should the hooch business fail him he could still make his fortune lecturing in Drury Lane Theater, London, on the life expectancy of the average Chicagoan. Lady Diana Manners, who discovered him in his soft-drink hideout, had suggested this to him. And he was proud of referring to her ever afterward as "My friend, Lady Diana Manners, who wants me to go on the stage. . . ."

When he was not discussing these prospects with his literary and business acquaintances Spike was engaged with his brothers in a beer business that was a great annoyance to Al Capone. Spike was shot at numerous times in line of duty but despite his considerable bulk never got touched. He never liked commentators to disparage the marksmanship of his Italian opposition. He preferred to think, rather, that some bodily dexterity of his own moved him out of the way of flying slugs.

George Stone, Chicago *Daily News* rewrite man whose desk was next to mine, used to discuss this phenomenon with me from time to time. George didn't think it was physical dexterity that kept Spike alive. He thought it was the use of blank ammunition by some blind man in the opposition. However, Spike came very close to elimination one day and George and I knew about it sooner than anybody else.

We were going to lunch when we came upon Mr. O'Donnell standing by a firebox on the La Salle Hotel corner. George greeted him and to make conversation asked how things were going.

"It's a funny thing, George," Spike said in a low monotonous voice. "I was standin' in front of a drugstore at twenty-fift' and Wentwort'. It was a beautiful morning, George. I never seen a morning like that out there. The sun was shining and all

the leaves was coming out where you could see 'em over behind the drugstore and there was a couple of little birds up on
the telegraph wires singing and singing."

George looked at him blankly. Spike may have been unpredictable but the last thing anybody would have expected to
find in him was an interest in the pastoral loveliness of a spring
morning at Twenty-fift' and Wentwort'.

"And there's a little kid playin' on the sidewalk," Spike went
on. "Right at my feet he was. He was riding one of them
kiddy cars. And he certainly was a nice little kid. I asked him
what his name was but I don't think he told me. While I was
lookin' at him a car come along. It was an open car with the
top up. Somebody yells at me 'Hello . . . Spike!' An' I got
just time to knock that kid flat and fall on top of him. Boy,
they sure give it to that drugstore. The front looked like they
run a sewing machine over it. They were certainly nasty,
them boys. . . ."

George looked at him curiously. "And when was this?" he
asked.

"This mornin'," said Spike sadly. "Down at Twenty-Fift'
and Wentwort' . . . about twenty minutes ago."

"Good-by, Spike," said George, with considerable intelligence, I thought.

There were times in the fabulous twenties when we were
convinced that chaos had come to stay, that there would never
again be a time in Chicago when hooch and murder would
not be the principal topics of news. The world belonged to
the "big-shots." Little children lisped their names and imitated
their exploits in play. Another generation, one felt, would be
erecting statues to Capones and Gennas and O'Banions in the

public parks. . . . And then, of course, it was all finished virtually overnight.

Just before Hitler went into the Sudetenland I came back to the office from an assignment in the Black Hills and ran into John Craig.

"I wish you'd run out to the Clarendon Hospital and look at a guy they've got. I wouldn't ask you to do it but there's nobody else around here who knows Louie Alterie by sight. And they think that's who it is. . . ."

I got my car and started north and rolled over in my mind this surprising statement. . . . I was the only one on the premises aside from maybe John himself who knew Louie Alterie and in his day it seemed to me that everybody had known Louie Alterie. Where on earth had all the other reporters of that day gone? I felt pretty old until I suddenly realized that Louie had gone out of town to start some unidentified racket in Colorado only about six years before.

What was even more surprising, as I realized when I put my mind to it, was that there should be any need to send a personal acquaintance of Alterie to identify him. . . . What had become of all the police?

When I got into the hospital it was as if a decade of my life had fallen away. For here was a scene that had been as unchanging as the Prohibition Act itself—the same little basement receiving room, blood-spattered and messy looking . . . a sheeted figure on an enameled gocart with a young little doctor and a young little nurse bending over it . . . the same languid cop in the open doorway with a green lawn, a sunny garden and a stretch of white back porches beyond him . . .

[216]

the same pile of shredded clothing tossed in the corner as it had been cut from the back of the man on the cart.

"What happened to him?" I asked.

"Sawed-off shotgun," said the policeman without changing his pose. "In his own doorway."

"Who is he?" I went on.

"Can't say," the cop answered disinterestedly.

I went over to the gocart and lifted the sponge from a face that was still recognizable although a couple of slugs had marked it. I put the mask back and answered the cop's questioning look.

"Yes," I said. "It's Louie Alterie."

And then came the day's principal shock. The little doctor who had been doing what could be done to save this often forfeited life stiffened up and pointed at the prospective corpse with his probe.

"And who," he wanted to know, "is Louie Alterie?"

I passed that one because what Craig had said had prepared me for it.

"Louie Alterie recently has been classed as a gambler," I said. "Before that he ran a hide-out for mobsters out in the Rockies. He was a killer with a long record. He was chief cannon for Dion O'Banion's mob." And only then did it flash upon me that a new day had dawned in the land.

"Who," the little doctor wanted to know, "was Dion O'Banion?"

I puzzled over that one as I went back to the office to write a lead on the fall of the mighty. Eight years had gone by since they shot Dion O'Banion while shaking hands with him in his flower shop across from the Cathedral . . . eight years and already one of the imperishable names of a nightmare decade had gone into the still more imperishable mud. I think of it whenever I see a new face in the rotogravure—Hitler, Mussolini, Rommel—

"Who was Dion O'Banion?"

20

REPORTER KNOWS ENOUGH TO COME
IN OUT OF THE RAIN

THE first night that the harried wife of Charlie Owen thought he had been killed by angry gangsters he was brought home by an appreciative chief of police. The second night that this horrible conviction rose in her mind about 3:00 A.M. he was returned to her by the highly polished gunman Dion O'Banion, himself to be killed by gangsters in the next few weeks. That will give you some idea of the stature of Mr. Owen if not of his charm.

Owen, as results show, was a spectacular and highly successful newspaperman. He got a governor of Illinois indicted. He cleaned up a ring of automobile thieves. He furnished the evidence in the first big attack of the community on the murderous cliques that were rising out of Prohibition. But he certainly was no example of the craft to be held up before earnest novices in schools of journalism. Nobody ever knew precisely where he was at any given time. He talked with a Southern accent in a mess of figures of speech and generalities that amounted to a code, and one who got his stuff into print had to be an interpreter as well as a rewrite man. Everybody loved him including the gunmen whom he gave plenty of occasion to kill him.

"It'd be a shame to knock him off," one of the murdering Gennas is said to have remarked to a pal in our circulation department. "He talks too good. . . ." Whether that was the reason or something else, he contrived to live a long time running with the hare and hunting with the hounds. Only once was he in any danger that he recognized for himself. . . . That grew out of his Southern sweetie-pie attitude toward humanity, his tendency to refer to all females from two to eighty years old as "honey." One evening in what he thought was an innocuous telephone conversation he said "honey" to Mrs. Dion O'Banion who related the incident to Dion who toured all the speak-easies of his acquaintance questing the hide of Mr. Owen. He cooled down a bit when he finally came upon Mr. Owen honeying an ancient beggarwoman but it is generally conceded that Owen's margin of safety in the encounter was as thin as O'Banion's temper—which was pretty thin.

Charlie Owen was probably the most unpunctual soul in a city of 3,600,000 people. So it was natural that he should own a watch accurate to within two seconds a month. He kept it that way, too, by plaguing jewelers all over the land. He had a way of demanding service on things he spent money for.

Once in a moment of blindness somebody in one of the bigger music houses sold him a radio set. Charley, who knew the press agent, made the firm exchange the set for another like it and that exchanged in turn for another and so for fifteen transactions, probably because he didn't like the program he could get over WGN. He had similar troubles with cars, parlor lamps, and toy trains for his little boy.

I recall one evening when, as he and I were waiting for a handout from some political committee temporarily officed in the Hotel La Salle, he suggested that we visit the phonograph shop across Madison Street. We found a tired girl getting ready to close the place for the day. Charles, as I remember it, was interested in a piece titled something like "Three Birds in a Tree" . . . the sort of title that somehow you didn't connect with Charlie Owen. The tired girl looked through the current catalog and failed to discover it.

"I seem to remember the piece, though," she said. "It may be in one of the older catalogues—and we have quite a stock of old records. . . ." She looked through some more catalogs and card-index files and then through shelf after shelf of dusty record envelopes, filling the place with a choking atmosphere of prewar soot and presently—after about half an hour—she found it. In triumph she handed it to Charlie who smiled his approbation.

"Will you play it for me, please, ma'am?" he asked. And she wound up a phonograph and played it. Charlie listened in rapture until it was finished. Then he beamed on her and tipped his hat gallantly.

"I thank you kindly, ma'am," he said. "I certainly always liked that piece." After which he put his hat back on his head again and walked out. I didn't stay to see what the girl did.

If one can derive any lesson at all from Charlie Owen's unbelievable career it must be that he travels farthest and fastest in this business who adheres to the theory that everybody's out of step but Mike. Mr. Owen's conversation was brilliant with the exposition of other people's oddities and foibles. He took it for granted that his immediate associates all lived where he did himself, somewhere in Cloud-Cuckoo land, and that all were as skilled as he himself in observing how ridiculous and incongruous was life in other localities.

I shall never forget the look of childlike amazement on his face as he came to John Craig, then his city editor, one dull, warm summer Saturday afternoon and told of a sort of Peter Pan adventure in the lower reaches of the mysterious News Building.

"The place was absolutely empty," he said. "There wasn't a soul in the joint except one little old lady who was asleep in an office with a sign on the door that said 'Wide Awake Club.'"

On the other hand he showed no such fine appreciation of the odd when he was asked to turn over his notes to the reporter who relieved him after a morning's testimony in the Len Small trial. Charlie had been listening carefully to a lot of complicated evidence about state budgets and expenses, political skulduggery and the like for something over three hours but there was only one line written in his notebook: "Charles Fitzmorris is Chief of Police of Chicago."

One school of thought has held that Charlie Owen hypnotized people from whom he was trying to get information, which may or may not have been the case. There was the time he was sent down to find out something from a man at the moment in a cell in the Joliet city jail. What Charlie wanted to learn is now forgotten but the prisoner knew what it was and he turned out to be coy about it. Mr. Owen, who had come into the cell at 10:00 A.M., was still working on his argument at 9:00 P.M. when somebody came around to turn out the lights.

[222]

Mr. Owen so far had not been able to convince the interviewee that he ought to talk.

The prisoner had a wild light of hope in his eye when the turnkey sounded taps but it didn't last long. Mr. Owen instead of turning to the door started to take off his coat.

"Move over," he suggested. "I'm staying all night."

"Okay," said the prisoner. "Just what do you want to know, and make it snappy. . . ."

And I remember another case where the nature of his charm might be difficult to describe. . . . With a customer as witness Charlie had posted a thousand dollars with a South Side druggist for payment to a man about town—or rather a man about that end of town—who knew where the body was buried or something similar. But there was a stipulation that the druggist would not turn over the money to anybody unless both Charlie and his customer were present. The customer meanwhile went out and got killed and the druggist saw a great opportunity. He was aloof when Mr. Owen came back to ask the return of his thousand dollars.

He cited the regulation and Mr. Owen cheerfully agreed that he was right about it.

"There's no reason why we should quarrel about such a little thing," he said. "We'll find some way out of it. I'll just report to my people that you're a friend of mine and a friend of theirs and then they'll go out and get something like a friendly writ of mandamus—all in fun, of course. . . ." And the astonished druggist opened up the safe.

Mr. Owen, so far as a voluminous record shows, met only one situation with which he was powerless to deal and possibly that wasn't his fault.

One day when Mr. Owen turned up indisposed, Mr. Craig assigned a reporter to put him into a hotel room until his condition should improve. The reporter, who was an economical person, decided that Mr. Owen's immediate need was not so much luxury as a bed and not a very expensive bed at that. And he thought he knew where to get it.

It is not generally known to the trade but there is a hotel in Chicago—a first-class hotel—where chorus girls can live at boardinghouse prices. A manager who got his start from the patronage of the theatrical profession remembered his obligations when it came time to put up a new building. He set aside one floor of small, simple, but comfortable rooms where the girls could house themselves respectably. Sometimes rooms on this floor might be rented to persons of good character other than chorus girls, so to this hotel and to this floor Mr. Craig's emissary brought Mr. Owen. He paid in advance for a room, took Mr. Owen to it and put him to bed.

One of the features of this floor was the absence of private baths. That came home to the reporter as he started back to his office. At the end of the corridor he noticed the labels on the public bathrooms and they gave him an idea.

He went across the street to Woolworth's, bought a ten cent screwdriver and came back. When he left the hotel for good he had the key to Mr. Owen's unlocked room in his pocket and on Mr. Owen's door there was a sign which read "LADIES."

John Craig rescued Mr. Owen about seven o'clock that evening. The floor was quiet and deserted. . . . All of the young actresses had long since risen and gone to work. But Mr. Owen who should have been rested and refreshed by several hours of sleep was sullen and irritable.

[224]

"Honest to God, John," he complained, "this is the damn-dest dump I ever was in. . . . Women running in here every two minutes. . . ."

Only once did Mr. Craig show any tendency to doubt Charlie Owen's judgment. For Mr. Craig knew Mr. Owen better than the rest of us and presumably knew what Mr. Owen's judgment was. The moment of mistrust came one day an hour or so after John had left Mr. Owen in Jack Farley's speak-easy. Mr. Owen called up to explain why he hadn't come back to work.

"It's the rain, John," he said. "I'll get going just as soon as it stops."

He didn't sound drunk so Mr. Craig took a quick look out the window and blinked his eyes to make sure that they were working properly. Out in Wells Street the sun was shining brilliantly and the dust was swirling from a pavement that hadn't been wet in a month.

Of course nobody knew better than John Craig that one should never be surprised at anything that Charlie Owen did or said. But if a sober Charlie couldn't do any better in the way of excuses than to think up a rainstorm on a bright day, then something must be wrong with him. Craig was actually worried when the phone rang again.

"I was going to ask you to send somebody down here with a raincoat and an umbrella," said Mr. Owen. "But I guess that's out. . . . Anybody would drown if he tried to get across the street. Don't you think so?"

"Of course," said John. "It's pretty bad all right. But just stay right where you are and I'll get somebody around to rescue you somehow."

He picked out the soberest reporter within reach and sent him up the street on a dead run to Farley's. In five minutes the reporter was on the telephone.

"I can't get into Farley's," he said. "The big water tank on the roof is busted and the front of the building looks like Niagara Falls."

"A great reporter, Charlie Owen," John Craig said as he hung up. "He's never wrong about anything, even rainstorms on dry days. . . ."

Walter Strong, who succeeded to the ownership of the *News* after the death of Victor Lawson, lingered with us long enough to start a long overdue program of expansion, put up a new building and junk a lot of archaic presses. He died before his influence as a publisher could be felt by most of the staff but not before he had left to the profession one graphic demonstration of what it means to be a newspaperman.

Strong's association with the editorial side of the business was limited to the memory of a few months as a cub in Beloit. But somewhere along the line between that time and the day when he took over the paper he picked up an understanding of the difficulties if not of the technique of producing the news. As a businessman with a hand in many enterprises he had a number of friends whose knowledge of the newspaper world was confined to what they had seen in the movies but who were loudly critical of it and particularly of that portion controlled by Mr. Strong.

It was their credo that all reporters, but particularly *Daily News* reporters, were careless. They suggested to Mr. Strong that he fire the whole lot and train a lot of earnest young men to a sense of responsibility—and more to the same effect. Mr. Strong listened to this line of conversation daily for several weeks as he rode the trains between his home and the office and eventually he got tired of it. He concealed his feelings however and when one day he sent out a lot of invitations to a banquet in the club rooms on top of the half-finished Daily News Building, the critics took it as a gesture of conciliation.

The job of getting to the party was something that most of the guests remembered long afterward, from the eerie trek in the dark over piles of gravel and lumber through what was to be the concourse, to a ride to the twenty-fourth floor in a wooden construction elevator. There were strange echoes in the big building. Hours afterward the guests were reminded of them.

The dinner, sent up from the Northwestern Terminal Restaurant, was good . . . the big room in which it was served gave no indication of the chaos that lay just outside. During the fish course a policeman came into the room, asked for Mr. Strong and whispered something to him. Mr. Strong looked disturbed. However, when he came back to the table again he was as genial as usual. About the middle of the ice cream somebody thought he had heard a cry for help somewhere outside. Mr. Strong said he thought it must be the wind in some of the open construction.

As coffee was poured, he stood up.

"Gentlemen," he said. "I have asked you to come here to-night . . ." But he didn't finish the sentence. A man at the middle of the table who hadn't spoken much during the evening and didn't seem to know anybody suddenly pushed back his chair, jumped to his feet, pulled out a pistol and fired point-blank at the guest sitting opposite. The guest fell over backward. A police whistle shrieked outside. The door opened and a woman was briefly glimpsed in the entrance. But only briefly. As she stepped across the threshold the lights went out and there was another series of shots and two or three more screams. An electric lantern flashed to reveal a brace of policemen and as that single ray of light died out the air was filled with a noise of clanking iron. Then the lights flashed on again to discover the petrified diners in a number of odd attitudes and to reveal that both the murderer and corpse had gone away. Where there had been a bedlam there was now a dead and terrifying quiet. Through it broke the voice of the host who oddly enough had begun to smile.

"Now, gentlemen," he said, "we shall see how good you are as reporters. A waiter will give each of you a pad of paper and a pencil and you shall write out in your own way a record of what you saw just now—or what you thought you saw— and when your stories have been read aloud I shall entertain further suggestions about the improvement of my staff. . . ."

The best brains of Chicago went to work then to prove what any cross-examiner knows about the fallacy of human testimony. Mr. Strong burned the manuscripts before his guests took their way sheepishly to the terrifying elevator. One wishes he hadn't.

21

REVOLT OF THE ANONYMOUS

〜〜〜〜〜〜〜〜〜〜〜〜〜〜〜〜〜〜〜〜

IT IS odd that the two people in all the folklore of American newspapering whom I understand best and know best are a pair I have never seen and whose names, for the purposes of publication, I have forgotten. For each in his own way represents the subconscious revolt of his kind against the anonymity with which this business is cloaked. I can understand them as no one can who has not spent a lifetime listening to other people's worries, cheers and bright ideas.

There was a sort of assistant filing clerk in the library—"morgue," to the trade—of the *Daily* ———, whose name in this account will appear as Peter Smith. Peter Smith wasn't the brightest morgue attendant in the business, but he was gentle, polite and willing to be as helpful as his limited capacities permitted and most of the men who had any dealings with the library were kind to him. Life for him became just what one might suppose he'd have wanted it to be if he had had anything to do with the making of it. He was allowed to pursue a routine that had nothing in it to excite him or remind him of mental shortcomings. Nobody crossed him, he crossed nobody. He became a silent, shadowy figure, differing from other shadows among the tall stacks of files only because he sometimes moved.

As is quite common even when one lives among friends nobody ever gave a thought to the life of Peter Smith outside the office. It was conceivable that he had such an existence— a bed somewhere and a source of meals—but beyond that speculation ceased. . . . Newspapermen generally are interested in other people's affairs only when they are assigned to be interested in them.

Even the men with whom Peter Smith worked in the library knew nothing at all about him as a human being—his emotions, if he had any, his hopes, his desires, his ambitions. He spoke to them oftener than to anybody else—which was seldom. He glowed appreciatively when they thanked him for something or included him in a joke. But he never came far out of his shy silence. There probably would have been no change in this situation if another Peter Smith hadn't committed a spectacular suicide in his former wife's apartment.

A reporter came to the library for the clippings, if any, on Peter Smith and was given two envelopes. One was filled with a lot of news about the Peter Smith who had killed himself— details of a divorce suit, threats against his former wife, public attempts at reconciliation, an arrest and a peace bond. . . . But the other, for all the need for immediate work on the suicide story, was what really caught the reporter's attention. There was no doubt about it. This was the envelope of Peter Smith, the vague-minded filing clerk.

"*Southland* Good Movie," read one of the clippings. "I think the picture *Southland,* starring Marian Bryce, was the best of its kind that I have seen this fall. It was beautifully photographed and splendidly acted." (Signed) Peter Smith.

There were other one-paragraph criticisms of a similar sort and a few paragraphs of social news:

"Mr. Peter Smith has returned to the Bronx after a vacation in Hempstead." "Mr. Peter Smith won a two-dollar prize in Wednesday night's Bingo." "Mr. Peter Smith, who has written many of our photoplay criticisms, writes that he was much pleased with the performance of Nora Watts in *Miss Adventure*."

All of them, as it was easy to determine from text on the back of one, had been printed in the *Bronx Movie News,* a sort of advertising program, distributed to the customers in certain neighborhood moving-picture houses. The reporter put them away and tiptoed out.

"I felt as if I'd been spying on a human soul," he said when he could bring himself to talk about it—without mentioning names—a couple of years later. "The last thing on earth that I'd do would be to pry into the secret of that little guy . . . and the worst secret I'll have to lug around from now on is his—that he has the instinct to get up, to be respected, to bust out of this damned silence. . . . Do you know what I mean?"

I said that I did.

The parallel case is that of one whom we shall call George Robbins who in his proper identity was, for many years, the crack rewrite man of the New York *Herald Tribune.* Mr. Robbins was a smart technician as goes without saying in the case of anybody able to hold that sort of job and become a star and in addition to that, it should be stated at the outset, he was a man of regular and temperate habits. He was probably the most dependable man in the *Herald Tribune* office. So finally he blew up. . . . And why wouldn't he?

It is to be noted that in all such cases as this the calm citizen about to go berserk always gives some hint of his intentions. Like a geyser he has an indicator which an experienced observer may read. So you wonder why his first pitiful outcry about a telephone interview was not properly interpreted. He had been asked to get plenty of detail about what one Mr. Jesse Weaver thought about the economic condition of the United States and he was clearly rebellious.

"I went to school with that lug and he doesn't know anything about anything," he said. "Why a guy ought to be an authority on banking and economics just because his grandfather died last week and left him a million dollars is something I can't figure. . . ."

But his city editor was obdurate, probably on the principle that the best interviewees are always lugs who don't know anything about anything. In deep gloom Mr. Robbins returned to his telephone, listened to Mr. Weaver and wrote an interview that made the interviewee sound like the greatest financial authority since Croesus. Then he went down to Bleeke's interesting barroom in the same building and took what steps he thought to be necessary.

Nobody noticed any change in him when he came back to his typewriter. There was nothing very important about any of the assignments passed along to him during the next couple of hours, so nobody pressed him for copy. Thus there was nothing to interfere with the complete surprise of the city editor when the bulk of Mr. Robbins' night work was brought over to the desk at once. . . . There were five stories, beautifully written as always, on a wide variety of subjects: Somebody had put forward a possible cure for cancer. The city was threatened with a milk shortage. A leading banker had suggested the issuance of scrip to tide over one phase of the depression. Sally Rand was about to take up skiing. The American Museum of Natural History had just placed on exhibition the skeleton of an eohippus. In none of them had Mr. Robbins deviated from the general theme but, as the city editor saw at the first glance, he hadn't changed the theories evoked by Mr. Weaver.

Roughly the leads went something like this: "George Robbins, the city's leading authority on cancer, today was asked by Drs. Goldsmith and Kelly to give them the benefit of his experience in laboratory experiments on the new electonic therapy. . . ."

"George Robbins, the milk expert, today was asked by the cows what he thought about the proposed milk shortage. . . ."

"George Robbins, the financier, today suggested that the way out of the depression was for each bank to issue a lot of two-dollar bills which nobody would want to spend anyway. . . ."

"George Robbins, the fan dancer, today instructed his manager to complete arrangements for a ski race at Bear Mountain course, the other contestant to be Sally Rand, for a side bet of a couple of baubles. . . ."

"George Robbins, the city's only surviving eohippus, told reporters today that he was leaving his fine berth at the American Museum of Natural History. 'I have ambitions,' he said, 'I can do it if I try. I'm going to quit being an eohippus. I'm going to be a horse.' . . ."

The city editor watched George almost enviously as he got his hat and coat and started for home. . . . It is so seldom that any rewrite man ever does what all rewrite men have always wanted to do.

There have been other notable outbreaks of self-determination in the newspaper business in all parts of the world, as interesting—some of them—if not as perfect technically, as Mr. Robbins' one-man uprising. There was the famous cable message credited to Glenn Babb when he was A.P. correspondent in Tokyo. Cablese, as few people save those unfortunate enough to deal with it know, consists of combinations of words to pass as single words when the tolls are figured up, as "Outoftowning weekend," for "I am going out of town over the week end." "He outwent," for "He went out." "George Californiaward," for "George is on his way to California. . . ."

Mr. Babb, one presumes, had been having some trouble convincing his office of something or other, else this story whose truth he will never admit would not have been tied to him for life. As the report goes he finally got tired of argument and sent the classic message: "Upstick job asswards."

There was also the classic gesture of the crew of John R. Walsh's Chicago *Chronicle*—the lads who had borne the heat and burden of the day for a dubious character and had been paid for it in shortweight gold. They put the *Chronicle* to bed for the last time after Mr. Walsh decided it wasn't worth keeping and, somewhat in the fashion of Mr. Robbins, they interviewed themselves. The paper as it reached the street that final morning was the world's outstanding collection of libel in retaliation for which the injured John R. Walsh could do nothing but sue John R. Walsh.

And there comes to mind a forgotten young man who one day became very tired of Victor Lawson and all his works and pomps. This young man whose name was Frederick Walker had received a public reprimand from his city editor for failing to get all the names in a West Side shooting case. Still indignant, he went out and got himself a job in a factory over on the Northwest Side and was starting back to town to turn in his resignation when inspiration came to him. He went into a corner drugstore, called the *Daily News* and furnished a dazed rewrite man with the most complete story of a cable-car wreck ever printed. A gripman had failed to release his grip, or clutch or whatever they called it, as he came to a cable vault. The car had somersaulted and the two trailers had been rolled over. Thirty people were killed or injured. And he had all the names and addresses.

The *News* had a complete scoop on the story of course. Mr. Walker had called only a few minutes in advance of a deadline and in those days there weren't so many facilities for checking on an accident as there are now. By the time the frenzied editors found out that there hadn't been any wreck all the home edition had been printed. The young reporter never came into the office to get what was left of his pay or to receive congratulations. He was sorry that he couldn't point out to the city editor how well he had learned his lesson about names in stories. Every name he'd sent in that afternoon had been correctly spelled and the addresses had all been right. He had been careful about that. He had filled up the casualty list with a roster of his friends.

22

MR. CHARLES LINDBERGH MEETS A
PHOTOGRAPHER

UNTIL the war took Charles Augustus Lindbergh and his opinions off the front pages he maintained the most whole-souled and unrelenting hatred of the press and its talented workers to be found anywhere in the United States. Probably he cherishes it still—when he has time to think about it—for Lindbergh, whatever else you may say of him, is no quitter. And what he was thinking yesterday he probably will go right on thinking today.

Lots of well-meaning people inside newspaper offices and out have tried to explain Mr. Lindbergh's so called phobia on purely psychological grounds—the resentment of a naturally shy and retiring personality at being forced into a continuous exhibitionism—the natural tendency to link newspapers and newspapermen with the most sorrowful moments in his life. And in their listing of newspaper sins they have made out a good case. Mr. Lindbergh could hardly be expected to cheer the photographer who forced the Lindbergh car off the road and drove a nurse into hysterics to take a photograph of baby Jon. No working reporter that I've ever met had a word to say for the monkey-house that Hauptmann was tried in. And it's likely that the old American principle of free speech wasn't too vigorously respected during Mr. Lindbergh's campaign for isolation. On the other hand, it is my own theory that not one of these things, however great its apparent influence, had anything at all to do with the case.

Mr. Lindbergh's trouble began simultaneously with that of Floyd Collins who got trapped by a rock in a Kentucky cave and died there. Floyd Collins, the groundling, was the last person you'd think of in connection with the almost legendary Lone Eagle. And yet their destinies were linked as those of few men are. It's startling to think of what a difference there might have been had Mr. Collins died in bed of measles . . . in the attitude of the press toward Lindbergh . . . in the attitude of Lindbergh toward the press . . . in Lindbergh himself. . . .

Floyd Collins, however, found his cave, crawled into it and was trapped. Miners working day and night drove a rescue shaft to the cavern where a boulder had pinned him. And the world sat back and watched a drama of ghastly simplicity. If the shaft reached him in time he would be brought up into the sunshine and live. If it didn't the pain and the cold and the fever of his broken bones would kill him.

The Chicago newspapers were well represented at the cave, particularly by cameramen, for the rescue drive among the natives of this region had become the most photogenic spectacle of the year. Chicago, and for that matter the rest of the world, was screaming for pictures over every long-distance line in that part of Kentucky. And with praiseworthy enterprise one paper, the *Herald and Examiner,* had arranged for the transmission of its photographs from the shaft head to West Madison Street by airplane. The pilot hired for this job by the *Examiner* with I.N.S. splitting the fee was a youngster in whom the city editor placed little confidence. His report to the city desk is well remembered.

"I guess the guy can fly a plane all right," he said. "He's been on the mail run between here and St. Louis. But whether he'll ever get back here or not is something else again and I'm not putting out any guarantee. . . . He's baled out of a couple of planes and the contractor who's got that mail route says he's expensive. . . . His name's Lindbergh—Charles Lindbergh."

The *Examiner's* progressiveness in chartering a plane came as a great surprise to the opposition for nobody had any inkling of what to expect until Lindbergh came down in a field near the cave and started to look for the *Examiner's* representative in the field. And in his search he had the misfortune to run into Mr. Leekie Steeger of the Chicago *Tribune*.

Mr. Steeger knew little about airplanes and he had never shared the confidence of anybody on the Hearst pay roll, but he was a smart observer. He knew from Lindbergh's costume that this was an aviator. He guessed that the aviator probably had been hired by some newspaper for moving something in a hurry. He knew that inasmuch as the telegraph was still faster than the airplane nobody would be in that much hurry to get a reporter into an office—so it had to be pictures. He knew that his own newspaper wasn't sending airplanes after his pictures. Therefore this was an *Examiner* job. He waved an arm at Lindbergh.

"You from the *Examiner?*" he called.

Lindbergh said that he was.

[238]

"Fine," said Mr. Steeger. "You certainly made good time. Get this stuff back to Chicago just as quick as you can make it. Every minute counts."

Lindbergh took a small package from him, ran back to the plane and took off. Early that evening he delivered a box of unexposed plates to the *Examiner's* picture editor. And it is said with some justification in our business that the smile which young Charlie Lindbergh gave Leekie Steeger as he turned to run for his plane was the last he ever gave in any circumstances to any member of the press.

By and large I suppose the photographers made no more history in our part of the country than elsewhere. The "Show-a-Little-More-Leg-Queenie" technique may not have been indigenous to New York but it wasn't overdone out in our neighborhood. Russ Hamm once created what promised to be the most serious international incident since the sinking of the *Maine* when he took a photograph of Queen Marie picking her nose. On the other hand he was the personification of gentlemanly solicitude when she wanted to know how they managed to heat the Northwestern Railroad station. I forget what his answer was but there was nothing flip about it.

We had a large photographer once on the old *Journal* staff who used to go about lifting automobiles off the ground by their front axles to determine whether Ford or Chevrolet was "putting more stuff into a car for this price." And it's odd that we never got any complaints about that one. He never had to knock people down or otherwise disturb himself. After a couple of seconds of automobile lifting he was able to get his own way in any assemblage. The *Tribune* once had a photographer who called all the North Shore society belles by their first names and could get order out of a Junior League show in a couple of minutes by swearing at it. We always felt that a man like that should have been something higher than a photographer—something, say, like the President of the United States. . . . We had commando operators like Eddie Johnston who could outslug any two bailiffs of his weight in the world. And we also had Clyde Brown whose poise and dignity could get him past the outer guards of any bank president in the country.

The first photographer with whom I ever worked in Chicago was W. B. Sato (sometimes called Bill), a native of Tokyo and founder of what he labeled the Japanese School of Press Photography in the United States. Sato was getting on in years when I was teamed with him, which is to say that he was over thirty-five. He had had a remarkable lot of experience, even for a photographer, and he had a sense of humor that probably came with it. We used to ask him repeatedly why he wasted his time making pictures of debutantes and prize dogs and elevated wrecks when he really ought to be photographing artillery and fortifications and such. And the joke never seemed to grow stale with him any more than with us. Always he would answer that he had done that small job in his early youth and now had to earn a living with such raw material as happened to lie at hand.

As a matter of fact he was an American citizen by some process I don't know much about. He had been cabin boy for Sampson or Dewey or one of the other important naval figures of the Spanish-American war and when he talked about domination of the Pacific it was American domination that he meant.

"I am just as American as John Delaney or Pat Sullivan or any of the Doherty's," he told me once. "I'm not as American as the Ginsbergs . . . they seem to have come over here earlier."

So there was just a bit of impatience in his welcome when one day he received a visit from Jun Fujita, one of his countrymen then trying to work his way through an engineering course at Armour Institute.

"I had a monopoly," he said later. "Before Fujita came around I was the only Japanese press photographer in town. But he came in and he asked me about the work. He said that he intended to be a photographer. I asked him if he knew anything about a camera and he said no, that he'd never been close enough to a camera to touch it. He asked me what kind he ought to get to take pictures for newspapers. And he went and got one. Then he brought it around to me and I showed him where the button was that you pushed. And I told him how you had to load the plateholders in a darkroom and how you had to pull the slides when you took a picture. . . . He didn't know anything, that boy. He didn't know anything.

"So he left me and he went across the street to the *Evening Post* and said, 'You need a photographer. I am a photographer. Why don't you hire me?' So they hired him. They think that because I am Japanese and am a photographer that therefore if he is Japanese he is also a photographer. And what they actually have got is just another Jap."

But he was wrong about that. Fujita may have had only one lesson but he didn't need two. He made one routine picture of a shocked policeman carrying a little girl's body out of the Eastland that still rates as one of the greatest newspaper photographs of all time. One naturally wonders what became of him.

There has always been plenty of high comedy in the photographic department. There is the classic case of Joe Benton—now happily extinct—who got overheated taking a picture of a shooting in Randolph Street. He walked into a firebox, cracked his head, shouted 'Who you hittin'?' swung his camera in a full-arm haymaker and cracked a policeman's horse right on the nose. It was generally conceded that he had set a new mark for the trade in being wrong on every possible count.

There was, of course, Sol Davis of the Chicago *Times* who pleaded defective hearing when warned not to take pictures in Judge David's courtroom and immediately blew the judge out of his seat with an oversize magnesium flash. There was Norman Alley—or somebody of his period—who knocked out a picture-shy gunman, photographed him while unconscious and thereby ruined his career. There was the more recent contretemps of infrared photography during a blackout test when two rubber-heeled cameramen crept up on each other in the dark and took each other's pictures.

And of course there was the incident never mentioned in the photographic department of the old *Examiner* about the two sturdy lads who tracked down Nona Vallette, a lovely blonde wanted for a careless murder. Two of them were sent because the picture editor knew the job was virtually impossible. Nobody had been able to find Miss Vallette, police, reporters, or even theatrical booking agents.

[242]

Miss Vallette, as Mr. Makaroff, the *Examiner's* roving city editor, put it, "was swallowed up just like she was swallowed up." So the task ahead of Messrs. Morris Kolb and Ernie Michels was one of those jobs that photographers dream about —plenty of expense money, plenty of excuse for visiting night clubs and no great disturbance in case of failure. It was all very fine indeed. And then one of these lads made the mistake of going to the address the picture editor had given them and ringing the bell. A beautiful blonde answered the door and said "Come in." So they went in. They weren't too pleased about it either. So far they hadn't visited a single saloon, let alone a night club, and the expense account looked as if it might stay frozen at a dollar taxi bill.

"We didn't expect to find you here," said Mr. Kolb almost regretfully.

"I just got in," said the blonde.

"You know they're looking for you, don't you?"

"Not any more. I went over to the Chicago Avenue station."

"Okay, then. You got nothing to lose. And how'd you like the pictures taken?"

The blonde posed sitting at a table, listening to a telephone, writing something on a piece of paper, holding one hand aloft as she might possibly have held it had she been a Spanish dancer. She treated them to a series of emotional close-ups. She changed costumes for them. She produced half a bottle of gin. All in all it was the most complete and simple scoop that either of them had ever had. With great regret they packed up their apparatus and went back to the office.

Of course it was the wrong blonde. It couldn't have been

[243]

anything else. But neither Mr. Kolb nor Mr. Michels was willing to concede the point without a struggle.

"But she'd been to the police," said Mr. Kolb. "She admitted they'd been looking for her. I ask you what other woman would the cops have been looking for?"

"Any one in that block," said the picture editor.

23

WEIRD BEHAVIOR OF OHIO RIVER
FLOODS

It may be hysteria bred of fatigue that builds up the most ludicrous stories in the world on the fringes of tragedy . . . or it may be fear or a sense of superiority or plain rebellion. It comes to my mind how easily we laughed at the world's oldest jokes while we sat in the mud under the German bombardment before Romagne. I recall how excruciatingly funny it was when a gunner's pants split as he was feeding the pompoms on a cruiser in the South Pacific. I recall also how pleased I was on one occasion when somebody sat down on a derby hat in the pew ahead of me in church. And it begins to seem obvious that laughter is beyond reason as humor is beyond definition.

In the course of a dozen years I covered numerous floods on the Mississippi, Ohio, Missouri, Kansas, Republican and Colorado Rivers and I came to hate this sort of assignment with a bitter unreasoning hatred. I came to know that there were never any extenuating circumstances to a flood. People were going to be homeless and wet and suffering—many of them ill and dying. There were going to be shortages of food, shortages of housing, bad water, bad roads, dubious wire service, foul living conditions. There would always be trouble with crackpot officialdom, tired and jittery militia, unsinkable drunks. There was pretty sure to be a Chamber of Commerce warning the press against "exaggeration" and just as certainly there would be a Red Cross chapter urging "full presentation of the facts." Tragedy and sanity infrequently dwell together— virtually never when the cause of the tragedy is high water.

To the Ohio flood of 1937 came most of the veteran trouble-chasers in the newspaper business. We waded into it at various points, journeyed by launch through the streets of Louisville and Paducah and eventually established headquarters in Cairo, Illinois. In this locale Ray Daniell (New York *Times*) and I turned in a peculiarly satisfactory performance not because we were anything unusual in the way of reporters but because our papers didn't circulate in Cairo. The first metropolitan journal to come into the place after our arrival was the Chicago *Examiner,* so as a matter of course Art Smith who represented the *Examiner* in Cairo was the first to receive a visit and threat of expulsion from a citizens' committee.

We won that encounter because the local patriots found us all together and were outnumbered. But that day when Mr. Daniell and I went north to Carbondale to leave some things where they wouldn't be harmed if the water should come over the Cairo wall we figured that something undoubtedly would have to be done. Mr. Daniell bought a red and green baseball cap at a Carbondale variety store as a present for Mr. Smith.

"If we can get him to wear it as a sort of badge things will be immensely simplified for us," he said. "The irate citizens will know just where their target is." But when we looked for

[246]

the cap sometime later it was gone. Apparently we'd left it in my car in the Carbondale garage along with my gasoline lantern and other useful equipment.

We returned to Cairo to watch the flood water creeping nearer and nearer to the top of the dike. And there we learned that Henry McLemore (United Press) and Stewart Rogers (*Daily News*, New York) were already on their way to take their places at our side. We could understand the solicitude they expressed in their message about it. We knew that the plight of people in places like Cairo or Louisville or Paducah always seems worse to people up in the dry areas than it does to folks who live on the river. What we didn't understand was a suggestion of how they intended to get from Memphis to Cairo. As nearly as we could translate it, they were coming by boat. We were too tired to figure it. We stopped at the first factor: the down current of the Ohio-Mississippi flood at that moment was something like seventeen miles an hour. And there were about two hundred miles of water between Memphis and Cairo.

Three days—or maybe four— later we learned the details of this expedition and we solemnly shook the hands of the survivors. And save for the fact that we saw these men and heard their story from their own lips we might have been excused for doubting that any of it happened. The weird folklore of the rivers contains no more bizarre incident.

Messrs. Rogers and McLemore arrived at Memphis the day we first heard from them and immediately took steps to get to the spots where the threat of the roaring water was more immediate. Straightway they looked about for a boat. For, as one of them explained later, when you are covering a flood it seems obvious that you ought to have a boat. But they didn't look for just any boat. What they wanted was a fast one—a cabin cruiser—and they knew that they'd have to pay plenty for one that filled the specifications. Eventually a lad was discovered who had a gasoline launch which he was willing to hire out for some exorbitant sum—I have heard $300 mentioned, among others. They tossed their typewriters into the little cabin, paid over the charter fee in advance and took off. The launch was reputed to cruise at twenty-three miles an hour but actually did about twenty-one. That, against a seventeen-mile current, gave them a net progress toward Cairo of four miles an hour.

At the end of eight hours they ran aground on a submerged railroad track and tore the bottom out of the launch. They had other harrowing adventures before their clothes were dry again but this they were willing to classify as the worst. They stood in water waist deep, clinging to the wreckage of a shed for six hours during which it seemed unlikely that anybody was ever going to see them. A fishing boat came along after while and they were picked up. The rescue boat couldn't get up as much speed as the launch but the river rat who owned it was a better navigator than the lad who had taken them upriver the first thirty miles out of Memphis. By zigzagging across currents and traveling mostly in still backwashes he was able to make noticeable progress—six miles an hour or better. There was a stove in the shack amidships where they dried their clothes. They were beginning to congratulate themselves on their luck when the skipper hit one current he hadn't seen and brought up squarely in the top of a tree.

It began to look serious then, Mr. Rogers later reported.

There was no food aboard. The skipper suggested that when morning came they might be able to shoot some rabbits in the surrounding treetops. He said that the rabbits naturally would climb trees when the water came up behind them. But this turned out to be like so many other things that people know about natural history—just theory. They discovered some snakes in the branches sticking up out of the river all around them, but not a single rabbit.

There they hung most of the day. Along toward midafternoon a Red Cross patrol boat came along and tried to pull them free. Failing in this, the latest rescuer took them aboard and sidled across to Fulton, Arkansas, which they reached just about dawn.

They weren't much the worse for wear. Despite their close race with death during the past forty-eight hours they were determined to go on. They admitted, as they filled themselves with hot soup and coffee at an all-night lunchroom, that the chances seemed to be much against their ever reaching Cairo. They conceded that nobody who hadn't experienced a Mississippi River flood could ever hope to imagine its horror and danger. But the greater the risk, the greater would be the story if they should live to tell it. They came out of the restaurant and automatically turned into the gray morning toward the river where, if their luck held out, they might find another heroic boatman who would consent to take them out onto the roaring waters.

But just as they were about to cross the street they leaped hastily back. A large bus loomed up in the gloom and stopped almost beside them. The sign on it was where they couldn't help but read it: "Memphis to Cairo . . . $1.50."

[249]

They got in.

There came a day when the tide of the Ohio began to fall away from the revetments on top of the Cairo dike and we started out, as is customary on such occasions, to follow the crest of the flood on its way toward New Orleans. Ray Daniell and I got a taxi ride to Carbondale, picked up my car and what baggage we had left in storage, and drove out through a wet night toward a bridge at Cape Girardeau and a passable road through Arkansas to Memphis. We pulled up in front of a leading hotel about 1:00 A.M.

In case you don't know it, the costume that one acquires in covering floods is *sui generis*. You pick it up piecemeal where you can and the fit of it is what it is. I for instance was wearing a corduroy coat such as used to be issued to W.P.A. laborers, a cotton flannel shirt, high boots and a pair of riding pants, the seat of which had some of the beauties and all the space of a kangaroo's pouch. Bellboys with no sense of discrimination brought up to our suite all the odd things that they discovered in the car. So presently I was able to add to my weird ensemble of clothes a gaudy baseball cap—the one we had bought as a badge for the hunted Art Smith.

In the debris that the boys had left in the middle of the floor, amid shovels, blankets, thermos jugs and the like, I discovered my gasoline lantern. And to make sure that it had not been damaged in transit, I lighted it. About that time there was a knock on the door. I asked Daniell who might be calling at that hour of the morning and, from the depths of the shower bath, he yelled that the house detective had probably seen us as we walked through the lobby.

But it wasn't the house detective. It was a tall blonde of

[250]

whom, unfortunately, I am able to give only the sketchiest description. For she took one look at me, standing there with the lighted lantern in my hand, her big blue eyes fixed in amazement, then terror, on my baseball cap. She gave one shriek and streaked down the corridor toward the emergency stairway.

There the story closes for lack of evidence and I am sorry. For many years now I have whiled away a lot of dull hours trying to guess what story she told her friends. . . .

"And I knocked on the door of the swellest suite in the joint . . . and there stood a guy in a teamster's coat and a baseball cap and wringing wet and he had a lighted lantern in his hand. . . ."

Further than that imagination fails to go.

24

THE WOMAN'S ANGLE

O~N~E of the things you notice when you attempt any classification of the esoteric literature of the newspaper business is the lack of the woman's touch or, as they used to call it in Hearst practice, the woman's angle. There never have been as many women as men in journalism but even so you'd expect a larger prorata representation of them in shop talk. It may be, as so many contend, that they are the saner element in the so-called profession. It may be that some latent chivalry among the males protects them. But whatever it is their position in the archives is almost negligible.

You'd wonder at that, considering the fine talents displayed by the one or two who *have* ranked themselves with the Charlie Owens and Hildie Johnsons and Lyman Mooses in some of the larger sagas of newspaperdom. The late Amy Leslie set an example for them decades ago with her review of a theatrical performance that hadn't taken place. And there was the statuesque brunette on the *Inter-Ocean* who explained her habitual tardiness by telling the city editor haughtily: "But I think it's so stupid to come to work at one o'clock." And there was a fair start toward a new school of journalism in the technique of a young woman who a year or two later carried the "stupid to work" philosophy to a fine conclusion by weeping on the shoulders of male reporters until they wrote her stories for her.

Perhaps one should not include Amy Leslie in this group study of female talent because after all she was competent and willing to carry her own share of the load. Her only show of occupational eccentricity occurred when she was very new in the business—in fact before she had any job at all. And she had a national reputation as a drama critic before anybody thought to mention it.

Amy had been a chorus girl in the *Black Crook* company along with a couple of other girls who later became famous in the newspaper business—not that there seems to be any connection. As a young married woman she was doing well as prima donna in an operatic repertory company which played Gilbert and Sullivan, the *Bohemian Girl* and such from coast to coast. She was called back to Chicago from Denver by the illness and subsequent death of her little boy and she never went back to the stage again. One day she read that her old company was coming to town to play *The Chimes of Normandy*. She visited the editor of the *Daily News* and asked permission to write a review of this performance and got it. She caught a severe cold on her way home and went to bed. But that didn't prevent her from writing the review. She had seen the company in *The Chimes of Normandy* dozens of times while singing the leading role herself, so she felt that she really didn't need another look. She sent her review around by a messenger along about midnight and didn't find out until the next afternoon that the company had been snow-bound outside of Omaha for twelve hours and wouldn't arrive until the next day.

The silly element in this story seems to have been furnished by the editor, whoever he was. He sent around a letter congratulating Amy on her fine review, never mentioning the fact that he hadn't printed it and that the curtain had not yet been rung up on *The Chimes of Normandy*. He offered her a permanent job which she took and the moral seems to be that in journalism the truth is mighty and will prevail.

There have been any number of smart reporters in the United States in the current generation who were also women. And conversely there have been a lot of women on newspapers in the same length of time who weren't reporters. We have had plenty of beauty-contest winners, husband shooters and the like who for a brief moment came slinking through the local rooms dripping memoirs and *Nuit de Noël*. We have had such phenomena as the tavern dice girl who became a reporter the night a tired city editor got drunk in her saloon. And of course there have been many who were what they were without any advertising or other assistance.

One day the diligent police of St. Louis picked up Marty Durkin or Dog-faced Louie or some other killer and shipped him back to Chicago. It is difficult to forget how he was met at the Union Station by the beauty and chivalry of the press. What the chivalry did about it is of no moment. But there was a smartly dressed and lovely-mannered young woman from Mr. Hearst's *American* who gave the interview its tempo:

"Oh, Mr. Durkin (or Dogface)," she said throatily. "What is your opinion of Chicago girls?"

On another occasion a beauty who should have been in *The*

Follies announced tactfully to the bereft husband of a murdered woman: "My city editor told me there ought to be a good sob story here." And they tell of another interviewing a former county clerk accused of having embezzled half a million dollars: "So then you didn't really take the money like they say you did, Mr. Sweitzer. And oh dear, what I could do with a new fur coat!"

Wherever two or more of the old time itinerant copyreaders are gathered together you hear stories of Laura, a telephone operator on the San Francisco *Examiner,* who was thwarted in love. Her personal tragedy somehow was never linked up with sundry other domestic breakups that developed among members of the *Examiner* staff. Even after there had been four divorces and a couple of suits for separation nobody put out any explanation except that most wives eventually get tired of living with newspapermen.

One day the wife of the sports editor was called to the phone by a woman who said: "Get a load of this!" Then there was a click and she heard her husband talking to another woman. "Okay," he said, "I'll leave them with Jake at the filling station. They'll be there at noon tomorrow." And the other woman said, "Thank you very much."

The wife was puzzled but not shocked by what she had heard. That night she asked the sports editor about it.

"It was your sister Bessie," he said. "She wanted two tickets to the ball game tomorrow and I said I'd leave them for her. . . ."

"I know that," said the wife. "I recognized her voice. But who was the woman who called me and told me to listen?"

Her husband was thoughtful but not for long. "It would have to be the girl on our switchboard," he said. "And the girl on our switchboard this afternoon was Laura. We'll cook up some new dialogue with Bessie and get a little more definite evidence. . . ."

Two days later the sports editor took his evidence to the publisher, one of Mr. Hearst's more famous aces.

"It's apparent that she's been getting the dope on everybody in the office," he said. "She's responsible for all these bust-ups. . . . She just hates all men and she's venomous."

"Humph," said the publisher greatly impressed. "I'm glad you told me about it. I certainly will do something about it. We can't let a woman like that run hog-wild."

And he did do something about it. He got himself a private phone that didn't go through any of the office switchboards.

One of the best among the girl reporters in recent years was Virginia Gardner who brought to the business a sharp brain, a deft literary style, the courage of a Marine top sergeant and a shy retiring manner that phonies misinterpreted with touching regularity. Her last contribution to a better and safer life in Chicago was an exposé (in the *Tribune*) of twenty or thirty quack doctors to whom she had gone demurely and convincingly for a diagnosis of ills she didn't have. Her stories about these experiences were starkly revealing but they lacked the wealth of detail that went into the memoranda which she delivered to the city editor for use in possible lawsuits. One morning she left such a record before going home for a two-day rest. When she returned she found a note from the city editor in her letter box:

THE WOMAN'S ANGLE

"DEAR MISS GARDNER:

"The matter contained in your memorandum of the eighteenth is frightening. I must ask you to be on the alert constantly in your dealings with these men. Unless you exercise the greatest possible vigilance you may be subjected to physical violence which, of course, would be a source of embarrassment to the *Tribune*."

Miss Gardner, who probably had not thought of this catastrophic possibility, thereafter walked with the greatest circumspection.

25

THE GREAT POOL-TABLE
PHILANTHROPY

~~~~~~

As MAY have been stated elsewhere in this record, there is no reason to suppose that delirium tremens is more an occupational disease of journalism than of, say, tuckpointing. Of recent years the cloying atmosphere of virtue has hung thickly over the local rooms of the land. It is even recorded that the warden of the Illinois state penitentiary complained to a startled editor that a reporter had visited his establishment in a state of inebriation. But, to be quite frank, it was not always so. Whether the newspaper business made its old-time votaries alcoholics in self-defense or whether old-time journalism was the product of alcoholics may long be argued, but there is no denying that mellow whisky and mellow journalism were somehow mingled and interdependent. The results of that relationship were just what you might expect.

One of the country's more prominent managing editors—a fine example of industrious sobriety if there ever was one—came out of that foggy period. Most of the earnest young men and women who work for him haven't the slightest suspicion, but for many years he figured as the hero of a barroom story so unusual that few contemporary reporters could take more than three drinks without recalling it.

This intelligent gentleman, long before he was a managing editor or even idly thought of as a managing editor, was a reporter on the careless staff of the Chicago *Daily News*. One evening, as was his wont, he got himself into a condition that witnesses described as "plastered." There was nothing unusual in that or even unfortunate. His condition caused him no pain nor mental distress. The only trouble was that he ran out of money along about midnight and couldn't find any source that he had left untapped. In this emergency he heard somebody mention the name of Victor Lawson, and that gave him an idea.

"Of course, Victor Lawson," he said. "The way to get money is to borrow it from people who have money. Victor Lawson owns my paper and he must have a lot of money. I'll go and see."

So he spent his last fifty cents on taxi fare out to the North Side and rang the door of Mr. Lawson's fine house. By one of those chances that newspapermen come to think are not chance at all, Victor Lawson came to the door himself.

It should be noted here that Mr. Lawson in politics and personal habits was strictly a teetotaler. And while he never interfered in the management of a local staff that might have in its composition a few thirsty ones it was a matter of common report that he abhorred alcohol and despised drunks. Despite all this he escorted his visitor inside and invited him to make himself comfortable.

"I'll not sit down," said the reporter. "I work for you. I need twenty-five dollars. Mr. Dennis [Charles E. Dennis, the managing editor of the *Daily News* at the time] told me once that you'd have it."

So far the tale is preposterous enough. But its finish lifts it squarely into the unbelievable. The dazed Mr. Lawson got the money, gave it to his erring employee, walked with him to the door and wished him a kindly good night. The reporter came to work the next day, reasonably sober and expecting to be fired. But nothing happened. Today's abstemious managing editor cannot even yet figure out why.

There are other stories of the same genre about the contemporaries of this genius and they are worth listing even though they lack a comparable cast of characters. There used to be a legend of an unnamed drunk who borrowed a dollar from Jane Addams. Some of the people who knew Jane best said that she would never have given cash to a man obviously looking for more drink. Others said that her experience with drunks was probably so academic that she didn't recognize this lad as a horrible example.

Denny Morrison, the able rewrite man, used to say that the softest touch in an alcoholic moment was always some public personage whose private life was as far from human ken as that of the Grand Lama.

"They're never hard to reach because everybody thinks they are inaccessible and so they don't need any guards. And they're so unused to having the bee put on them that they haven't any defense mechanism."

His own choice for the operation, a civic leader in the more rarified elevations of the social stratosphere, furnished a hundred dollars' worth of proof for his theory. It is worth mentioning however that the plan doesn't seem always to have worked. Mr. Morrison at a later date wrote a lot of advertising material for the Nippon Yusen Kaisha line's San Francisco office and in part payment received a round trip ticket to China and a certificate entitling him to all the courtesies of the ports served by the line. He spent what cash he had on a farewell party and went aboardship about 3:00 A.M. A few hours later he awoke in a deck chair to find himself at sea and without funds aboard a Dollar liner. The gift of tongues deserted him and he stoked his way around the world.

There used to be a rule in physics—maybe there still is—that for every action there is an equal and similar reaction. That being the case it is only natural that if the newspaper business makes expert biters it must correspondingly produce a lot of bitees. That great truth and the fact that Walter Howey, the Hearst miracle man, is reported to have only one eye combine to make memorable the story of a trip to Milwaukee made by the late Gilman Parker, one of Mr. Howey's pupils and principal admirers.

Mr. Howey at the time was publishing the *Herald and Examiner*. Mr. Parker was theoretically a reporter. The expedition to Milwaukee came about because Mr. Parker in making a round of the local bars had come upon some unidentified character who wanted to go to Milwaukee. Mr. Parker went along, lost his new-found friend and reluctantly came back to consciousness on a bench in a railroad station. In his emergency he paid a visit to the managing editor of the Milwaukee *Sentinel*.

He had never in his life seen this managing editor nor did he know anything about him. But his need was immediate and he couldn't try out Mr. Morrison's system of borrowing from the more lofty citizenry because he didn't know any of the more lofty citizenry.

The managing editor was really his only chance. He probably would have collapsed before he could find another victim. But it all worked out well. The managing editor looked at Mr. Parker's soiled person, critically at first, and then, as Mr. Parker's battered charm unwound itself, with deep sympathy.

"I don't deserve decent treatment," Mr. Parker said convincingly. "It isn't that I went out and got drunk and wandered away from my assignment . . . that's bad enough, God knows, but it's not the worst. I'm ashamed of myself because I've thrown Mr. Howey down. Mr. Howey trusted me. He gave me a job when I needed it. He gave me responsibility. . . . And then I go out and do a thing like this. . . ." Mr. Parker broke into tears. The managing editor was visibly touched.

"You've got the right stuff," he said heartily. "I think I can see why Walter Howey would have faith in you. And don't worry, he'll be glad to get you back."

So then the managing editor took over the great work of rehabilitating Mr. Parker. He took him out to the press club and administered a pick-me-up. After that he offered breakfast, a haircut and a shave, a clean shirt, and a loan of ten dollars. Mr. Parker said truthfully that he had never met such generosity before and for a moment he was tearful again.

The managing editor smiled.

"I've fixed it up," he said. "I've written a telegram to Mr. Howey and I'll send it from the office downstairs. I'd like you to look at it. . . ." Mr. Parker looked.

"I am ashamed of myself," he read. "I don't ask my job

back. I want only the chance to set myself right in your eyes."

"Swell," said Mr. Parker. "I can do only one little job of copyreading on it. . . ." He pulled out a pencil and crossed out one letter . . . the "s" at the end of "eyes."

While we are on this interesting subject we should give a thought perhaps to one of the last of those giants who made the alcoholic era what it was. This one was named George Rowe— or something similar—and his sin was not so much drunkenness as a sort of general helplessness. Nobody ever knew where he was going to be at any particular time on any particular day— not even in what town. He was definitely the most undependable specimen produced by a craft that specialized in his like. In addition to that he was one of the best rewrite men who ever contrived pieces for a newspaper. It goes without saying that he was immensely popular. He had all the ingredients for popularity.

Mr. Rowe, at the time of this history, was one of the more temporary liabilities of the Chicago *Daily Tribune*. He was well paid—better than most men in similar jobs on the other newspapers in the town. He had a modest flat up on the near North Side and no family to support except a wife. It was hard to see how anybody in his position could get himself classified as the head of one of Chicago's fifty neediest families. But George achieved this with virtually no effort.

Almost before his friends on the *Tribune* knew what was happening, his furniture had been repossessed, his telephone cut off, his light turned out. He hadn't any gas or coal. He had no credit at the grocer's. He and his wife were sleeping—when and if they slept—on the bare floor of the flat. They weren't eating at all.

When word of this disaster was brought to Mr. Rowe's employers and associates there was immediate action. The employers filled Mr. Rowe with nourishing food such as good hot soup. The associates filled him with nourishing drink. The city editor or somebody sent a deputation out to the Rowe flat to transfer Mrs. Rowe to a warm hotel pending some more permanent adjustment. And then, unknown to Mr. Rowe, the reporters, photographers, rewrite men, copyreaders and editors took up a collection to pay off all the debts that had brought their comrade to such a pass. The loot totaled several hundred dollars. Mr. Rowe was close to tears when they gave it to him.

The presentation, if I remember correctly, was made about a week before Christmas at a time when the streetcars were filled with singing newsboys and you had to shout down a quartet of carol singers every time you wanted to give an order in a department store. The spirit of the season was rampant in the land and Mr. Rowe's redemption seemed to be its finest manifestation.

The *Tribune* staff allowed Mr. Rowe to be the administrator of the happiness which they shared vicariously and distantly. They never even looked in on it until the night before Christmas, and then they weren't crass about it. They sent a couple of gentlemen with nice manners and plenty of finesse up to make sure that the Rowes were actually living their own lives once again—gentlemen, as Charley Owen later remarked, who knew enough to take their hats off in the house. These worthy visitors got to the Rowe address without any difficulty. With a little more effort they found the right doorbell and rang it. Mr. Rowe, who was taking a night off, came to the head of the stairs to invite them in with hilarious enthusiasm.

They felt then that their work was done. They'd been asked to find out whether or not Mr. Rowe was happy and they had found out that he certainly was. They felt a little sheepish about intruding further but Mr. Rowe was insistent. They climbed the stairs and followed Mr. Rowe into his flat. . . . At any rate they took it to be his flat. They couldn't see very well because the lights were out but the sound of their echoing footsteps told them that there wasn't any carpet on the floor. Mr. Rowe led them blindly through a couple of doors and then they found themselves in what had been a parlor. A dozen candles were burning brightly in bottles on the mantelpiece. There was no furniture in the place except for one piece that stood squarely in the middle of the floor. That one was a billiard table.

"Sorry about the lights," Mr. Rowe apologized. "But when I got around to paying the Edison Company I was out of money. I wasn't able to get the furniture back from the guys who took it but that doesn't make any difference. I figure we can get along this way until I make enough money to buy a lot of new furniture. And as for the telephone I don't need it, really. Nobody ever calls me except the office and it's easy for Bob Lee to send a boy over if he wants me. . . ."

The spokesman of the visitors' committee gasped.

"But the billiard table," he mentioned. And Mr. Rowe beamed.

"Yeah! It's swell, isn't it?" he said. "I just got it. They made me pay $600 cash for it but it's really worth a thousand. And it's just what I wanted. I figure that if I have a billiard table at home and an icebox I won't go out nights and I'll save a lot of money. . . ."

The emissaries of the joyous Yule went back to the *Tribune* office to make their report and there were one or two reporters —newcomers—who expressed surprise. There were no more collections to restore Mr. Rowe to solvency. Wiser counsel prevailed and somebody got him a job in New York. It was a cheaper solution.

26

THE QUIET AND ALOOF

You sometimes hear the suggestion among the more meagerly informed members of the newspaper profession that the Chicago *Tribune* must be turned out by a lot of scholars and gentlemen totally unlike those who turn out the less well-advertised journals of the country. The argument persists that the austere policies of the exalted front office must produce a highly rarefied atmosphere in the local room . . . that *Tribune* reporters, militant—not to say fanatical—crusaders for a better and Republican world, walk in silence and alone . . . that dignity envelopes them like an ermine cape and that human foibles are far from their ken. And don't you believe it.

Out of the *Tribune's* atmosphere came George Rowe, the pool-table fancier whose exploits have been recounted. Walter Howey, the generation's finest exponent of pyrotechnic journalism, was primarily a *Tribune* product, and it cannot be said that he ever wrapped himself in silence or walked very high above the earth.

There is record of a *Tribune* reporter who came to cover the rumbellion at Iron River, Michigan, in the uniform of a

Russian colonel. And surely nobody has yet forgotten the ubiquitous and talented Dick Little.

It wasn't so long ago that the President of the United States came to Chicago to make his speech about the quarantine of aggressor nations and incidentally to open a bridge across the historic river. And one recalls the big sign that filled the eyes of Mr. Roosevelt or whoever else stood in the speakers' stand: "THE TRIBUNE, AN UNDOMINATED NEWSPAPER." It seems to have a bearing on the subject of this discussion, for a week later it prompted the President to make some inquiries about the alleged sublimation of the *Tribune's* staff. He was about to go away somewhere and he called Walter Trohan out in front of the assembled White House correspondents who had come to bid him farewell. "I hope you'll pardon my curiosity," Mr. Roosevelt said. "But I just wanted to take a look at an undominated reporter."

John Kelly who once represented Colonel McCormick's interests on the police beat has gone into retirement, but his memory lingers on. There was nothing silent or aloof and plenty that was human about Mr. Kelly. He was a crack police reporter, a hard-working liaison man between the *Tribune's* editorial Shangri-La and actuality, but oddly enough he is remembered by his friends less as a journalist than as a poet. The world at large is probably not aware of it but he was once laureate of the First Ward, the sweet singer of Alderman John Coughlin—and a very good one, too.

Mr. Kelly was not chosen for this job. He elected himself after Bathhouse John—as Alderman Coughlin was more generally known—broke into ministrelsy with a ballad entitled "Sweet Midnight of Love." It was Mr. Kelly's fair contention that the alderman needed help in his poesy. This Mr. Kelly was willing to provide. So shortly, with or without the alderman's consent, numerous lyrics began to appear under his signature. On the whole he seems to have been pleased with the result, for he never made formal complaint about it, and until the day of the alderman's death few had suspected Mr. Kelly's long-distance collaboration. Unfortunately most of this anthology has been lost, but some of it remains in a mind that has the futile knack of absorbing such stuff. One simple lament will do as a sample of the general tone and dignity of all the work:

"In her lonely grave she sleeps tonight
  By the side of the Drainage Canal.
Where the whippoorwill weeps in the twilight hour
  They've buried my Darling Sal.
A mile this side of Willow Springs,
  Not far from the Alton track,
They've buried my Sal, my dear old Pal,
  But these tears won't bring her back."

Whatever the internal theory about what reporters ought to be like, whatever the effect of editors to classify them, the *Tribune* always has had considerable luck in getting the right man to cover a wide variety of jobs. The highly literate James O'Donnell Bennett could, when asked, write a finished review of *The Streets of Paris* at A Century of Progress. The gentlemanly Phil Kinsley, fresh from a scientific assignment, found nothing distasteful nor beyond his experience in swapping insults with bereft gunmen at Huey Long's funeral. Larry Rue, the least gullible man in the business, could support the *Trib-*

une's isolationist policy in London and make friends in the war ministry while doing it.

I first saw the *Tribune's* Arthur J. Evans in Cuba in the revolution that drove out Machado. He was riding in an open automobile in the Parque Fraternidad, calmly smoking a cigar and staring up at the rooftops in a detached study of the snipers who were trying to kill him.

Art Evans was one of the smartest political reporters in the country and for years he had been doing a good job with the *Tribune's* Washington bureau. He got the Cuban assignment because he was closer than any other available reporter to good airplane transportation. And he was so pleased at getting it that he forgot about personal danger or discomfort.

"It's fun to get out in the open and cover a story again," he said that night. "I think I'd rather have a lot of misguided patriots shooting at me than have to go on forever writing guidance for patriots. . . . And besides these guys are rotten shots."

The youngsters used to tell him how old he was—although he had few years over some of us—and he would smile tolerantly while scooping them. Once when he was covering one of the numerous Huey Long dust-ups a girl from one of the Baton Rouge papers came to the Heidelberg Hotel to interview the visiting reporters. Allen Raymond met her in the lobby and advised her against disturbing these gentlemen, most of whom had gone to bed.

"After all, there's no necessity for it," he told her. "I've been traveling with these fellows for a month and I know all of them very well. I know just about what each one would say. So it probably would simplify matters if I were to give you all the interviews. . . ." The girl thought this would be a good idea. Raymond outlined each story for her, suggested some leads, and thought up several anecdotes. Apparently he was well equipped for this diversified task, for the young woman got no complaints, not even from Mr. Evans who read the next morning under his signature: "I have never covered a case of such importance as this since the time I was assigned to the Hayes-Tilden controversy."

Evans proved on numerous occasions that a reporter's most valuable asset is *sang-froid*. If he's able to write a few sentences in English so much the better. But as Mr. Evans himself put it, "You can talk yourself out of a bad situation where you may never get a chance to write."

Not so long ago reporters, particularly reporters with Middle Western accents, were a little sour toward assignments in Harlan, Kentucky. Harlan had no censorship but it had a definite news policy—Speak No Evil—and it had a lot of deputy sheriffs with high rating as marksmen. After a couple of reporters had been shot in Harlan's main street their successors never came to town without fearing the worst.

The attitude of the private citizenry toward the visiting press reflected that of the county officials. It may not have been antagonistic but it was surely not friendly. And to try it out one day came Mr. Evans.

His particular assignment was an election in which there promised to be some test of strength between the element represented by the coal operators and a hitherto inarticulate mass aligned more or less with the cause of labor. Incidental to this immediate event Mr. Evans' further assignment was to observe the mores of the community. And the community, resentful as always, knew that was Mr. Evans' job quite as well as Mr. Evans.

He walked about the town on the evening of his arrival, conscious of hostile glances. But he encountered no overt act until the next day—election morning—a few hours after the opening of the polls. A large, official-looking man stopped him and asked in a voice that was dangerously pleasant:

"You're a reporter from up north, ain't you?"

Evans answered just as pleasantly:

"Yes. I'm from the Chicago *Tribune*. My name is Evans."

The big man looked at him from under half-shut eyelids.

"Well, sir," he said, "who's going to win the election?"

Art shook his head sadly. "I can't tell you that," he said, "until I find out who's counting the votes."

There was just a second of silence and then the big man guffawed.

"Well, if that don't beat all!" he roared. "Brother, you're all right. . . . You just come along with me and I'll get you a shot of the best whisky you ever put a lip over. . . ."

The story was around town in ten minutes, of course. And experienced Harlan correspondents will tell you that the present openhanded friendliness of Harlanites toward newspapermen dates from that morning.

Taken by and large, the *Tribune's* city editors don't seem to have been any special breed of cats either. . . . There was the one already mentioned who took to his bosom the overwealthy princess of Jarputana. And lest you think he was unique, there was the one—his name stands in shadow—who paused in the day's occupation to give good advice to a murderer.

There is some excuse for him, perhaps, for the murder, despite the fact that all the world was talking about it, was strictly a New York product. Veronica Gedeon, an artist's model, had been slaughtered in her apartment along with her mother and somebody else, by an erratic boarder named Robert Irwin. Irwin had moved out of New York without bothering to sort the corpses and the police of the hinterlands had received calls to be on the lookout for him. They were still looking for him, it is to be presumed, when he got tired of it all one Sunday afternoon in Chicago. He walked into a telephone booth in the Morrison Hotel and called the city editor of the *Tribune*. The city editor may have been new to his job but it is apparent that he was not new to the newspaper business and that he understood the finer nuances of "the rib." So when Mr. Irwin said that he was Mr. Irwin and that he was wanted for the murder of Veronica Gedeon, the city editor laughed unpleasantly.

"Go home and sleep it off," was his advice. "We're too busy here to monkey around with low wits. . . ." Or words to that effect.

Mr. Irwin had another nickel left and with that he called the *Herald and Examiner*. The *Examiner's* city editor was less coy. He held the murderer in conversation while a reporter traced the call and another reporter went over to the Morrison to take charge of Mr. Irwin when he stepped out of the booth.

The moral of all this seems to be that if a murderer calls at your door and says he's a murderer, he may be telling the truth . . . and it's best not to tell him he's drunk until you've got him inside.

27

TEN CENTS FOR WOLFBANE

MR. GEORGE DIXON, the eminent sociologist of the New York *Daily News,* once suggested the founding of a school of journalism in which the compiling of expense accounts and the avoidance of libel suits would be the principal subjects. He does not seem to have gone far with his idea for the reason that folks who matriculate in schools of journalism have their own ideas about what they ought to study. By the time they get to work on a newspaper staff and realize the unimportance of the old curriculum it's too late to do anything about it. For instance, as Mr. Dixon points out, they have learned to spell all names correctly, whereas the misspelling of names is a sure protection against suits for damages. And as for expense accounts. . . .

It is an axiom of the trade that nobody ever came out even on an expense account. If you're careful and honest you always spend more than you can account for. (Lionel Moise once spent seventy-five dollars on the thirty-five-mile trip from Chicago to Gary, though it must be admitted he spent the money before he found out where he was going.) If you're careless this evaporation of company funds may easily class as an expensive luxury. One recalls the famous remark of Doc Dwyer to Colonel R. R. McCormick in the midst of a hopeless struggle with this mystery. "All I know, Colonel," he said, "is that I take just exactly as good care of your money as I do of my own." If you are overscrupulous about protecting your own interests, you may have some trouble adjusting the publisher's return on his initial investment. Too much zeal may bring demands for refunds from auditors with results as disastrous as if you had displayed no zeal at all. There is a neat balance in the properly prepared expense account. The fine judgment required to arrive at it is a gift that has never been promiscuously distributed.

In the first place an expense account should have verisimilitude. In that respect it is unlikely that anybody will ever improve on the widely quoted record of Mr. Gene Fowler on the occasion of his hunt for some lost aviators in the arctic wilds of Northern Canada. Mr. Fowler appears to have lost the daily notes of expenditures which all reporters keep with meticulous care. Lacking such important data he made no effort to get an expense account together until after his arrival in New York. Then, of course, he had trouble remembering things—particularly three thousand dollars' worth of things.

Little by little he worked it out . . . all the charges for pemmican and whale blubber on which northbound correspondents have frequently existed for days and days—snowshoes, skis, parkas, sleeping bags, dog sled, dogs. . . .

He was still a couple of hundred dollars short when he came to the dog item. But in putting the figures down on paper he was reminded of other things. . . . There had been a death in the dog team, he recalled—Pogo, the lead dog, had gone west.

That accounted for the delay at Skoogiac and the expense of sending three men in a kyak for an Eskimo dog doctor of some repute. . . . But the dog had died anyway and had been buried after the consumption of a lot more whale oil and pemmican. And still that left Mr. Fowler $60 short.

There is no telling what a lesser genius might have done in such an emergency but Mr. Fowler was no lesser genius. Just when things looked blackest his memory rescued him. Once more he saw the touching funeral of the dog at Skoogiac and heard once more the moaning in the arctic night. As in a flash he saw what he had done with the missing money. And he set it down where all the auditors might read: "Flowers for bereft bitch . . . $60."

Dimly one recalls that John Ashenhurst, one of the Chicago *Evening American's* aces, covered a flood in the lower Mississippi Valley and turned in a bill to his office for a pair of binoculars and a bicycle which he had bought to help him in his work. It's a pity that the record at the moment does not show how he used these unusual tools or how much Mr. Hearst's auditors allowed him for them. One of his successors in flood investigation for the *American* had a harder time getting paid for a more logical claim regarding things you need for looking at a flood.

The victim of a tighter supervision over outgoing funds in the *American* office was Mr. Fred Hurley whose trouble may be said to have started somewhere in the neighborhood of the Brown Hotel, Louisville, in the flood of 1937. He struggled with the rising waters for a week or so and returned with a fine cost sheet on which he had noted such items as the rental

[276]

TEN CENTS FOR WOLFBANE

of boats, automobiles and airplanes and the purchase of such necessaries as clothes, tents, food, umbrellas, etc.

In other words everything seemed to be in perfect order until Harry Reid, the current city editor, happened to notice a reference to a diving suit.

"Fred," he inquired, "what about this diving suit?"

Mr. Hurley looked at him pityingly. "What about it?" he repeated. "Why, it was a diving suit. I got it to go down in the Ohio River looking for things. You know . . . looking for things in the flood. . . ."

"Of course," said Mr. Reid. "I understand all that. I wasn't asking you about what you use a diving suit for. What I wanted to know is where is it."

Mr. Hurley looked at Mr. Reid with an odd light in his eye, for it was unusual for city editors to be interested in the whereabouts of diving suits.

"It's at home," he said. "I couldn't see any reason for wearing it down to the office."

"Fine," said Mr. Reid. "You can bring it down tomorrow morning."

Mr. Hurley for the first time in a long career looked nonplussed.

"Bring it down?" he questioned. "What for?"

"Because you are through with it," mentioned Mr. Reid. "And of course you understand that, now you are through with it, this diving apparatus is the property of the *Evening American,* or more properly, of Mr. Hearst."

"What does Mr. Hearst want with it?" asked Mr. Hurley.

"That we won't go into," stated Mr. Reid. "The point is that I want it here on my desk tomorrow morning at 8:30 o'clock.

[277]

We advanced you the $635 that you spent for it and we want it. Do you understand what I mean?"

Mr. Hurley got the general idea that Mr. Reid wasn't fooling, and with some indignation he announced that he would bring the suit in the following morning. But he didn't. Whatever his impression of the urgency of the situation, he forgot. He was almost apologetic about it when he so informed Mr. Reid. Mr. Reid looked at him icily.

"I'm not going to take any runaround in this business, Hurley," he said. "You'll have that suit in here tomorrow morning or you're fired. I don't care much which."

Mr. Hurley cursed but that didn't alter matters. He felt, despite all bluster, that he was definitely on a spot. He would have to turn up on the morrow with a suitable diving suit or else. And the worst feature of the unpleasantness was that Mr. Hurley didn't have any diving suit. The entry had been merely a synonym for "miscellaneous," a word which auditors had come to frown upon. But how was he going to explain that to a pigheaded guy like Reid? Throughout the day Mr. Hurley dragged his feet, and the expression on his ghastly white face was that of a man who had looked upon Death.

In the morning Mr. Hurley came to work at ten minutes to nine and he dumped onto the desk of the city editor a diving suit complete with lead-weighted shoes. For just a moment Mr. Reid seemed surprised.

"Very good," he said after while. "Put it in my locker and I'll try to think up a lot of aquatic assignments for somebody."

Mr. Hurley did not seem to be pleased. "Do you mean you want to keep it?" he inquired uneasily.

"Of course," answered Mr. Reid. "What did you think I wanted to do . . .?"

"I beg pardon," said Mr. Hurley and his voice was hardly more than a whisper.

Three nights later the diving suit was mysteriously stolen out of Mr. Reid's locker. The scrubwomen and night watchmen were under the impression that somebody from the *Examiner* had taken it, but the only basis for their theory was that they had seen somebody carrying what they thought to be a drunken man in the direction of the *Examiner* stairway. They had paid little attention, for it was not, one suspects, an uncommon sight.

Mr. Reid discovered his loss just about the time that he noted the absence of Mr. Hurley. A moment later he had heard the story of the drunken man who was being carried somewhere and then the telephone rang.

"This is Captain Anderson of the Coast Guard," announced the caller. "One of your men borrowed a diving suit from us to have some pictures taken or something three days ago. He said he'd return it right away and it's not back yet. . . ."

Mr. Reid sighed as one does who recognizes defeat.

"I think you'll be getting it back this morning," he said. One gets to be clairvoyant when one is a city editor.

Throughout a long career most of which has been spent in close collaboration with the comptroller I never lost hope that someday I might write a place for myself in the lore of expense accounts with a bit of repartee of that sort which newspapermen remember longest because they envy it most. It would certainly be grand to coin a phrase like that of Richard Henry Little anent this fascinating subject. Floyd Gibbons, director of the Chicago *Tribune* Foreign Service, sent a telegram from Paris to Little in Russia: "Why is it that your expense accounts are larger than those of anybody else on the staff?" And Little answered: "I'll bite, why?"

And there was the similar case of Junius Wood, also in Russia, who was asked by the auditors to itemize his food bills. The auditor queried peevishly: "What makes you think we will pass a bill for caviar for breakfast?" And Junius made his classic reply, "Eggs is eggs."

I never succeeded, of course, in equaling the works of these masters. In point of fact I became involved with the auditors only three times in thirty-odd years. The first episode had to do with a cashier of the old Chicago *Daily Journal* who chased me back to Gary, Indiana, to get a receipt for a two-dollar hotel bill. My carfare as I remember it was around a dollar.

Years later I spent an interesting summer in Havana superintending a lot of revolutions and like many of my kind forgot to keep books. After three months I came home to find the accounting department on the verge of something and a harried managing editor somewhat impatient at my carelessness.

"They've been howling for an expense account until my ears ache," he said. And I nodded sympathetically.

"How much did they give me?" I asked. And he said, "Three thousand two hundred and eighty-six dollars and twenty-two cents."

So I filled out a blank:

EXPENSE ACCOUNT

Department: Foreign Service. *Name:* Robert J. Casey.

[280]

Days	*Description*	*Total*

I went to Cuba. I stayed there three and a half months covering three revolutions. I spent $3,286.22. I wish to God I knew where.

Yours very truly,

ROBERT J. CASEY

I have since been told that this was a highly unorthodox procedure but I don't know. The dazed comptroller took it in to Colonel Knox. He looked at it and said: "Of course he doesn't know where he spent it. . . . They were shooting at him with machine guns." And he okayed the account.

The third episode was hardly of the same dimensions. I had been assigned to cover a feature story of a wolf hunt by the farmers of southern Illinois and was about to leave the office when I learned that the expense account for this undertaking was limited to $10. The reason for that as I later found out was that the city editor had originally asked the Statehouse reporter at Springfield to cover it and for a trip of a few hours south of Springfield the ten dollars seemed adequate. But having accepted the assignment I couldn't with any grace unaccept it. So I drove to Springfield, rented a taxicab for the rest of the journey and saw the shooting of a dog in what turned out to be a case of mistaken identity. Then I turned in my expense account:

Wolf Hunt

To rent of Packard car, Chicago-Springfield	.02
Gas for same	.01
Oil for same	.05
Garage for same	.01½
Tip to attendant	.00½
Rent of taxi Springfield-Litchfield	.04

Oil .01, Gas .02	.03
Newspaper to get news of wolf	.02
Rent of Horse Litchfield-Hillsboro	.01
Rent of Bicycle Hillsboro-Schram City	.02
Rent of Roller Skates Schram-Irving	.01
Garage for taxicab	
Barn for horse	
Rack for bicycle	
Hay for horse	
Oil for bicycle	
Grease for skates	
Rent of opera glasses to look at wolf	
Membership public library to get book to study habits of wolf	

. . . and more of this for 175 items which, unfortunately, added up to only $9.90. I decided that itemization had gone far enough. So instead of splitting up the remaining dime I gave it all to one entry: "Wolf-bane. . . .10."

The cashier had no quarrel with this document. He paid my $10 and hung the account on his wall where it stayed for many years. It was a fine example, he said, of how an expense account ought to be written—so full of detail, so patently honest. I was glad, of course, because he was glad. On the expense account covering my next assignment I made one notation: "Ballance due on wolf hunt . . . $37.78." And I got that, too.

28

A SNEER FOR THE CYNICS

When I was sidling through Coppens' rhetoric at St. Mary's, Kansas, untold years ago, a worried English teacher advised me—along with the rest of the class—to keep out of the newspaper business.

"Newspaper writing," was his refrain, "will ruin your literary style. And the routine of journalism will make you cynical before your time."

I remembered that. Whenever I felt that newspaper writing was ruining my style I tried to be worried. But I never really felt concerned about becoming cynical before my time . . . not in any such atmosphere of sweetness and light as clung to the old *American* office or for that matter in any of the other pleasant and uplifting local rooms through which I wandered during my eventful years.

What place has cynicism alongside such a reporter as Joe Vennick of the vanished *Evening Post?* Mr. Vennick came to the high point of his emotional career when covering the murder of a young woman. Good reporter that he was, he got to the telephone first and his competition had to run two blocks to find similar accommodations. But when Mr. Vennick got

[283]

his city editor on the phone and started to tell his harrowing story he was overcome with grief and unable to break through his own sobs with any coherent speech.

His opponent, being less sensitive, was able to inform a re-write man what was going on and scooped Mr. Vennick by a noticeable margin . . . which seems a great shame.

There was also Mr. George Wharton of the A.P. (in the event you are making up case histories of noncynical, senti-mental people). Mr. Wharton had been saving what money he didn't need out of an A.P. salary to buy a flivver. He had gar-nered just about enough to turn the deal when his wife fell down the front stairs and broke her leg. The flivver money went for surgeons, crutches and such. All of which made no appreciable difference in the gay manner of Mr. Wharton. The joyous Yuletide was approaching and frequently he talked of a suitable gift for the little woman. He seemed to be having a lot of trouble picking something that would be adequate and at the same time express a little of his own feeling. So, in the end, he gave her the doctor's receipted bill for her leg.

Going over this list, I seem to remember the genius who used to hide his poker winnings in his wife's pocketbook overnight.

As a sort of reverse to this medal comes the memory of Henry Paynter who always kept a $10 bill sewed up in the lin-ing of his coat for use in a moment of emergency. Once when he was stranded in Milwaukee or Madison, he cut into the lining and found out that his wife had been there ahead of him. Being a wise girl, she had discovered a long time before that a dollar bill inside a coat lining crackles just like a $10 bill.

And I recall how Jack Diamond paid $10 to a creditor—not by mail or messenger as a less thoughtful person might have done, but by telegraph. Jack paid the $10 to the telegraph company plus the charge of a quarter for transmission across town and he filled out the form in good order except for one point. He came to the item: "State some detail by which payee may be identified." And on the dotted line he wrote: "He is a deaf-mute."

Not quite in the same category, but similar, is the story of Ben Hecht's prompt answer when Maxwell Bodenheim telegraphed a request for $50. Ben sent him a check for $50 by return mail but neglected to sign it.

It is encouraging to recall how the ravens or something fed the needy of the newspaper business—which is to say nearly all of it—in those days.

Bill Hedges, later to be prominently identified with the rise of radio broadcasting in the United States, was riding home on a crowded streetcar one night when he felt somebody jostle him. He smiled to himself as he recognized the accepted technique of the pickpocket and he waited to grab the stealthy hand that would presently be slipping into his overcoat pocket. He wasn't worried because there was nothing in the pocket. So he continued to read his newspaper until sometime later a noisy argument on the back platform made him aware that a detective had just arrested a pickpocket. Bill sighed almost regretfully at having missed his chance to grab the man himself. Then he reached into his pocket for a handkerchief and found somebody else's pocketbook, a wad of money and a watch. . . .

Mr. Charles MacArthur, when he was doing odds and ends for the *Herald and Examiner,* was another upon whom the manna descended whenever he had need for it. Not once but many times before a representative of the Black Watch offered him a sort of permanent subsidy, strange people had given him food and drink. But never had he attended the sort of reverse-English Barmecide feast that he shared with one John O'Fallon on a January night in 1916.

The dinner was impromptu. Mr. MacArthur on his way to an assignment stopped at Mangler's restaurant for nourishment of one sort or another. In a corner he discovered Mr. O'Fallon who had a drink in front of him and seemed to be going to sleep. In a flash it came to him that Mr. O'Fallon needed cheering up, so he slipped into the opposite chair.

"How about having dinner with me?" suggested Mr. MacArthur heartily. Mr. O'Fallon blinked owlishly.

"Okay," he said. "I'm having dinner. Thanks." Then he fell asleep. . . . Just about that time a waiter arrived with the "Evening special, $1.25, including soup, steak, salad, two vegetables, dessert and coffee." Paying no attention to Mr. MacArthur, he spread it out in front of Mr. O'Fallon. Mr. MacArthur pulled the dishes over and began to eat.

Forty-five minutes later Mr. MacArthur finished his meal, put his napkin on the table, selected a toothpick and walked out. Soon afterward Mr. O'Fallon woke up, looked at the empty dishes, signaled the waiter and paid his check.

"When food's tashteless as this is," he said, "itsh time to go home."

Mose Lyon of the *News* was another of the favored ones. The ravens never came very near him but he had a lot of other friends called copyreaders who tided him over his frequent difficulties. He was appreciative, too. I still can see his indignation one day when a cafeteria checker charged him for a surplus pat of butter or an extra slice of bread. Loudly disturbed, he took the matter up with the manager and got a five-cent reduction, after which he came back and threw the check in front of me.

"They're not going to cheat my friends," he said.

. . . Cynics, one judges, are unfortunate folk who just don't meet the right kind of people.

29

THE WORLD AND JUNIUS B. WOOD

THE book of Junius B. Wood for some reason or other has not yet been written, and, what with the press of other business, it is not going to be written here. The information contained in this chapter does not in any way purport to be a final report on Mr. Wood because no compendium under half a dozen volumes is ever going to do him justice. Rather it is a compilation of footnotes for a future historian who can find additional data in the conversation of almost any newspaperman of this generation.

Junius B. Wood was perhaps the greatest foreign correspondent who ever lived—and the greatest pain in the neck to doddering officialdom. He wrote more—and possibly more interesting—letters than Madame de Sevigné, most of them in bitter complaint about rules governing swimming pools in the District of Columbia, the duty on matches at Shimonoseki, the operation of hotels in Moscow. He is mentioned with love and reverence in the memoirs of the Abbe children (*Around the World in Eleven Years*) and is sometimes mentioned by acquaintances as the sort of acid gent with whom no stuffed shirt could ever be friends.

In addition to that, in a highly legendary trade he has become a legend. The folklore that has grown up about him would make a new edition of Bullfinch. The saga of his prowess is sung regretfully wherever his kind gather in the anterooms of foreign ministers or censors. That his ghost lingers in the world's press bureaus from Shanghai to Albany would be remarkable enough even if the man were not still alive and as impatient and as vigorous as he was in the beginning.

Contrary to the general belief, Junius Wood was not born at the end of a cable in some dangerous and distant hole in Europe. He was not always a foreign correspondent. In point of fact he was once a pretty fair political reporter, a realist among the eager-eyed young romantics who covered the City Hall beat in Chicago. And if in view of his later record you find this incongruous you may puzzle yourself further with the fact that in this phase of his career he made friends who mourned his absence during all the long years of his new life. . . . He never came back to the old home grounds, from Moscow or Singapore or Berlin or Sydney, that he failed to visit Hinky Dink Kenna and other politicians of that school, all of whom held him in considerable awe. Historians who argue that Mr. Wood never had any friends are definitely in error. Mr. Wood had quite as many friends as he had enemies—and frequently they were the same persons.

Now that Henry Justin Smith is gone from us it is hard to discover just how this able City Hall reporter was detached to cover the landing of the Marines at Vera Cruz . . . but anyway he was. He got to Vera Cruz in good order well in advance of the riot, saw the Marines come ashore and witnessed the killing of Chicago's personal hero, Sammy Meisenberg.

The management of the Chicago *Daily News* was well pleased with him on this occasion. Henry Smith congratulated him and got the ways cleared for what was to have been a graphic, step-by-step account of Private Meisenberg's sad progress home. Then something went wrong with Mr. Wood's schedule and also, apparently, with Mr. Wood.

Mr. Meisenberg reached Chicago all right and was laid out in state in the rotunda of the City Hall. Thousands of citizens passed by the bier and patriotic novelty vendors sold mourning buttons in Mr. Meisenberg's image and likeness—"Hair yar! Pitchers of de herro! Onny ten cents!" But Mr. Wood was not present among the mourners nor among the reporters who preserved so much of the record of this tearful field day for posterity. Nobody knew where Mr. Wood was, least of all Mr. Smith.

The first inkling the office had of Mr. Wood's changed attitude toward the hero-burial program came in a cablegram from Mexico City. . . .

"My war petering out. Eye going cover this war just breaking in Europe. . . . Send three thousand Laredo, Texas."

To this Mr. Smith is said to have replied: "Come home."

With anybody else, perhaps that might have been the end of it. Mr. Smith thought that was the end of it, notwithstanding his acquaintance with Mr. Wood. But two days later came another cablegram:

"Going cover war in Europe. Cancel money order sent me here. Send three thousand Houston, Texas. Arrange permits me to land England France."

And in effect Mr. Smith replied to that: "If you didn't receive my telegram I didn't receive yours. Come home."

There is no need to reproduce the entire file of this correspondence. Save for the date lines—Jacksonville, Florida; Richmond, Virginia; Washington, D.C.—they were virtually the same. There was one difference in Mr. Wood's Washington message. He began it petulantly: "Why don't you answer my messages?" From New York he delivered the information that, having failed to get either assistance or advice from the home office, he was sailing for Southampton immediately aboard the *Baltic*. He mentioned that he had made all necessary arrangements with the State Department and the British and French Embassies and that he would be pleased to find about six hundred pounds awaiting him on his arrival in England. So the Chicago *Daily News* (that is to say, Victor Lawson, who already had a high-priced foreign service) capitulated. Credentials were forwarded to make Mr. Wood's self-appointment legal and somebody else took over the telephone at the City Hall.

One draws the veil over quite a number of intervening years during which Mr. Wood finished the war as one of the sixteen correspondents accredited to the United States Army and moved on into Japan. Little happened to him there except the backwash of the big earthquake which occurred while he was doing something in Harbin. But what did happen was strictly according to the specifications of the Wood saga.

Junius had left Tokyo on an assignment early in August 1923. Mrs. Wood went to live in a hotel in Kamakura, a resort on the beach south of Tokyo, and was still there when it was shaken down in the big earthquake of September first. Mrs. Wood escaped with a few scratches, was picked up by a U.S. destroyer and taken to Shanghai, but there was no record of her rescue. In constantly increasing fury, as the ship steamed on toward China, she was reviewing what had happened to her, placing the responsibility, and stiffening her silence. Like many another person in the world by that time she had come to believe that Mr. Wood was capable of anything and resourceful beyond calculation. Perhaps he hadn't exactly been the cause of this earthquake which had slaughtered so many thousands of Japanese. But certainly he had gone away and left her to face it alone. He hadn't been around when she was trying to find her shoes in the wreck of the hotel. He hadn't been around when she was standing with other refugees in the water on the beach. . . .

Junius Wood arrived at what was left of Kamakura a few days after the earthquake, found some of his wife's clothes in the wreckage of the hotel and feared the worst. In the meantime she had made a connection with the *President Garfield* sailing from Shanghai to Seattle and, still wrapped in silence, had taken a passage. She was in San Francisco and in a slightly more forgiving mood when Junius heard anything about the matter. The incident is cited because of the widespread belief that this is the only time he ever lost an argument and a sort of secondary credo that he might have had something to do with the loosing of the Yokohama earthquake.

He went elsewhere from there. To China, South America, the Balkans, Germany, Russia. And in Russia he stayed for a large part of his fantastic career. He plagued the Bolsheviks— who liked him none the less for it. He maintained a highly critical attitude toward the great social experiment until the day Moscow bade him a reluctant good-by. He was ordered out of the country on five hours' notice and the same evening

was given the job of reorganizing the state police system. Perhaps one should say something more about the police system. . . .

One day there came to his room at the Metropole Hotel a
smart young man from the Gay-Pay-Oo with the order of evic-
tion.

"You have written defamatory articles about Russia," the
young man said. "You have told nonsensical untruths about
the government. So you will get packed up now please and
leave with me to take the next train."

"Okay," said Mr. Wood cheerily as he started to haul his
suitcase out from under the bed. "But I wish I had longer to
stay here and argue with you about what you've just said. I
may have written nonsense about this country but it has always
been the precise truth."

The young man bridled. Junius began to whistle a gay tune.

"You have insulted the branch of the service in which I have
the honor to be," the young man said. "You have stated that
there is nepotism in our police department. You have said that
we are more inefficient than the capitalists."

"And what's wrong with that?" Mr. Wood wanted to know.
As the visiting detective stuttered over his answer Mr. Wood
began to sing "My Bonnie Lies Over the Ocean" loudly if not
entirely on the key. He tossed a couple of suits into the case,
dumped some underwear and a shaving kit out of a dresser
drawer and closed his typewriter. The young man from the
Gay-Pay-Oo was beginning to run a noticeable blood pressure.

"Sir," he said huskily, "you don't seem to realize what has
happened to you. You are being sent out of the country."

"So what?" or words to that effect, asked Mr. Wood.

[293]

"You mean you can laugh at such a thing as this?"

"That's what I'm doing, isn't it? Listen, comrade: Suppose you had been sent to Siberia for six or seven years and then all of a sudden some dumb second lieutenant of police came into your shack and told you that you couldn't stay in Siberia any more, that you'd have to pack your suitcase and get going for Moscow. Would you be crying about it? Don't bother to answer. I'll tell you. . . . Well, as far as this assignment is concerned I've been six or seven years in this town which is my version of Siberia. And now you come in and tell me that I have to go home. You fix it up so that even my paper can't make me stay in this Godforsaken place! Tovarich, I certainly thank you. . . ."

He threw the last of his linen into the suitcase and snapped the lid. "Okay," he said. "Let's go."

The man from the GPU had lost his early eagerness.

"There is something very wrong here," he decided. "You actually want to get out of the country. You must have a reason for that . . . a real reason. So you will come with me, yes. But not to the railroad station. You will come with me to headquarters."

So they went to the gloomy bourne of the GPU, Junius still whistling, his escort growing more indignant, and presently they came before a dour Commissar who wanted to know what all the fuss was about. The young man told him. Junius Wood had maligned the GPU. Junius seemed to be pleased with his order of expulsion. The Commissar looked at Junius sadly. He had known him for many years and had been irked by him in a thousand ways and yet, in a way, he knew it was going to be more lonesome for official Moscow when this incredible man should go over the border.

"You said many unkind things about our police," he said. "You have broken all the rules under which correspondents are tolerated here. You have said that my staff consists of a lot of incompetents. . . ."

" 'Incompetent slobs' was what I said," Junius corrected him. "I wish I could give you the exact equivalent in Russian . . . but no matter. Tell this guy to take me to the railroad station."

"Do you really think they are incompetent?" the Commissar asked him gently.

"It saddens me to think how incompetent they are," Junius assured him. "They are mostly peasant boys who don't know the difference between arson and arsenic. They may be able to recognize a murder when they see one because they have plenty of opportunity. But they don't know what to do after they see it. They're somebody's relatives and that is all anybody can say for them. . . ."

"They are new and eager but perhaps a little inexperienced," admitted the big chief. "But who are you to criticize them? You are a journalist. You write things about politics. You do not know anything about criminals."

"I was a police reporter for three years in Chicago," stated Mr. Wood with great dignity. "What I don't know about crime isn't worth knowing. . . ."

"And maybe you could install a system in this office that is better than the one we have now . . . ?"

"With one hand tied behind me and both eyes shut," replied Mr. Wood.

"Then," said the Commissar, "you have a job. Pushkin com-

rade, have somebody take Mr. Wood's luggage back to the
hotel. He is staying with us. . . ." So Mr. Wood stayed and
revised the tables of organization and the operating system of
the police department. And he stayed in Russia until nostalgia
caught up with him at last many years afterward.

With such a beginning it was inevitable that numerous apoc-
rypha should have arisen like the cycle of Dorothy Parker
stories to keep his name from being forgotten in the outside
world. There are sundry yarns (such as the one which says
that he nagged the Rumanian government into breaking off
relations with us) that we have no time to go into. But there
is one which, despite no better ancestry, has a literary beauty
of its own. Fact or fiction, it is still a little gem for the collection.

Mr. Wood, early in his career in Moscow, took out a membership in the journalists' union not as any philosophical
gesture but as a practical investment. So he was not without
official assistance when the water tap in his hotel bathroom
got out of order.

The bathroom setting of this narrative gives it an air of verisimilitude above all other detail for it is a matter of authentic
record that another bathroom figured in another incident in a
hotel in Manila. In that case somebody had objected to Mr.
Wood's use of the typewriter in his room after midnight. No
one, however, could object to his taking a bath after midnight.
So he did regularly every night with particularly fine effect
inasmuch as the shower-bath rooms in the Manila Hotel used
to be lined with tin and separated from the main corridor at
the ceiling by an open grillwork of brick. When, after four

nights, he turned off the water and resumed his typewriting nobody objected.

The behavior of the Moscow tap, however, seems to me something over which he had no control. When he first noticed it, a few weeks after his reinstatement with the police, he mentioned it to the concierge of the hotel with the suggestion that maybe a new Fuller ball would fix it up. At the end of a week he mentioned it to the concierge again. And thereafter he mentioned it daily for a month. By that time his patience was at an end and more in sorrow than in anger he sat down and wrote one of his famous letters to the head of the journalists' union.

"I live," so went the complaint, "in a hotel which is largely patronized by foreigners. Very few of these foreigners are, like myself, paid-up members of a soviet. They have no interest in the glorious advance of Russia except inasmuch as it affects the jobs that they have been hired to do here—the building of factories, the opening of mines and oil refineries and such. It is only natural that they get their ideas of the efficiency of this country from what they see in their daily life—to wit, in their hotel.

"I have complained repeatedly to the concierge of my hotel about the dripping tap in my bathtub and always he has treated my complaint as a matter of no consequence. The tap still drips after all these weeks and unsympathetic members of the foreign colony are beginning to laugh at the progress of my pleading. They are beginning to believe that all of Russia is only a reflection of this stupid fool who has the interests of neither his country nor his union at heart. I ask you that something be done about it."

And, so the story goes, something was done. Shortly thereafter an investigation squad from the GPU came over to the hotel, took the concierge out and shot him. The tap still leaked.

Whether or not you consider the government's prompt disposal of the water-tap problem as a mark of respect to a comrade you'll be a long time searching the record before you find any sign of unusual favors toward Mr. Wood. That he was *persona grata* with the police department did not mean, for instance, that he was any more than tolerated by the press-relations bureaus, censors and such. With the Foreign Office in particular he was for a long time nothing more than "one of those foreign writing nuisances," which classification entailed much personal hardship.

The Foreign Minister may not actually have undertaken the chastisement of the press as part of his official duties but it must be conceded that if he had worked at it he could have achieved no more brilliant result. For instance, it was the policy of the Foreign Office never to issue a statement to the press during the day or even during those hours of the night when ordinary people might be expected to be up and about. Generally the handout, bulletin or whatever it was, was issued about 3:00 A.M. after the eager correspondents had been told to get around to collect it at 1:00 A.M. The intervening two hours were usually spent by the visiting reporters jumping up and down in the snow outside the entrance of the building in which the Foreign Minister lived. When, finally, a concierge got around to opening the door and admitting them to the building, they still had to climb up five flights of stairs and do some more waiting in a cold hall before the precious blurb was placed in their hands.

[298]

This, of course, was a highly unsatisfactory system but even the frozen-footed correspondents admitted that it had its points. At the end of the wait they were able to meet the Foreign Minister face to face and at least indicate something of what they felt. They realized just how good a system it had been one night when after the usual dance in the frozen snow the door opened and the porter stepped outside.

"You are not to come up," he said. "The Minister of Foreign Affairs has sent these things to you. So you will take them, comrades, and good night to you all."

Mr. Wood took his along with the rest and sat up the rest of the night fixing a lead for it that is still memorable wherever newspapermen gather to discuss the problems of reporting in Russia. Mr. Wood's dispatch began:

"MOSCOW, January 25—According to a statement issued last night by the janitor of the Foreign Office . . ."

The next time the correspondents went around to the flat of the Minister of Foreign Affairs they did not have to wait in the snow.

30

SOCIAL STATUS OF A CORNCOB PIPE

~~~~~~

ONCE every four years Junius Wood came home from the farther rims of the world to cover the national conventions for the Chicago *Daily News* and to add new cantos to the saga. There was nothing about him to suggest his close association with the dreadful Reds except a fur cap which he didn't wear in convention weather anyway, and an addiction to a Russian ersatz pipe tobacco called *mahorka. Mahorka* at its best smelled something like burning brake lining and Mr. Wood consumed it in a corncob pipe which carried no odors of frankincense and myrrh even when unlighted. It might be well to mention that Mr. Wood's addiction to corncob pipes if not to *mahorka* had caused him trouble even in Russia. Corncob pipes never appealed to the Russian taste which is singularly unparticular in other things. As a consequence they are among the things that you can't buy in a Moscow commissary and as soon as Mr. Wood had burned out the supply he brought with him from the States, his plight became dire. In his emergency he ordered a supply from a firm of backwoods corncob pipe fitters in the hills near Springfield, Missouri. And in due time they arrived in Moscow.

STATUS OF A CORNCOB PIPE

The customs agents in Moscow are, one may judge, just about the same as customs agents everywhere. When they don't know what a novel and apparently dutiable article is they make a guess. The enclosed bill, setting forth that Mr. Wood had paid somebody in Missouri $4 for fifty pipes, did not enter into their calculation. Probably nobody in the office knew what four dollars U. S. currency would amount to anyway. So, while Mr. Wood waited, they made an appraisal: "Toys, hand-carved . . . duty one hundred rubles" (or, unless you did business with the black market, approximately fifty dollars).

Mr. Wood made a noise about this that was heard halfway around the world and in the end was granted a review of his case when he was able to demonstrate that you could actually smoke *mahorka* in one of the things without its exploding. Thereafter he was allowed to import corncob pipes at a nominal duty and was invited—nay, encouraged—to smoke them in all public buildings, government offices or other places where people might be interested in scientific phenomena.

Back in America it became a source of great inconvenience to Mr. Wood that numerous hotel managers declared flatly—the pipe, plus *mahorka* was unfit for smoking in highly polished lobbies. Mr. Wood was disposed to argue the point. Sometimes he won, sometimes not. But when finally he came to the Ten Eyck Hotel in Albany, preparing to accompany Al Smith on a presidential campaign tour, he found a manager with a disposition as inflexible as his own. The late James O'Donnell Bennett, his companion on this expedition, was much pleased. One suspects that he didn't like Junius' pipe any better than anybody else. Junius, as was his custom, accepted what seemed to be an uncompromisable verdict with philosophy. However, he did not share Mr. Bennett's opinion that there was something funny about it.

"This is only the beginning," he said. "This manager has never really had a chance to smell *mahorka* at its best and he must be won over. But I'll bet you ten dollars that I shall smoke this pipe loaded with *mahorka* in this lobby tomorrow night at eight o'clock and that except for possibly one gentle suggestion by the management, there won't be any interference."

Mr. Bennett took up the bet and the money was duly posted with another correspondent. The next morning he met Mr. Wood for breakfast.

Perhaps I should digress here to mention that Mr. Wood's Jovian ire was most likely to rise as he was taking his meals. He was always something of an epicure. He knew what he wanted. And, as the saying goes, he raised hell if he didn't get it. So Mr. Bennett's first inkling that something was wrong with his arrangement about the pipe came when Mr. Wood accepted an annoying flaw in the service virtually without comment. Mr. Wood had ordered two-minute eggs. The waiter brought in a pair that were obviously hard-boiled and cold. Mr. Wood in his gentlest voice called the waiter's attention to the discrepancy. The waiter apparently had an answer right out of the hotel's book.

"Well, suh," he said, "them's what we calls two-minute aigs heah. . . ." Junius, with a sad smile, ate his eggs.

Came luncheon with a similar incident. Mr. Wood had ordered blackberries for dessert and he got black raspberries. Once more he called the waiter to look at the evidence and the waiter, now more sure of himself, said: "Well, suh, them's what we calls blackberries heah. We been servin' 'em foh blackberries." And again, to the astonishment of Mr. Bennett, Mr. Wood accepted the ruling.

At 6:30 that night they sat down to dinner in the same dining room. There was little reference to the ten-dollar bet although Mr. Bennett did ask coyly if Junius had his pipe with him. The dinner seemed perfect—even with Mr. Wood's specifications—and there was no word of criticism from anybody until the cheese was served. Mr. Wood, among other talents, has a great skill in judging rare cheeses and with an expert's care he had chosen an old Cheshire. He mentioned as the cheese was set before him that it was not Cheshire but Cheddar. And as before the waiter assured him that the hotel management thought it was Cheshire. Mr. Wood abandoned the discussion, finished the Cheddar and drank his coffee.

It was just eight o'clock when they entered the lobby. Mr. Wood selected a seat in plain view of the alert manager, pulled out his corncob pipe and a bag of *mahorka,* filled up the bowl, tamped it, struck a match and leaned back luxuriously as clouds of rubbery smoke began to seep through the potted palms. The exasperated manager came on the run and his voice was harsher than on the preceding evening as he repeated his ruling:

"It is against the rules for you to smoke that pipe in the lobby, sir . . . And we must insist . . ."

Mr. Wood looked up at him in what looked like a mixture of astonishment and indignation.

"You are acting under a misapprehension," he said quietly. "In a hotel where hard-boiled eggs are two-minute eggs, and blackberries are black raspberries and Cheshire cheese is Cheddar cheese, this is a cigar." The manager opened his mouth once to say something but gave it up. Mr. Wood with a seraphic smile signaled to the young man who had been holding the stakes.

It was sometime during the campaign that Junius Wood arrived in Chicago long after the last edition of the *Daily News* had gone to press. He got out of a cab in front of the tottering old building in Wells Street and started down the dimly lighted passage in front of the cashier's department toward the stairs. He'd gone only a few steps when a watchman stopped him and, incredible as it may seem, asked him who he was and what he wanted. Despite Mr. Wood's innate modesty he was naturally a little flabbergasted at that. He felt, justifiably, that the watchman might have seen enough of his photographs to recognize him. Here he was, the friend of kings, the deviser of the Russian police system, probably the most famous correspondent in all the world, and on his home threshold he had discovered the one cop on earth who didn't know him.

Patiently Mr. Wood explained who he was and the reason for his late arrival but the watchman wasn't convinced. He reached under a counter and got out the office directory in which—inasmuch as Mr. Wood's normal habitat at the time was Russia—he had no place.

"Sorry," the watchman said. "If you was in here it would be all right for you to go up to the editorial department. But you ain't down here and I can't do nothing about it."

"Okay," said Mr. Wood. "Think nothing of it." And he went around the corner to the Hotel La Salle and telegraphed his story—three thousand words of it—at overhead rates to the managing editor in care of the Head Janitor.

STATUS OF A CORNCOB PIPE

I have many lovely memories of Junius as we traveled the convention circuit together back in the days when they nominated Al Smith in Houston. We drove thousands of miles over theoretical roads in my car and whether he lacked experience in automobile riding or had no nerves, he thought my driving was excellent. Only once did he show any emotion. He had gone to sleep at the time when, to avoid a steam roller on a fresh earthen fill, I turned down the bank and brought up in front of a culvert about two feet high. He woke up and appraised the situation instantly. "My God," he said, "do we have to go through that?" . . . I remember his wordy quarrel with a flip but careless waitress in a Houston hotel. I remember an exchange of invective that nobody could follow without a thesaurus. But more particularly I remember the amazing sequel of the argument. The next morning Junius was late for breakfast and the waitress came to me much disturbed. "Your friend," she said, "what happened to him?"

I said that he'd gone over to the Elks' Club to get his mail— which was the truth even if she didn't seem to believe it.

"Okay," she said. "I was afraid maybe I hurt his feelings the way I talked to him yesterday."

I spooned my porridge in a sort of daze as I began to realize that most of Junius' relationships were quite like this. The people he fought with so glibly unaccountably loved him for it. For some reason that I have never determined I never fought with him myself. . . . Possibly I foresaw that it would be a waste of time.

Junius was in Germany in the early days of Hitler when he finally decided that he had had enough of exile. The Chicago *Daily News* contributed somewhat to his decision although not so much as some people have supposed. Somebody had inaugurated a policy of economy in the foreign service, one of the features of which was a sort of rationing of cable space. Each correspondent was told to limit himself to a certain tentative maximum of words each month. This plan, it was pointed out, would enable the auditors to calculate with some accuracy in advance the amount of cable tolls that would presently have to be paid. Mr. Wood did not seem to hear suggestions that in emergencies he need not stick to the schedule. Along about the middle of June 1934 he sent a cable to the office that his quota of words for the month had been exhausted.

"You will be hearing from me," he said, "on the first of July."

June 30, you may remember, was the day of Hitler's blood purge when he wiped out all present or expected opposition by murdering all dissenters. The A.P. and U.P. filled the office of the *Daily News* with thousands of words about this barbaric hecatomb. But there was no word from Junius Wood—not a bulletin, not a schedule, not a hint that he was still alive.

Managing Editor Hal O'Flaherty cabled an inquiry. He probably knew in advance the answer he was going to get:

"My cable quota exhausted. Will cover this story in detail next month when business office authorizes cable tolls."

Mr. O'Flaherty cabled back in effect: "Don't be silly."

And that seems to have been the wrong suggestion.

"What do you mean, silly?" demanded the outraged Mr. Wood. "You know the rules as well as I do. If you can't make up your minds what you're going to do I can't do it for you. As for me I can't write news on a cash register. . . ."

There was further interchange during which Mr. O'Flaherty

was unable to see the important principle involved in Mr. Wood's action and Mr. Wood declined to entertain suggestions that he forget the cable restrictions or else put the bill against his July quota. Toward the middle of the day Junius resigned. This time he meant it.

31

THE CENSORS—FRANKIE AND MAXIE

SAVE for the censors the current war doesn't seem to have brought many new problems to the newspaper business nor to have produced any new kind of newspapermen. In journalism if nowhere else the more things change the more they are the same thing. Yesterday's reporters turn out to be today's reporters also and the stories cling to them as they always clung. The interesting people in other words continue to be the interesting people.

I stood one morning in the bar of the Savoy Hotel, London, with Ray Daniell of the New York *Times* and listened to the clunks falling along the embankment. Except that it was noisier and we had a better hotel to loiter in, the situation didn't seem to be very far geographically from the dangerous days of the Ohio River floods. We were trying to appraise our present situation when a bellboy came. The censor wished to speak with Mr. Daniell. So, on the bar phone, Mr. Daniell talked with the censor.

The problem reminded me in some vague way of Cairo and its Chamber of Commerce and the local concern that nothing but favorable truth should go abroad. The censor had taken note of Mr. Daniell's story in which Mr. Daniell had described the night's raid on London. Mr. Daniell had said that one of the largest night bombing forces yet turned loose by Germany had come up the Thames estuary and had been intercepted by night fighters and that the R.A.F. had won. The censor, on the whole, was pleased with the story, but didn't Mr. Daniell know that it was forbidden to mention the names of rivers in dispatches. It would be necessary to eliminate the name of the Thames.

"Okay," said Mr. Daniell. "Make it the Amazon."

"The what?" said the censor.

"Yes," said Mr. Daniell. So the copy was duly altered and sent to the cable office and an hour later copyreaders in the *Times* office were elated to find out that a German bombing party had come up the Amazon estuary, that it had been intercepted by night fighters and driven back, and that London was saved.

I had my own experience with what seemed to be typical American minds the next day. Somewhere in my lead I had quoted "bombs bursting in air." The censor quarreled with that. There hadn't been any bombs bursting in air, he said. And if they had burst in air, that would have implied some sort of time fuse which might well be a military secret. I told him patiently that this was a line from "The Star Spangled Banner," and that the next line, "gave proof through the night that our flag was still there," would be understood by every American who might read my dispatch. He cheerfully removed his objection.

"I didn't know that," he said. "I'm getting more American every day."

William Stoneman, who was a good police reporter, has long been one of the best foreign correspondents on an American pay roll without changing his technique. His international scoop on the resumption of relations between the United States and Russia was one of the most remarkable beats since the invention of movable type. And his success with it was due not to any advance information but to impromptu ingenuity.

Every correspondent in Moscow knew that Max Litvinoff was to go to Washington to negotiate a new status for the Soviet government in the United States. But that was all the good it did anybody. The censorship had been clamped down immediately the story began to circulate, and the correspondents sat down to argue and chew their fingernails or wait for the lifting of the ban. . . . All but Bill Stoneman.

He got into a *droshky* and rode out to the suburbs where he knew there was a branch telegraph office. There he addressed a full-rate message to Hal O'Flaherty, 400 West Madison street, Chicago:

"Maxie meets Frankie next month Pennsylvania Avenue. . . ."

The message went without delay and was promptly dissected by O'Flaherty, Paul Mowrer and Carroll Binder. Pennsylvania Avenue could mean only Washington. That identified Frankie as FDR. The leap from there to Maxie was simple.

Mr. Stoneman got another bit of interesting intelligence past some determined English suppressionists by means of a similar technique. He knew that an unadmitted censorship was editing all outbound news concerning the affairs of Edward VIII, the temporary king. But he didn't quarrel with a situation that he couldn't improve. Instead he accepted the dicta from on high and omitted all mention of royalty from his dispatches. He took new interest in the affairs of commoners—not only the commoners of London but of sleepy little towns in the midlands—their problems of living, their love affairs and their marriages. As a part of this series he apprised his editor that a divorce had been granted by one of these courts in the hinterlands to one Simpson, an American. And of course the censors at the cable end in Manchester passed it. They weren't interested in the affairs of anybody named Simpson.

Mr. Stoneman is the man who was congratulated by Her Majesty the Queen on the brilliance of his dispatches from Hell's Corner in the Straits of Dover. He is likewise the man who battled toe to toe with the censors as leader of the American correspondents in London. He stands higher in the respect of British brass hats probably than any other reporter with whom they have come in contact. But he is also the lad who crawled into the wreckage of his bombed flat to rescue a pet turtle; who fed shillings into a slot machine in an Oxford street pub during the Burlington Arcade fire in the hope of hitting a jackpot before the building came down. He is definitely one of the more interesting of the interesting people.

32

SPARROW ROBERTSON AGAINST
THE REICH

~~~~~~

IT SEEMS a long time now since the Anglo-American Press club of France met in Drouant's and discussed such journalistic matters as *chateauneuf du pape, ananas au kirsch* and caviar. It seems a long time since there was any press in Paris, or for that matter any Paris. The one thing that keeps that worried but gay period between wars from dissolving like a dream is the green and ever fragrant memory of Sparrow Robertson. For Sparrow stayed on when others left. As virtually the sole representative of a once flourishing American newspaper business he took his responsibilities seriously, continued the performance of his routine duties in the fashion of a stop light we once saw working under the crest of an Ohio flood, and treated the Nazis with just the right shade of contempt. He died before the war had taken any turn for the better, which is a pity, and without knowing that for once he had become the most talked-of reporter in the world—which is close to tragedy.

Everybody who read the old Paris Edition of the New York *Herald Tribune* will remember Sparrow's column of sports news. For the most part it mentioned such of Sparrow's "sporting and social friends" as might be found of an evening at "The Silver Ring," "Tommy's California Bar" or "Johnny's under the Sink." At times it contained some reference to Longchamps or Le Boxe or the Davis Cup or something else recognizably sporting, but not often. And there was generally a bit of reminiscence about "My old pal, John Doe," or unnamed fiends who wouldn't believe that they "couldn't do this to me."

Sparrow's philosophy was simple. The world consisted of "my old pals" or people who "try to push a guy around." His friendships apparently were undying, and enmities—if you could call them that—came to an end on his declaration of principle: "You can't do this to me!"

Robertson was not always a sports writer, if indeed he ever was. The legend has it that he made shoes for track athletes in Boston, got to be a timer in foot races and came to Europe with one of the earlier Olympic teams. The contestants of the team went home and were forgotten but Robertson stayed in Paris to remind an astonished world continuously of his presence. There was a clause in the will of James Gordon Bennett affecting him—or at any rate his pay and tenure of office were as much a part of the title to the Paris Edition of the New York *Herald Tribune* as the good will and presses. It is unlikely that he ever made very much. It is certain that he never wanted for anything. His "old pals" in the restaurant and hotel business were many and faithful.

His column, according to some schools of literary thought, wasn't very good. And occasionally one heard part of Paris asking the other part if Sparrow knew where the body was buried. But, as a matter of unsentimental fact, more than one of a procession of editors found out that Sparrow was actually an asset. More than one tried to edit the column—to put it into English as the saying went. Not a few tried to leave it out altogether. Both practices brought quick notice and loud howls from the circulation. Whatever the rating of Sparrow's column, whatever the mental status of the circulation, there it was. The people somehow liked to read Sparrow Robertson. Some of them wrote letters to the editor to say that his like was to be found nowhere else in the world. And that was probably true.

International affairs never bothered him much despite his constant meddling with them. Paris was to him just a beautiful place to live in. France was a very nice country whose natives spoke an odd language that he never bothered to learn. The war, when it came along, was a sort of childish nuisance that he felt might well have been avoided if a few of the politicians had really put some thought into the matter. He complained bitterly at times about the military use of the track at Chantilly. It saddened him to think that there wasn't going to be any Olympics—with their side-line pageants of international amity—for some years to come. But the actuality of the war, its imminence and its dangers, never seemed to touch him.

When the disheartened French troops came back across the Seine and Paris poured out onto the roads to be bombed, trampled upon and machine-gunned, he sighed deeply and went out through the deserted streets toward the Paris *Herald* office. Long since the presses had stopped. The long city room was empty and silent. There were hoods on the typewriters for the first time since they came over from New York. All the tables were clean. All the desks were closed.

With a world cracking all about him, Sparrow sat down at his desk, put a piece of paper in his typewriter, and turned out a column in which his disdain for war was almost godlike.

"Until last night you could see quite a lot of the old-timers meeting their sporting and social friends in O'Neill's. This was the place where the crowds went to when they went. . . ."

"My old pal Bill Feeny who used to run the travel bureau in the Rue Scribe has closed his office temporarily and is vacationing in the Pyrenees. . . ."

"Some people have been piling their bicycles in the Rue Castiglione until I can't get into my hotel. They can't get away with that. They can't do this to me. . . ."

"My old pal Joe Ford who represented the New York Pantheon attractions is visiting friends in Marseilles. . . ."

Sparrow tore the copy out of the typewriter and hung it on the city editor's spike. The city editor wasn't there and even if you failed to recognize the war socially you couldn't help but realize that he wasn't likely to be there. On the other hand, an assignment was an assignment, and Sparrow's assignment was to write and deliver this column once a day.

Sparrow lived at the Hôtel Lotti which is a long walk from the *Herald Tribune* office. So, when he walked along the Champs Elysées the next morning there was no way to avoid seeing the tide of Germans spreading out over the city. However, that day and the next and many days after he wrote his column as he had always written it—"My old pal!" "They can't get away with it!" And, as always, he hung it on the city editor's hook. When the hook was completely filled he transferred an empty one from another desk. In the meantime he lived at the Lotti and got his food from a friendly Italian cook.

The sundry bistros where he could meet his sporting and social friends were all shut up except the Silver Ring which had been set aside for the entertainment of German officers. Sparrow's world apparently had retired somewhere behind closed doors and he hadn't much contact with the seething world beyond the Place Vendôme except in occasional meetings with French barmen and concierges who knew him but whose language he had never learned to speak.

Still, life wasn't so bad as it might have been for an idealist such as Sparrow. There weren't any patrons in the Lotti for the first few days except him. After that a few nondescript Germans and their wives came and went without bothering him any. There was still a little food in some cache that the Italian cook knew about. So Mr. Robertson settled down to be patient until the weary years should bring an end to this war as they had to the last one. And then the Luftwaffe arrived.

Sparrow was aware of the Luftwaffe for the first time when he came down from his room for breakfast and found the lobby filled with the military. The civilians, the fat women, the thin red-lipped blondes had gone. A major met him as he came into the room and spoke to him in French.

"You can't get away with that," Sparrow told him tersely. "Try some other language."

The major spoke in German and after that in fair English.

"The general regrets," he said stiffly, "but this hotel has been taken over by the air corps as a headquarters building. You are the only civilian left in the hotel and we must ask you for your room."

"Oh no!" replied Mr. Robertson unabashed. "You can't do this to me. I am an American. I am a tenant of the hotel. I haven't any interest in your war whatever and I am going to keep my room."

The major looked at him blankly and saw a little old man approaching his eightieth year who was either the bravest person in Paris or the most ignorant.

"But, sir," he exclaimed in exasperation, "you are making trouble."

"Why not?" demanded Sparrow. "It's my room." And he went out to deliver his copy that never would be printed to a city editor who wasn't there. When he came back he met not only the major but an apoplectic colonel, apparently an adjutant, who spoke politely enough but with a hint of an explosion in every word.

"Apparently you have not understood," he said, "but we really must have this room. You can't live here in the air corps headquarters. Don't you see that? It's just impossible."

"Hell," said Sparrow graciously, "I'm not particular. Nothing bothers me. Air corps or singing blondes, it's all the same. And this is my home and I'm staying here. Get down your boss, the general or whoever he is, and tell him that."

"He will very likely kill you, you stupid pig," mentioned the colonel. But he gave some directions to an orderly. As nearly as Sparrow could make out with his fragmentary knowledge of German, the colonel was asking for further instructions in the quelling of a riot. By way of answer there was a fanfare abovestairs and a general, stooped under the weight of his medals, made a slow and impressive descent.

"Pig-dog," breathed the exasperated colonel, "you have disturbed the general so that he has come here to see this nonsense for himself. He will kill you."

But Sparrow was paying no attention. Smiling in a sort of incredulous rapture he was gazing at the ornate figure descending the stairs. And the sharp black eyes of the general were fixed on his and on the general's face was a similar expression. Then suddenly he spoke:

"Sparrow!" he roared.

"My old pal!" bellowed Sparrow. . . . He had recognized the general as a nice old guy he had met at the Olympics somewhere . . . Berlin it was, in 1936.

"These guys . . . my room . . ." he began. By that time his old pal the general had put an arm around his thin little shoulders. "I'll get you a better one," he said. "It's going to be fine having you here. . . ."

Sparrow died in the spring of 1941. Maybe the daily trip to the city editor's desk over near the Arc de Triomphe came to seem futile as the permanence of the Germans seemed more and more certain. The Luftwaffe turned out for him in fine style and his old pal the general delivered a suitable eulogy: "He was a nice little guy."

33

MESSRS. FISH AND THE TALKING DOG

THERE used to be an actor of singular talent on the rolls of one of the departments in the County Building . . . may still be there, for all I know, unless somebody has killed him. He was short, swart, fat, bucktoothed, unshaved and poorly clad, all of which may have made some difference to him as a tax collector or whatever he was in civil life but certainly didn't interfere with his act. This genius, whose name was something like Dubinsky, had only one role: the uncouth foreigner. He spent a large part of his time going about annoying court attachés who couldn't understand him, walking on the feet of exasperated aldermen, bellowing double-talk in the ears of information clerks.

His acting job is best described as "the giving of the rib." And he was so adept at it that half the officeholders in the building had been his victims and the other half just hated him on general principles.

He would come roaring into the office of some ward heeler's nephew frothing at the mouth and spitting bubbles of mild soap and his charge, "You ruined my sister!" could be heard well out on the road to Dubuque. There was a lot of conversation after this disconcerting bellow, conversation that was loud and horrible even if nobody was ever able to make out a word of it. Stooges would intervene just as Dubinsky seemed on the verge of throttling the clerk or sometimes when the clerk was about to throttle Dubinsky. And while he left no corpses in his wake you could always tell where he'd passed by the look of panicky hatred in the eyes of his carefully selected audiences.

Dubinsky was the greatest of his kind and that is why he has been picked here above all other professional ribbers to prove a point about the interesting people of the newspaper business—that in addition to hearts of gold they also have nerves of brass. For Mr. Dubinsky's one failure in a long, triumphant career, was when he left the judges and States' Attorneys and bankers of his early successes and tried to disturb the *savoir faire,* to shake the poise and dignity of an intelligent police reporter, one Otto Markheim.

Mr. Dubinsky wasn't the only one who made a mistake in Mr. Markheim. The distinction was shared by all the reporters present at the time in the City Hall press room. In secret caucus they had unanimously elected Mr. Markheim as "the likeliest fish" for the experiment. They assured Mr. Dubinsky that while he might possibly be able to distinguish between heat and cold, that just about ended his intellect. "A set up," they assured Mr. Dubinsky. "He'll be a perfect scream. . . ."

Mr. Markheim was reading a newspaper at a desk in the middle of the room when Mr. Dubinsky came like the echo of a land mine.

"You ruined my sister!" he screamed. And Mr. Markheim looked up at him nervously.

"What's her name?" he wanted to know.

MESSRS. FISH AND TALKING DOG

It comes as a natural corollary that in a business where there are such agile mentalities as that of Mr. Markheim you will find also a quota of earnest jokers, recognizable as such even when they fail to carry sneeze powder and exploding cigars. There is an old Madison Street saw to the effect that a man who is too sly to be tricked is the sliest of tricksters. So there is a large file of literature on the subject in every local room.

There were the helpful lads on the *Evening American* who taught Mr. Ivan Heidelbaum, the ghetto chronicler, how to spell. Mr. Heidelbaum one morning blurted out to a crowded local room: "How do you spell pinochle?" They told him. And he wrote the lead that still hangs on the bulletin board as a perfect specimen: "Mr. Kleppermann," Mr. Heidelbaum wrote, "has reached the pinochle of success."

There was the battle of the pneumatic tubes that made the County Building press room uninhabitable for days. One of the bright lads in the press room sent a mouse over to the boy who looked after the tubes for the City News Bureau. The boy shot back a pound of cockroach powder.

There was of course the youngster on the *News* who tried to put limburger cheese in the hat of a rewrite man who had been snappy over the telephone, and made the mistake of putting it in his own.

In a similar vein of innocent merriment were the pranks that grew out of Henry Justin Smith's superstition about pins. Whenever he saw one he'd stop to pick it up and batteries of pin-scatterers made life a lucky hell for him every time he'd start out to the composing room before an edition.

There were the patient workers in the old *News* office who devoted the better part of an afternoon to cutting the bottoms

out of a thousand envelopes which the Associated Press correspondent used to send his copy through the tubes to his office.
They say it was worth the sacrifice to see his mounting rage
as he would slap a fold of paper into one after another and
watch it come straight through.

There were the sleepless ones of the detective bureau press
shift who found that a man named Upjohn had a telephone
and thereafter called him in relays all night long inquiring:
"Are you Upjohn?"

There was—how could any newspaper historian forget it?—
the incomparable double-action "rib" inflicted on the trade by
John R. Walsh who was a theoretical banker as well as a theoretical newspaper owner. Mr. Walsh eventually went to jail
because his bank fell down on top of him, although many people thought keeping up the Chicago *Chronicle* was the greater
felony. The thing that his employees wished to see him hanged
for never came out in the evidence. . . .

In those days there was a considerable circulation of gold
coin throughout the country and there was likewise a considerable business in the sweating of it. Every gold coin that ever
came out of the mint was certain to show considerable wear
in the course of a year unless it went directly into somebody's
sock, and it was only natural that despite the constant watch-
fulness of tellers the banks every now and then found themselves stuck with a lot of short-weight gold. This was a source
of great concern to most of the bankers of the town but apparently nothing more than a minor annoyance to Mr. Walsh.
He paid off the *Chronicle* help with it. The *Chronicle* help in
turn pushed it back on Mr. Walsh's bank—through the aid

of proxies unknown to the tellers—and thus were discovered the principles of perpetual motion.

There was the case of the late Dempster MacMurphy, the business manager who installed a deaf secretary to deal with people who came to sell him things or interest him in causes. (Though maybe that should be reclassified under the head of efficiency measures.) There was the speech in French which Howard O'Brien made one night to a gathering of the yearning souls who contribute verse to newspaper columns—a speech which consisted entirely of the text of the advertising posters on the wall of the Tavern Club's French bar. There was the old friend of John Boettiger who sent him a telegram on the occasion of his second marriage: "Save Sistie for me!"

There were hundreds of such episodes in the still unwritten book of Chicago but even as you lay them out for inspection you realize that they are, after all, puny efforts compared with those of the brethren in, say, New York. New York people seem to have a greater gift for elaboration, richer imagination —and possibly more time—than the rib impresari of the Middle West. . . . There is the story of Mr. George Dickson and Mr. Fish.

Mr. Dixon was sitting that night on the city desk of the *Daily News* (New York) when he came upon a typographical error in an early edition of the *Herald Tribune*. There was a small headline, something like: HAMILTON FISH WARNS UNIONS. Which would have been all right except that the story underneath it read something like this: "J. B. Cadwalder, assistant curator of the Shedd Aquarium, Chicago, today issued a new bulletin on the care and feeding of tropical fish. . . ." Mr. Dixon, aware that such disasters always come in pairs, looked farther and on page 18 found another headline: "FISH SENSITIVE SAYS EXPERT." And another story which in effect went: "Reds in control of labor unions are to be the chief concern of Hamilton Fish. . . ."

Mr. Dixon then picked up the telephone, called the city desk of the *Herald Tribune* and identified himself as Mr. Fish. Vaguely through a fog of humming noises he could hear the thin voices of several slightly nervous men. The city editor shifted him to the managing editor and presently he heard a pleasant voice in apology.

"I know what you are calling for, Mr. Fish," this editor told him. "We have corrected the mistake and it will not appear in other editions."

"I can't understand it," said Mr. Dixon. The editor laughed unconvincingly.

"It's no surprise to people in this business," he said. "You see, Mr. Fish, the difficulty is that the text of a newspaper article—which we call the 'story'—is not set up by the same printer who sets up the headline.

"In order to identify each head with its proper story we attach to each of them what we call the 'slug-line,' a key word which can be easily read by the printer who assembles the type. As it turned out we had a story about tropical fish and the key word for a story like that was, of course, 'Fish'. Then, from a different source we got a report of your address, Mr. Fish, and as a slug we used your name. . . . So you see there were two stories on the bank slugged Fish and two headlines slugged Fish and the printer made what I think is an understandable error."

[324]

"Oh, that will be all right," said Mr. Dixon and he went back to work.

At midnight Mr. Dixon had finished his shift and was relieved by another bright young man named Dolan. He reported to Mr. Dolan all that had gone on during the night including his complaint to the *Herald Tribune* about the Fish story. Mr. Dolan reached for a phone and called the *Herald Tribune*.

"They'll be changing shifts now," he said. "And I think we ought to carry this further."

After a while the *Herald Tribune* city editor answered him and Mr. Dolan identified himself as Mr. Fish. The city editor —like Mr. Dolan only recently arrived at work—began an explanation.

"I saw that error on my way down to the office, Mr. Fish," he said. "And I think I can tell you how it happened. You see on a big newspaper the body of a story is not set up by the same printer who sets up the head. So to identify them and make it possible to link up each story with its proper head we give each of them a slug line. . . . ." He paused and Mr. Dolan could hear a lot of muttering voices. When the city editor spoke again there was something queer about his voice.

"Mr. Fish," he asked, "didn't you call us about this error earlier this evening?"

And Mr. Dolan's answer was filled with dignity as he replied: "I should like to ask, sir, to whom you think you are talking?"

"Why," said the city editor, "Mr. Hamilton Fish . . ."

"But this is not Mr. Hamilton Fish," roared Mr. Dolan. "This is Mr. Tropical Fish."

SUCH INTERESTING PEOPLE

Out of New York, also came the story of the talking dog and you might sense the hand of Messrs. Dixon and Dolan in it, too, save that the case was on record before their time. The late Edward Dean Sullivan, who saved the story for a possibly unworthy posterity, was sitting in a police press room in lower New York with sundry other characters, on the day when the talking dog first came in for editorial attention. The day city editor of the *Journal* called up his correspondent on the premises and said that a tipster named Jakey Kitz had found a talking dog at an address far down on the East Side.

"And what do you want me to do with a talking dog?" the *Journal* man inquired, for it was a hot day and thinking was difficult and futile.

"Interview him, you dumb sap," ordered the city editor. "Ask him what he thinks about Prohibition or the Einstein Theory. And get going." The reporter scratched some notes on a bit of copy paper, found his hat and got going.

As he had mentioned previously it was a hot day, a day scented with burning asphalt and distant fish, a day, in a word, such as you'll find only in downtown Manhattan on the fag end of a heat wave. There was no more hope for a crosstown streetcar then than there is now and taxis hadn't yet become numerous. The reporter took his coat off, hung it over his wet shoulder and walked. In about an hour he arrived at the address Mr. Katz had given his city editor and rang the bell. A bearded Pole came to the door and the reporter looked at his records and asked for Mr. Jarek.

"Jarek, he's gone," said the man in the door.

"Where?" inquired the *Journal* man.

"Staten Island ferry."

[326]

"Going to Staten Island?"

"No. Got friend there. Gateman. Name Pulaski."

"Did he take his dog with him?"

"Sure, take dog."

"I hear this dog talks. Is that so? Does this dog talk?"

"Sure. Smart dog."

So the reporter about-faced and bored through the quivering heat another two or three miles to the ferry building. After some time he found Mr. Pulaski and sought news of Mr. Jarek.

"Gone to Joe's Place," said Mr. Pulaski. And he named an address across town and farther north. The reporter felt ill.

"Did he have his dog with him?" he asked mechanically.

"He always has dog," said Mr. Pulaski.

"Does the dog talk?"

"I didn't ask him. . . ."

The reporter stumbled out into the breathless afternoon. In one blistering hour he reached Joe's place and repeated his question. But Jarek was gone. He had taken his dog with him. Joe didn't know much about the dog but thought that maybe Mr. Jarek had taken him home for a language lesson. . . . Of course it was possible that Jarek might stop at the Visnuski Arms on his way. And Joe described how to get there.

The reporter went to the Visnuski Arms and from there to a speak-easy a mile and a half back in the direction of the ferry. From the speak-easy he went to the home of another pal of Mr. Jarek and there got positive information that Jarek and the dog that Kitz the tipster had discovered were on the way home. It was about time. The sun was going, leaving the heat behind, and the *Journal* man had just about walked his last step.

He was so tired that he refrained from all emotion when at last he discovered Mr. Jarek sitting on the front steps of the house he had first visited. The dog, a large collie, was asleep at his feet.

"You Mr. Jarek?" asked the reporter. Jarek nodded.

"I'm from the *Journal*," said the reporter. "This the dog?"

"This the dog."

"Does he talk?"

"Sure he talks."

"Okay. Tell him to say something."

"Okay, Yippo—I call him Yippo because that's his name. Okay, Yippo. Tell the gent'man your name."

Yippo stretched, blinked an eye and said "Woof."

"How old are you?" asked Mr. Jarek.

"Woof," said Yippo.

"Where do you live?"

"Woof."

"Who's mayor of New York?"

"Woof."

The reporter turned from the dog toward Mr. Jarek.

"His vocabulary isn't so hot, is it?" he asked.

Mr. Jarek looked pained. "He's a dog. He ain't a college professor," he explained and the reporter, painfully dragging his feet, moved on toward a drugstore which might be expected to have a telephone. In a few minutes he was talking once more with the day city editor.

"You find the dog?" came a snarl over the phone.

"Yes. I found him."

"And he talks?"

"Yes. He talks."

[328]

"Good! Come right on in and write your interview. We'll splash it all over page one . . . biggest dog story of the year . . ."

"Wait a minute," said the reporter sadly. "I didn't get any interview with the dog."

"Why not? Didn't you say he could talk?"

"Of course he can talk," said the reporter patiently. "He can talk just like I told you. But only a sonofabitch like Kitz could understand him."

From the same locale and from an inventive brain that did much to set the style for a whole generation of inventive brains in New York journalism comes the story of the mysterious fire aboard the French cruiser *La Gloire* as she lay at anchor in the Hudson. . . .

It is not, of course, necessary to introduce Frank Ward O'Malley. . . . You remember the story of how the city editor called him over and said: "Look here! I've got a swell head-line: 'Hokus Pocus in Hohokus.' Get a story to fit it." And how Mr. O'Malley went to Hohokus, New Jersey, and got the story as ordered. . . . Well, that's the man.

Mr. O'Malley seems to have got along with no particular effort against the competition of his time, and few of his contemporaries recall that he was ever in any great disfavor with his editors and employees for his unconventional approaches to the news. But whether their acquiescence came before or after the demonstration of *La Gloire's* fire, information is lacking. It is said, however, that shortly before that catastrophe some managing editor had been discussing with Mr. O'Malley —in a purely academic way, of course—the close relationship between truth and the news, and implying that error in the printed word could be ascribed only to the deliberate intent of the writer. Mr. O'Malley had taken the position that facts are sometimes deceptive in their very nature and that human interpretation of them is bound to have its defects. He was still brooding on this matter over a glass of beer in a saloon overlooking the broad river when his eye suddenly lighted on *La Gloire*. With no hesitation whatever he went to the telephone and called the City Press and after that most of the managing editors in New York, including his own. His speech in all instances was the same:

"Zees is Capitaine Rolland of *La Gloire*. Eet is not true we have ze explosions, ze fire on my sheep. Eet is not ze trut' we have feefty men keel. . . ." And in all cases he hung up the receiver before anybody could ask him for details.

His telephoning finished, he returned to his beer and passed a pleasant afternoon gazing out over the waves and watching boatload after boatload of his colleagues being pushed away from the gangplank of *La Gloire* by a lot of irate and mystified Frenchmen who thought probably that the gangs of New York were trying to take over their ship. He was pleased to note, some hours later, that the stories of the incident in all the newspapers confirmed his theory that fact may somehow contrive to get itself all mixed up with fiction, and vice versa.

Taking inventory of all these tales one is forced to admit that they fail to prove much about the newspaper business except the opening thesis that in it you meet such interesting people. Mr. O'Malley may have taught us that editors are just as gullible as their three-cent customers. The associates and patrons of Jake Kitz proved in a way that talking dogs are still unable to read newspapers. But there is at least one "rib" in the catalog of this business that started out with a definite purpose and was carried to its end as a purely philosophical demonstration. One refers to what has sometimes been called "Pittsburgh's public hanging," and this fine exhibit was not the work of any inspired Manhattaner but of a native.

Every wandering reporter who was abroad in the land in 1936 knows Jim Daschbach of the Cleveland *Plain Dealer* because—what with the Republicans, Dr. Townsend, Father Coughlin, Gerald Smith and Whatsisname Lemke—all the screwball news of that summer was centered in Cleveland. The reporters from the outland came in to find that Mr. Daschbach, with the sharpest gift for harassing interview in the United States, already had the situation well in hand. They marveled at his technique, sought his hand in friendship, and thereafter let him do all the work. He gets Christmas cards from virtually everybody of note in the United States except maybe Lemke, Townsend and Father Coughlin—especially not Father Coughlin.

Such a person naturally came in for some investigation by the visiting press who wanted to know where he got the ability to think up just the right word to lift a smug crusader's blood pressure and posterior at the same time. And they discovered in him a very good reporter who had become realistic about bunk at an early age and had worked out a theory that the majority of human beings don't know what they are doing and a slick minority know only too well. It was in demonstration of this theory that the Pittsburgh incident occurred. . . .

Probably the most honest man who ever found a place in Pittsburgh politics was Eustace A. Morrow, for many years City Comptroller. Unlike most Honest Johns in the public eye, Morrow was one whose books balanced when he went out of office and he is something of a legend among students of municipal politics. During his term of office he was easily the most popular man in Allegheny County—with his own party because he lent an air of verisimilitude to an otherwise bald and unconvincing narrative, and with members of the opposition because they were smart enough to recognize a popular choice.

Aside from his status with the electorate, Mr. Morrow hadn't any active part in the episode of Mr. Daschbach's contriving. He never knew anything about it until everything was over. The inspiration came for the most part from publication in a local newspaper of a report that thirty thousand signatures had been set to a petition for a new city hall or a new bridge or some such thing. Mr. Daschbach, reading this thing in the City Hall press room, was outraged.

"Petitions don't mean anything," he said. "People will sign anything."

A rival from the newspaper that had been advocating the petitioned improvement took an opposite stand and Mr. Daschbach made a concrete proposition.

"Look," he said, "I'll bet you $10 I can go out here on the street and get fifty signatures to a petition that no man in his right mind would sign . . . you to be the judge of whether I win or not." The other reporter took up the bet, Daschbach prepared his petition on the customary forms, took it out in front of the city hall and began to shove it in front of people mumbling something about Eustace A. Morrow. . . .

In less than an hour he was back in the press room with fifty signatures which he presented to the idealistic young man on the opposite side of the argument. The idealistic young man paid the $10 bet without demur. The fifty names had been appended to a petition to have Eustace A. Morrow publicly hanged at Fifth and Smithfield Streets the following Monday at 2:00 P.M.

34

LAST HEGIRA OF BILL McGEEHAN

~~~~~~

I HAD gone down to Brunswick, Georgia, to cover a murder on St. Simon's island and had run onto Colonel Huston, one-time owner of the Yankees, and so heard for the first time the story of the funeral of Bill McGeehan. The murder was weird and mysterious and filled with characters out of *Wuthering Heights* but somehow the detail of it escapes me now. It was a bit of incongruity in the still and beautiful setting of this historic island whereas the last rites of Bill McGeehan, for all their incredible circumstance, were not.

The saga of McGeehan needs no repetition here—not in this generation. He was one of the most widely read sports writers in the United States, the possessor of a distinctive literary style, and a gay insouciant character to whom other newspapermen gave instant and undying affection. It has been said that his passing was recorded with more columns of obituary notices than that of President Harding. And the most amazing thing about that statement is that it might very well be true.

Friendship with Colonel Huston, begun in his early days as a baseball reporter, brought McGeehan to Georgia in his final illness. He had had some vague intention of sitting around

under the trees, perhaps fishing a bit or lounging in the big
hotel on Sea Island. Instead he was taken directly from the
train to a hospital. He didn't like it. After a week of fretting
he began to demand loudly that he be allowed to return to
New York. And in that emergency Colonel Huston demonstrated why McGeehan had rated his friendship higher than
that of thousands of others. He had another bed set up in
McGeehan's room and got into it. And there he stayed for
better than a month.

"It's bad enough to be sick without being lonesome, too,"
he told me afterward, "and the hospital food wasn't so bad
once you got used to it."

McGeehan got over that attack—probably just in time to
save the life of the Colonel—and for several months after that
he lived in a cottage near the old Episcopal Church on St.
Simon's, doing some of the things he had intended to do and
reconciling himself to the knowledge that he would never be
able to go back to New York. When he went to bed that summer he had a premonition that he would not be getting up
again and he told the Colonel so.

"This is the last of the ninth," he said. "And if they peg
me another fast one I'm out. But I wanted to tell you that I
don't want to go away from here. I want to be buried in the
churchyard over there under the live-oaks."

McGeehan died a few days later and Colonel Huston remembered his last request. He told Mrs. McGeehan about it.
But she seemed to be in a state of distraction and probably
didn't hear him. She announced that she was going to have
Billy's body cremated and take his ashes back to New York.

A Brunswick undertaker was called in. There would be no

difficulty about the cremation, he said, except that the nearest crematorium was in Jacksonville, Florida. She could have the body shipped there, if she wished, or she could send it there by hearse—which would be a little more expensive but quicker.

So the funeral was held and the coffin of Bill McGeehan was taken from the church and placed in the hearse, after which the mourners went their various ways and the hearse started for Jacksonville.

The chauffeur, substituting for the regular hearse-driver who happened to be ill, was a youngster who had some local fame as third-string pitcher for the Brunswick High School team. The baseball field was near the end of the causeway from St. Simon's—where the hearse had to pass on the way to Jacksonville. The youthful driver slowed down to look at the stands as he passed. Savannah was playing the locals for the state high-school championship that day and a record crowd was already turning out although the game wouldn't start for an hour and a half. Sadly he turned away and went southward with Bill McGeehan.

In the meantime the widow, returning to her empty home, suddenly remembered what Colonel Huston had told her. And in new paroxysms of grief, she called up the crematorium in Jacksonville and canceled her order. Thus, when the young hearse-driver arrived an hour later, he was told to take his passenger back to St. Simon's. With no great reluctance he turned around.

The game was in the fifth inning when he next came even with the scoreboard of the Brunswick baseball field. Savannah led the locals three to two. The boy looked out over the water toward St. Simon's and back into the hearse at the coffin. Then he turned in at the side gate where the ticket-taker let him pass without paying. He parked his hearse under the main grandstand directly behind home plate, found a seat on the Brunswick High School bench and watched the game until the locals won it with fine flourish in the ninth. Then he took Bill McGeehan home.

"There was a little row about it," Colonel Huston told me. "Of course somebody spread the news. You can't very well take a hearse into a ball park without being noticed and criticized. But I think all the hullabaloo was silly. I asked the kid about it and he said that he didn't mean any disrespect. He said that of all the dead guys in the world Bill McGeehan was the least likely to object to being laid out in a ball park during a championship game. And I agreed with him. It was just what Bill would have wanted."

35

LITTLE BULL AND THE RAIN MAKERS

~~~~~~

ONCE the good people of the United States had nothing to worry about except the depression and the drought. I don't recall that the Sioux Indians did anything about the depression. It wasn't anything that an Indian was likely to notice. But after the Dakotas and for that matter most of the Mississippi and Missouri Valleys had burned up for two straight years they intimated that they were tired of the white man's nonsense. They dug out their old ceremonial robes and called conclaves at which all surviving medicine men tried to recall the lore of the sun dance. After a couple of rehearsals Chief Little Bull, relative of the late Sitting Bull, announced that he and a troupe of carefully chosen dancers would revive a lot of the old rites and make some rain near Belle Fourche, South Dakota, on the following Sunday afternoon and at Fort Berthold, North Dakota, a couple of days later. I was assigned to cover these experiments and to lend to Little Bull all possible aid.

It was a long ride from Chicago to the Cheyenne reservation where the Indians assembled for their first sun dance in fifty years, and it was hot and dusty. For a hundred miles after you crossed the Missouri at Cheyenne Agency there wasn't a single sprig of green. The dust hung over the prairie in a yellowy haze. The fields were brown. The trees along the washes that sloped toward the Missouri were blackish gray. And the whole landscape quivered in the indescribable heat.

Into this came Little Bull and his ancient braves. All through the terrible afternoon they stomped and wavered and sang their chants, and the dust rose higher and made them look like something in a shadow play. And to render the aid that I had been assigned to render, I stepped out of my car and opened an umbrella.

The Indians were pleased with the umbrella. They said that it showed the right spirit. But nothing came of any of this. When the sun had gone down over in the neighborhood of the Black Hills, a flat, brassy disk, the Indians packed up their equipment. The spectators started out through the dust for home. Most of them had not expected any rain anyway.

The experiment in North Dakota had no more success. I wrote a dispassionate report of the proceedings and prepared to go back to Chicago and then I got a telegram advising me that the President had left Washington in a special train to investigate conditions in the drought area and suggesting that I join the party at Bismarck. So I went to Bismarck.

Save for the fact that the Indians didn't take part in it the scene here was just about what I had seen in Little Bull's conclaves—the dust and the heat and the despairing faces of men who wondered how they were going to support their families through a foodless winter. Hundreds of farmers—many of whom hadn't been able to find enough water to wash in for a couple of months—crowded the streets around the railroad station. When the President's train rolled slowly in, there was no stopping them. They spread out across the platforms and across the track, where they closed in in the wake of the train and marched forward with it in silence. Out onto the observation platform stepped the President, noticeably impressed.

If he had wanted to see the effects of the drought he need travel no farther than this. It was in the hundreds of soiled, sweaty, disheartened faces that peered up at him through the swirling dust. In deep emotion he held up his hand and made a speech that was obviously unrehearsed.

"My friends," he said, "I see you today in pitiful trouble. But you must not despair. Your government has not forgotten you. Your government is constantly mindful of you. Your government knows that something must be done for you. Your government *will* do something for you. . . ." He stood for a moment with his hand upraised.

Then the heavens opened and there was the most terrific cloudburst that North Dakota had seen in twenty years.

Mr. Ted Alford of the Kansas City *Star* made the keynote speech for the occasion.

"Humph," he said. "Little Bull couldn't make rain but Big Bull certainly can."

I don't really know why I have set down this story here unless to justify a hitherto unexpressed belief that the miracle workers are never very far from the newspaper business, in or out of it. It isn't that only the miracle workers can succeed in it, it's that only the miracle workers can survive in it. As John Craig once said when his secretary asked an office boy to save her the trouble of looking at the clock, it takes all kinds of people to make a newspaper office and they're all in it.

If there were giants in the old days in journalism there are no fewer now nor will there be tomorrow. There was a New York correspondent of a Boston paper whose technique came right from Macbeth's witches. He got an important interview with Governor Curley in New York, then slipped a bit of chloral into the Governor's drink so that he wouldn't be able to talk to any of the local boys when he got to Boston. There were the godlike boys who in ages past and present of the newspaper business refused to recognize disaster socially. The news editor of the Houston *Post* put the first story of the *Titanic* on an inside page. The news editor of the Chicago *Tribune* put it on a spike where it stayed until some underling rescued it. The editor of an Arkansas newspaper threw away the bulletin on the blasting of the *Maine*. His only explanation was that he didn't believe it.

Of similar altitude above realities was Mr. M. X. Forrest of New Orleans who covered the disinterment of a Civil War cannon and some ammunition in front of the cathedral. That night after a few drinks at the press club he could think of nothing else. A voice within him told him what he must do and he did it. He meandered down to the cathedral, loaded up the cannon and touched it off. Then he retired from the scene through the nave of the church and out through the sacristy, joining a crowd that had come to investigate the explosion.

Across the river in Algiers a milkman sitting at his breakfast table was just about to put a cup of coffee to his lips when it was taken out of his hand by a cannonball. If he reads this he will probably know for the first time just where the cannonball came from.

Mr. Lyman Moose, of whom much has been written here,

tossed several miracles—those already described and one that just comes to mind. Mr. Moose was working in San Francisco and one day came to work an hour late. He informed the city editor that a ferryboat had jammed into a slip—and somehow failed to make his story convincing.

"Write a story about it," the city editor said. "A lot of people are going to be interested in a story about why the ferry was an hour late. . . ."

A lesser genius might have surrendered. But not Lyman. He called up the press-relations department of the ferry company and explained his predicament. The matter was referred to a vice-president who issued a formal statement apologizing for the lateness of the ferry. And there are no wonders greater than that anywhere at all.

In the old days delegations of the newspaper literati and similar odd spirits from other professions used to lunch—just why I was never able to determine—at Schlogl's, an ancient German restaurant in Wells Street. Heavy oak chairs and tables and an ancient oak bar made up the furnishings of the place. There was about as much light as you'd expect to find in a crypt—and there were other resemblances.

Schlogl's was first made famous by Harry Hansen who wrote that baked owl was the *specialité de la maison*. I never saw any owl in Schlogl's identifiable as such but I shall admit that would be no reason for doubting the veracity of Mr. Hansen. My argument with the management was not over the owls *per se* but over the condition of the chinaware. The chef, so I have been told, was excellent. The raw material brought into the kitchen was of the best. The waiters—particularly Richard, the one who took care of us—were easily the best in Chicago.

But there seemed to be a house rule that they had to hire blind dishwashers.

My protests about thumbprints on plates continued regularly to the point where I was eating nothing but canned sardines and hard-boiled eggs, both served in unbroken packages. But I gave up one day when I cracked my egg and discovered on the white albumen the blackest thumbprint I had ever looked at. I realized that a genius who could get his fingerprints inside the shell of a hard-boiled egg probably could transmit them to me through the air. And amid the cheers of all my companions I apologized to the direction and all the help.

The old building in Wells Street was torn down and we had moved to other and possibly less interesting restaurants before I learned that people whose thumbprints you find inside eggs are not to be trusted. The prints turned out to have been made by Henry DeVries, a chemist who always ate at our table. He had spent a night treating the shell with wax and leaching a dye through the pores.

Most modern miracles I suppose have some explanation as simple as that. Maybe if you had access to the meteorological records of North Dakota and knew something about the law of averages you could explain Mr. Roosevelt's success in rain-making. It is sometimes less easy to explain the commonplace. There was for instance one of our best reporters who got a bit tight one wintry afternoon, squatted down at the entrance to the City Hall and held out his hat for the largesse of passers-by. Of course everybody who tried to rationalize his conduct started off with the premise that he'd been drinking. What they couldn't account for was why his alcoholic subconscious mind should have made a beggar out of him. Not until he was drunk

again did anybody get the answer and then it was quite understandable.

"Beggars get a lot of money," he said. "And you don't have
to have any special training to get to be a beggar."

Just as simple is the explanation of the mysterious case of
the Beeville (Illinois) *Enterprise.* . . .

A facetious linotyper on the *Enterprise* (circulation 700) set
up a humorous vulgarity on a breakover slug one afternoon
and got fired before anybody noticed it. As a matter of fact
the entire edition had been printed—and all the paper in stock
used up—before anybody noticed it.

The young editor had no gift of miracles but he had ingenuity. He took a safety-razor blade and laboriously cut the
offending slug line out of every one of the seven hundred
printed copies of his newspaper. The result was novel. The
Springfield *State Journal* took editorial notice of it.

"The Beeville *Enterprise,*" said this comment, "is the only
weekly in Illinois with a hole in it."

36

END PAPER

~~~~~~

EVERY now and then when you come back to the country from wars and similar distractions somebody will tell you that a great change for the better has come over American journalism. That half-mystical, half-material association of wills— Alcoholics Anonymous—has put more saloonkeepers out of business than Prohibition. The juvenility has gone from the conduct of the earnest young workers who fill the local rooms. Journalism at last has become a serious profession and Peter Pan is no longer on the payroll. Nobody's likely to shoot cockroach powder through the pneumatic tubes any more. No reporter is likely to come rolling in to hold a lantern in the managing editor's face and complain about the lack of honest men in the world. Nobody's going to annoy the police any more or dive into fountains in hotel lobbies . . . or at least that's the theory of it.

Once in a while, however, you begin to have some doubts. . . . So many things in the local room look as they always did before the world became adult and virtuous. So many things that you hear in conversation sound so much like things that you've heard before. . . . A couple of days ago Pete McEvoy, who once made an indifferent electorate aware of Dr. Townsend and who now is a sergeant in the army, wrote to me about a mutual friend who knows all the policemen in Washington, D.C.

Recently, according to Mr. McEvoy, this friend was arrested for menacing traffic while in a dizzy condition. He was locked up in the Eighteenth Precinct jail. Shortly thereafter another reporter—also a mutual friend—got arrested in the Ninth Precinct. He called the office to get into touch with the man who knew all the policemen, and so was connected with the Eighteenth Precinct and explained his trouble. The occupant of the Eighteenth Precinct cell was much disturbed.

"Arrested for intoxication!" he repeated with an air of disbelief. "That's certainly an outrage! What do you want me to do about it?"

I was carrying the sergeant's letter into the local room to share it with our local of Alcoholics Anonymous when I heard Clem Lane, the city editor, mumbling wrathfully in his beard.

"And what does he think of my intelligence?" he wanted to know. "I could take a bum excuse for the eighth time he was late . . . but the lug brings in his alarm clock to show me how slow it runs. . . ."

And down the hall Howard O'Brien, the eminent columnist, was looking at an advertisement for a drill press and lamenting the fact that recent bills had made the price of $29.75 look like an extravagance. The telephone rang and the chairman of the Men's Club of St. Paul's Episcopal Church asked Mr. O'Brien to speak to his organization on the following Wednesday.

[346]

"We haven't much money," this gentleman said. "So we pay a fixed fee of $25."

Mr. O'Brien laid down the picture of the drill press.

"Make it $29.75 and I'm yours," he said.

So I went back to my desk and looked up maps and time tables reassured. Everything changes and nothing changes. And the most fey of all professions will maintain its integrity without any help from me. . . . It's still fascinating to be a newspaperman—the interesting people are still interesting.